ALL MY YESTERDAYS

Cecil Lewis was born in Birkenhead in 1898, joined the RFC in 1916 as a pilot and was awarded the MC. After the war he went to Peking to teach the Chinese to fly. All this is recorded in *Sagittarius Rising*, recognized as a First World War classic. Returning to London he became one of the five founding members of the BBC and Chairman of the Programme Board from 1922 to 1926. He went on to write books and radio plays, directed the first two films made of Bernard Shaw's plays, was called to Hollywood where he got an Oscar for his script of *Pygmalion*, went on to beachcomb in Tahiti and returned to flying duties in the RAF in the Second World War. In 1947 flew his own aeroplane to S. Africa where he farmed sheep. Returning to New York to work for the United Nations in 1951, he was subsequently invited to join the staff of Associated Rediffusion when commercial television was set up in London a year later. He retired to Corfu in 1968.

Also by Cecil Lewis

Non-fiction

THE UNKNOWN WARRIOR
BROADCASTING FROM WITHIN
SAGITTARIUS RISING
THE TRUMPET IS MINE
FAREWELL TO WINGS
TURN RIGHT FOR CORFU
NEVER LOOK BACK
A WAY TO BE
GEMINI TO JOBURG
SAGITTARIUS SURVIVING

Fiction

CHALLENGE TO THE NIGHT
YESTERDAY'S EVENING
PATHFINDERS
THE GOSPEL ACCORDING TO JUDAS
THE DARK SANDS OF SHAMBALA

All My Yesterdays

AN AUTOBIOGRAPHY

Cecil Lewis

ELEMENT

Shaftesbury, Dorset ● Rockport, Massachusetts
Brisbane, Queensland

Published in Great Britain in 1993 by
Element Books Limited
Longmead, Shaftesbury, Dorset

Published in the USA in 1993 by
Element Inc
42 Broadway, Rockport, MA 01966

Published in Australia in 1993 by
Element Books Limited for
Jacaranda Wiley Limited
33 Park Road, Milton, Brisbane 4064

Cover design by Max Fairbrother
Designed by Roger Lightfoot
Typeset by Footnote Graphics, Warminster
Printed in Great Britain by
Dotesios Ltd, Trowbridge, Wiltshire.

British Library Cataloguing in Publication
data available

Library of Congress Cataloging in Publication
data available

ISBN 1–85230–405–7

Contents

Prologue vii

1. Roots 1
2. Growing Up 9
3. Into the Air 15
4. Back to the Middle Ages 31
5. Straight and Level 45
6. Broadcasting? What's That? 53
7. Truth and Beauty 63
8. My Eminent Friend 73
9. Drama in New York 81
10. Dreams in Italy 85
11. Elstree to Hollywood Jungles 91
12. Dusky Paradise 101
13. Mother Love 111
14. A Fight for Life 119
15. Seen from Africa 135
16. Work in Progress 151
17. Time to Retire 167
18. The Fifth Way 189
19. World to Come 197

To my beloved wife
and her lifetime of care and love

Prologue

I T is some years since I happened to come across an account of a strange fish, *Anableps anableps*, which inhabits the swamps and estuaries of the northern coasts of South America. It feeds on the weeds and small creatures which lie on or just below the surface of the water. To do this it has itself to swim snakelike on the surface. But this leaves it exposed to the sea-birds that prey upon it. To meet this perpetual crisis – life from one element, death from the other – Nature has endowed it with special equipment. It has double vision. In two rather protuberant sockets in its head lie four eyes; the upper pair look up into the air, the lower down into the water.

This miraculous provision to meet two opposing sets of conditions is, as far as I know, unique in Nature. Yet I do not find it fanciful to see in it a striking parallel to the human condition. A hundred poets, philosophers and mystics have testified to man's propensity to look up and look down, to look out and look in, to be forever divided within himself. We are, it seems, two-natured: what we do bears little relation to what we are. Our imposing public façade all too often masks a sorry tenement of doubts and fears, vanities and grudges. Whether we have dared to look at ourselves so frankly or not, we cannot fail to see the conflict, approaching chaos, in the world around us: race against race, religion against religion, class against class, have against have-not. From what does all this spring – since the outer always reflects the inner – if not from the desperate dichotomy that plagues us all?

It is comparatively easy for 'great' men to give an account of themselves: a great patriot, Churchill; a great lover, Casanova; a great revolutionary, Marx. Such men start with the odds in their favour. But the 'ordinary' man, such as myself, faces a task far more difficult and subtle. The lack of any singleness of purpose precludes a high narrative line. A weathercock life is apt to leave nothing but a ragbag of trivia. However, taking inspiration from *Anableps anableps*, another approach is possible: a sort of inquiry to discover what, if any, is the relationship between outer and inner, higher and lower. To see this perpetual crisis as a continual fluctuation, like a pendulum forever swinging between what could be and what is, this might be the beginning of a search leading a man towards a deeper understanding of his own reality. Such a possibility attracts me. For it is, I am convinced after a longish life, lack of self-understanding that bars the path, like a sword turning every way, between man and his own possibilities.

Of course such an inquiry is, in fact, doomed to failure from the outset; nobody below the level of a saint can expect to 'see life steadily and see it whole'. But in that direction at least lies a challenge. So, having issued it to myself, there is nothing left to do but have a go.

1

Roots

M Y father was a Congregational minister. His father was a Congregational minister. In the little Derbyshire village of Tideswell, all dour slate and stone, my paternal grandfather (whom I never knew) cared for the flock who worshipped at the 'Congry' and brought up a family of four on £80 a year. The children evidently had some initiative and ability. The only daughter, Mary, emigrated to South Africa to enter a nunnery. At the turn of the twentieth century such a step for a young spinster was an unheard-of adventure. However, the Mother Superior, after giving her a short trial, decided hers was too turbulent a spirit for such seclusion and turned her loose in the veld. She never came back to England, having fallen in love with the primeval emptiness of the place, and finished up, still a spinster, as librarian of Pretoria University. Her brother, Uncle Bo, was less adventurous and got no further than being a bank manager in Manchester, but Tom, his elder by two years, was my favourite. A huge bumbling giant of a man (all the family stood over 6 feet), he used to blow into my childhood like a whiff of the good whisky that he loved. His immense gusto and appetite for life, his broad North Country accent, his ribald humour, his endless fund of stories, all this intoxicated me. He lived in Peru, where he managed a large cotton mill and asserted that he settled all strikes by knocking the ring-leaders' heads together. On his rare visits home, he flung open the doors of our quiet household to the romance of 'foreign parts' and when his wife died, my grandmother, at the age of eighty-four, quietly got on a ship (she had never been abroad in her life) and set off for Lima where she managed his household for some years.

I still have a photo of this remarkable little lady, the only one of my four grandparents that I knew. She is sitting erect in a wicker

1

chair in a garden. Her staid black dress with lace fichu at her neck, her lace cap, her folded hands, her enigmatic smile, all give an air of being self-contained and content. This is what they were like, the women who raised our fathers. I remember no words that she ever said to me, but I can still hear the warm assured tone of her voice. She never left the North Country after her return from Peru and I was already launched into my broadcasting career when she died in 1924 at the age of ninety-six.

In the seventies of the last century it was often assumed that the eldest son would enter the Church. More reason for it still, if the family was in it already. So my father, prising open the door of his life with scholarship after scholarship, mastered Hebrew and ancient Greek and soon found himself ordained as a Nonconformist clergyman. In fact, I do not think he was religious in the strict sense of the term. For a man to shift the centre of gravity of his life so that it is really 'not of this world' implies a striving towards quite another set of values. But that is setting the sights too high, perhaps. My father was a thinker, a philosopher and a preacher – qualities quite sufficient to equip him for a career in the Church. Anyway, the gun of his career was laid, the shot fired and the trajectory took him swiftly up from the obscurity of Frodsham and Chester to the London suburbs and finally to the most coveted living in the West End – The King's Weigh House, Grosvenor Square. There the shell exploded.

The deeply rooted rituals of Catholicism and Greek or Russian Orthodoxy permit the congregation to take part in a mystery, apprehended but not understood, a vision of an altogether different state to which they may aspire but never reach, which calls to some hidden depths in their natures and reminds them that the sources of life do not lie in this material world. The Nonconformists, as the word implies, reject such an endless repetition of dead forms and insist on the power of the priest to exhort and teach his flock and to lead them to heaven – as if he knew the way, God help him, and were the guide on some personally conducted tour.

My father being already 'advanced' in his views, even for a Nonconformist, had reduced the rituals to zero. He preached most beautifully – this was what filled his churches – bringing a simplicity and warmth to everything he said, he read the lessons, prayed and pronounced his own benediction. It was the beginning of the personality cult, the one-man show. But he had already sensed, in this first decade of the twentieth century, that the Church was losing its grip. The future, he was firmly convinced, lay outside it. The word of God could be preached anywhere, on street corners, in the woods, by the shore. Why was a church necessary? And why should a man of God be paid for his services? Why had money to do with the spiritual health of mankind? The two were in head-on opposition. So he planned to become an itinerant preacher and leave the material side to look after itself. It was wildly idealistic, of course; but there was an element of sanity in it. In the East, where poverty, godliness and the begging bowl go hand in hand, it would not even have caused comment.

———

ALL this inner searching went on below the surface. My mother and I were quite unaware of it. But a member of his congregation was not. She was a wealthy woman and offered to provide my father with a roof till this new life could begin. They left on a walking tour in Italy.

So at the height of his career, at the age of about forty, he deliberately renounced all his achievements to become an outcast in the only world he knew. He had made himself a pauper and become utterly dependent on a woman, who now she had 'got' him, soon reminded him that he had compromised her, that she had given up everything for his sake and that, besides, she was supporting him. The dream had turned to disaster. Moreover, the First World War had broken out. The old world was breaking up. On both sides divorces were arranged. They were married.

Whatever had passed between my father and mother before this break had been carefully kept from me. But at thirteen I had sharp eyes and ears and from odd words and glances I felt something was wrong. My mother was a courageous gay little woman and it took a good deal to get her down. I saw that she suffered without really understanding the cause. Besides, I had been quietly sent off to boarding school to keep me out of the way and I learned of the break in a letter from my mother. She went through the crisis alone, packed up the huge London manse and retired to our little cottage at Hindhead. She came from a well-to-do family of millers and had modest means of her own, just enough to live on. She had married my father before his career had begun to develop and all these 'advanced' ideas of his were quite beyond her. I took her part, for, after all, the facts were clear: Father had left us and what was my mother going to do with the rest of her life?

I need not have worried. In the middle of the First World War she married again and was more happy and contented with her second husband than she had ever been with my father. He was a valuer of country properties for Knight, Frank & Rutley. No desire to turn the world upside down worried him. In fact, his career depended on things remaining firmly as they always had been. But the war, willy-nilly, marked the end of all such stability and after ten years an ulcer, unrecognized by the local GP, perforated. Emergency operations came too late. In a week he was dead.

Then indeed my mother's life was over, or so I thought, for she was well over fifty and this second blow (which affected and aged her greatly) seemed to condemn her to a vista of empty years. So when she announced a year later, rather shyly and apologetically, that she was going to marry a third time, I cheered. Such resilience, such vitality! How gay her laugh was! How eagerly and freely she grasped the opportunities that opened to her! Her third husband, a retired officer from the Indian Army, simply worshipped the ground she walked on. He kept the garden and washed the car, she cooked and housekept impeccably, as she had always done, the silver and the old oak shone. The little house was a sort of jewel fashioned out of a mutual care and respect for stability. Modest and ordinary, perhaps, but nevertheless basic, the corner-stone of any society.

Her third stroke was serious and I hurred home from Italy to find her propped up in bed, gaily asking for a glass of champagne. The doctor would not allow it until it was too late and then, alas, it was bitter. She began to sink and sighed deeply, 'I'm a long time dying.' Then we thought she slept, but her breathing was heavy and troubled. Without opening her eyes, she whispered: 'Hold my hand, darling. I'm a little frightened.' Soon, mercifully, she sank into a coma. After two days I gently roused her to tell her that I loved her. A smile lighted her drooping head for a moment. They were, I think, the last words she heard in this life. At dawn next morning she was gone.

When she had been laid out, I went in to take my leave. A light cambric covered her face and I stood there quite overawed by the presence of death, unable to lift the handkerchief. But, as usual, I need not have worried, for when at last, summoning my courage, I did so, I drew breath in amazement. I looked on the face of a young girl. All the wrinkled cares of a lifetime had gone. So must she have looked when my father married her, when I, her only son, issued from her body. It was the last gift of a generous heart to leave me remembering her so and I kissed her, consoled and reassured, feeling in some strange way that she was safe.

MEANWHILE my father was sweating it out in luxury, moving from one beautiful country home to another, travelling all over Europe and wasting year after year of his life in a sort of gilded prison. Although after the war those high ideals of his were more than ever necessary, they had died in him. He was older. The woman who was going to liberate him to follow them kept him penniless. If he wanted a new pair of shoes or an ounce of tobacco he had to ask her for the money! It was an intolerable situation, yet he seemed drugged, hypnotized, paralysed and unable to make any move to free himself. Perhaps, because he was very quiet and patient, he felt he was somehow paying for his mistake. So he stuck it out for twenty years – twenty years of what should have been the core of his active life.

Then, when he was over sixty, he happened to escape for a couple of weeks to go skiing in the mountains There he met a young woman, Joan, thirty years his junior. In a flash the whole ghastly nightmare of inaction and boredom was swept away. No grandiose ideals haunted him now. All he asked was to be able to exercise such rusty talents as still remained to him. He managed to get one or two articles published and followed the vein. The young woman came to live with him and slowly he begun to regain his self-respect.

To give an idea of how all his talents were pent up in him, one example will suffice. I was at this time in a position of some influence in the BBC. I had the idea of introducing a short mid-week lay sermon to bridge the gap from Sunday to Sunday for those who felt a need for such things. One five-minute script a week was required. The programme was not to come on the air for another six weeks. When I suggested to my father that he should take it on, he jumped at it. The entire material for a year, fifty-two scripts, was on my desk before the programme started! This little feature, the Philemon Talks, lasted for several years. The scripts were collected and published and the attendant publicity gave my father the opportunity to consolidate a modest place in this field of journalism. He maintained it for the rest of his life and at the age of eighty-four was still earning £1500 a year.

This Indian summer of his grew into a time of great warmth and contentment. Joan bore him a daughter whom he lived to see married. Although his wife refused all ideas of divorce, his young inamorata changed her name by deed poll to Lewis and the two lived together as man and wife – as indeed they were – until the wife died and they were able to legalize the situation. Today such scruples may seem ridiculous, but we all tend to live by the code in which we were raised and so this was natural and right for them.

The stream of articles continued – pieces on country folklore, on words, on customs, on philosophy, on religion. They poured out from the little book-lined study and brought in correspondence from all over the world. But finally there came a day when head and fingers could no longer communicate and the last sheet of paper, the saddest piece of paper I ever saw, held nothing but a jumble of disconnected letters. But even for such an inevitable emergency he was prepared. In the bottom drawer of his desk were found a stack of articles which could continue to appear under his name when he could no longer write them – his contribution to the housekeeping, he called it. There was no need of this, for Joan had more than enough for them both; but if a man has had to ask for 'pocket money' for twenty years, it is apt to crystallize in him a determination never to be so humiliated again.

———

THERE were two strange things about the end of his life which I feel I should not omit. I was hard at work in London and could not get down to Somerset often. His condition slowly deteriorated and the last time I was to see him alive he lay in bed, quite paralysed, his very blue eyes looking steadily out of the window into the summer garden. He had already lost the power of speech, only his hands moved, clasping and unclasping over his breast. I sat down beside him and, taking his hands, tried desperately to help him, to give him some of my vitality and strength. How powerless we are to help one another, I thought, how tragic, how terrible, how sad it is, the end of life. Suddenly he spoke, enunciating the words calmly and clearly, the tones of his voice as they had always been.

'I have never been happier than I am at this moment.'

I was stunned. I could not believe he had really spoken. Then, as the words rang in my head (they still do), I marvelled that when everything we call 'life' had ebbed away there could remain inside such serenity, such peace. He taught me then, in those last words, that below the surface, beneath all the lifelong busyness of men, there is something else which, if we can find it, is always there to sustain us through every peril – even the terror of death.

The other happening was, in a way, stranger still. Shortly after his death, I went on business to Russia, Scandinavia, over the Pole to Japan and back to Hawaii, California and New York. I had to try – according to an old custom long since fallen into limbo – to remember each day, for forty days, something good about him to help him through a dark period for his soul. I had kept this tryst as well as I could and was returning across the Atlantic by night. We were at 18,000 feet, the plane was almost empty and, unable to sleep, I wandered down after midnight into the little bar which graced the aircraft of those days. Quite alone there I was listening to the roar of the motors and peering out close to the window, abstractedly thinking how tired I was, how far I had come in so short a time, how glad I should be to get home. Then suddenly I focused on the reflection in the black glass. It was not my face that looked at me, but his. He had, as it were, vested himself in my form and was gazing steadily back into my eyes as I gazed into his.

I knew then that I should always find him in me; his gestures, his turn of phrase, his patterns of thought, the tones of his voice, they are all there. I find them every day. He sustains me. I sustain him. The chain-stitch of life cannot be broken.

> The truly wise mourn neither for the living nor
>   for the dead.
> There never was a time when I did not exist, nor
>   you, nor any of these kings. Nor is there any
>   future in which we shall cease to be . . .

Worn out garments
Are shed by the body:
Worn-out bodies
Are shed by the dweller
Within the body.
New bodies are donned
By the dweller, like garments . . .
Death is certain for the born. Rebirth is
   certain for the dead. You should not grieve
   for what is unavoidable.

Bhagavad Gita (The Song of God).
Translation: Swami Prabhavananda and Christopher Isherwood.

2

Growing Up

I have departed from a strict chronology in sketching in the background in which I was raised because it is, after all, a sort of nest which, even if we have nests of our own, we never leave. But in childhood this nest was my world. A jumble of impressions rise up out of those early years: the anaesthetist flapping a white towel dipped in ether before my face when I was circumcised; hearing the first wheezy music from the black wax cylinders of a phonograph; this somehow mixed up with terrifying stories of poltergeists; the huge sacks of flour that arrived regularly from Chester and the marvellous smell flooding the house as my mother baked our daily bread (and small mouse with currant eyes for me) on the big black-leaded stove. But most of all throughout my childhood the sound of my father's footsteps, pacing up and down, composing his three sermons a week. He did this at a high-standing desk on a little Blick typewriter which today would be a museum-piece. Seeing him there high above the congregation in his white surplice he seemed set apart, a being of quite another kind, and, as his only son, small wonder if some of this rubbed off on me. He never forced religion upon me in any way, but because he read most beautifully the words of the Bible became, as it were, absorbed into my consciousness and set standards for the majesty of fine language which was a heritage in itself.

Later there are memories of quite a different kind: seeing my parents wheeze away up the road on the first White Steam Car; watching them as they listened to our church organist initiating them into the mysteries of Wagner's themes in the Ring of the Nibelungen; and later still learning from my father, on the Hindhead links, how to swing a golf club (he was a scratch golfer and collected rows of cups). It was one afternoon coming back from the links that he found an opportunity to explain to me the difference between men and women and the means whereby the propagation of the species takes place. I was awed and shocked. Being about thirteen at the time, nothing of this kind had ever occurred to me. But of course the thing began to go round and round in my head. I was consumed with curiosity, not about the sexual act, but, having no sisters, as to what the female form was *like*.

We had at that time a pretty young serving girl called Lily and, my father and mother having some business in town, I was left alone at the little cottage with Lily to look after me. I remember clearly her plump cosy figure, the black dress she wore in the evenings, her white apron, her starched collar and cuffs. I don't suppose she was more than eighteen, and yet, it seems to me now, she may have had some acquaintance with that lowest common denominator of all human experience. Anyway, with the devastating practical directness of a child, I asked Lily if, since she was a girl, she would let me 'have a look'. She affected to be very shocked ('Get along with you!') but I persisted, coaxing and wheedling her to get what I wanted, but never, of course, touching or kissing her, for I had no idea that that had anything to do with it. After some days of this ('Oh Master Cecil, you are a tease!') she consented to allow me to come to her room when she had retired. In my pyjamas, holding the little candlestick in one hand, for this was long before the days of electricity, I knocked and went in, to find Lily safely in bed. After more pleading, she allowed me to pull down the bedclothes, to see her long nightdress covering her feet.

'I'll catch my death!'

'Quick then!'

As modestly as the situation would permit, Lily pulled up her nightdress to reveal all. She was a dark girl.

'Oh! Lily! It's just fur. Black fur.'

'Course it isn't. Silly.'

So, slightly opening and raising her plump legs, Lily revealed to me, peering closer, candle in hand, that Mecca for which empires have been lost and dynasties overthrown, which has launched a thousand ships, sired ten thousand murders, inspired a hundred thousand love songs and spawned a few dollars' worth of Big Business.

At thirteen it left me absolutely cold. I stood up.
'Thank you very much Lily,' I said, and went to bed.

———

I do not think it was only to keep me away from their domestic crisis that my parents sent me away to boarding school. At Dulwich and later at University College School I had learned absolutely nothing. But they must have already noticed that I was not unintelligent because of my avid interest in everything that was in those days called 'scientific'. I liked making things: I turned screws on my lathe; I invented ingenious devices for putting the gas out after I was in bed. I had already developed a passion for anything to do with aeroplanes. What I needed, my father evidently thought, was a school where these inclinations could be developed. So he announced that he was sending me to Oundle.

Lavishly endowed by the Grocers' Company, which had fostered the school since the Middle Ages, Oundle was at the time the only 'modern' school where the laboratories and workshops were given pride of place. The school buildings were scattered through the little town and under the vigorous and able direction of the Headmaster, Dr Sanderson, a big building programme was in progress. The great hall was already built and the wings, housing the art room and library, were a-building. New science blocks were also completed before I left and throughout those years, even as schoolboys, we all had the feeling of participating in quite a new attack on the principles of education. 'Beans', as the Head was affectionately called, was a rotund but vigorous man. His mortar-board squarely planted on his big head, his robes flying in the wind, he was everywhere, directing, encouraging, teaching and, it seems to me now, always succeeding by a wide tolerance and humanity. He overawed us, of course, but we did not fear him.

What a programme of work we were put through! Up at 6.30 – a cold bath was obligatory – early-morning runs, morning prayers, lessons till lunchtime, games twice a week, drilling for the OTC, two Sunday services, it seems we never got into much mischief because we were always too busy! The curriculum was wide – not only physics and chemistry, long periods in the labs or workshops, but mathematics, optics, mechanical drawing, literature, art, divinity, French and German – we were kept hard at all these and, as my young head was just beginning to work, I found study exhilarating and shot up to reach the Upper Sixth at the age of sixteen. To Oundle I owe not only a basic 'scientific' attitude to life, but a grounding in poetry, art and music – for all of which I developed a passion. If there was anything wrong with such a curriculum it was to encourage in me a tendency (which no doubt already existed) to be interested in too many things. Of course, to be broadly based, ready to cope with any situation, is what a whole man should be; but we were just entering the period when to be successful it was necessary to specialize. This partitioning of knowledge into smaller and smaller boxes is all of a piece with the fragmentation which is now taken for granted in every aspect of modern life. I do not think there is much future in it. Knowledge divides: only understanding unites.

Those three years at Oundle were all the education I was ever to have, the only carefree years in the whole of my life, and I look back on them full of gratitude and appreciation.

———

So, at sixteen I stood 6 feet 4 inches, a thin, stringy, beanpole of a boy, so weak I could not even pull myself up on a horizontal bar. Work some red lead into my hair and daub me with iodine and I could have passed for a Masai. But I had simply outgrown my strength. I was not gawky or ill-proportioned. When actual strength was not concerned, I could hold my own, getting school colours at fives and stroking the house on the river. In the rough and tumble of study ragging, I was let alone because of sudden violent outbursts of temper which intimidated anyone who ventured to attack me. But I was never really social or popular; something held me aloof.

What was the seat of this inner loneliness which I feel sure, to a lesser or greater degree, comes over all young people before the prison of adult life finally shuts them in? It seemed to me then – and I see no reason to change my opinion – that music, art and poetry were all like disembodied voices, influences, calling some message, some command that could not be understood precisely, yet inspired a man to search for something; something nobler and higher to be found only in the mountains above the plains of life. It was as if creative men and women had had some revelation, held the key to some secret, knew the path towards some mystery they could never reveal, but was surely there. A phrase of music or a line of poetry was enough to set me vibrating to this question. It took me deep inside myself and set me apart, for I wished also to join the community of lonely ones who sang of this El Dorado of the spirit. But how could I sing if I did not know where or what it was? This secret longing has haunted me all my life. I thought it made me 'different' for, in the pride of youth, I imagined that nobody had ever felt as I! It quickly earned me the nickname of 'Cocky' Lewis; but I had no feeling of superiority. It was simply that just below the surface lay these muted calls which I did not wish to stifle and yet were too private to communicate. Better in such a case to keep myself apart.

But all this unresolved wonder was soon to be swept into the wings, as, at seventeen, the curtain of my adult life swung quickly up, not to a roll of drums, but to a more ominous and sinister sound, the roll of guns.

———

THE only boy with whom the camaraderie of school spilled over into the holidays was Maynard Greville. His background and upbringing were utterly different from mine, for he was the second son of the Countess of Warwick and was accustomed to life on a lavish scale. It was an exciting experience for me to scramble over the walls of Warwick Castle and go fishing in the river below, not then covered, as it is now, with a foot of detergent foam. When the place was alive with family friends and house guests, it was very different from the dead showpiece you can visit today. The ten-foot logs glowed in the enormous fireplace of the hall, which was as big as a church, and Maynard put the wind up me by giving me an oak-panelled bedroom complete with four-poster where, he said, I should hear the ghosts clanking their chains down the stone corridors (I didn't). Returning to London, he on his Indian motor bike, I driving one of the family cars, an old Belsize, we set our speedometers to compare distances to town. When mine read two miles more than his, he alleged it was because I had my arm round my passenger, the younger Selfridge daughter, and couldn't steer straight.

But at Easton Lodge, the other family seat in Essex (later handed over as a sort of country club to the Labour Party), an incident occurred which was decisive. I arrived before Maynard in the late afternoon and the Countess, doubtless to get me off her hands till dinner time, gave me a shotgun and packed me off into the park: 'Bring me back a pheasant for supper.' I knew nothing about shooting and had never handled a gun in my life, but when I saw a rabbit in a small clearing, I aimed and fired. The little animal, for it turned out to be a baby, rolled over and started screaming. I never knew that rabits could scream. It was horrible. It went on and on. What to do? Wring its neck? But I had no idea how to wring a rabbit's neck and I couldn't bear the idea of touching it even. So, in a panic, I came close to the poor writhing thing and blew it to pieces with the other barrel.

It was a bad beginning. I had only just left the house and felt I could not return at once, so I reloaded and wandered along through the park to pass the time. Suddenly a cock pheasant got up right in front of me. It lifted very steeply, as pheasants do. I wheeled round and when it was almost overhead, fired. The beautiful bird fell dead at my feet. I was amazed. It was a fluke shot of course. The bird lay there in the bracken, quite still. The wonderful plumage, the shining blues and reds in neck and head, a moment ago it had been alive, and now ... Very gingerly I picked it up by the legs and started to walk back. I hadn't gone 50 yards when a sudden final death spasm shook its body. I dropped it as if it had stung me and stood looking at it for a long time. What had I done? I was revolted at myself. This was what they called 'sport'. I have never handled a gun or shot an animal since.

3

Into the Air

I N August 1914, a dreadful paroxysm, like a sudden fit, burst over the Western world. A small bomb incident, which would hardly make the front pages of newspapers today, set off a holocaust exceeding anything then recorded in history. It seems, in retrospect, to have been a sort of mad death-wish disguised as patriotism. If ever the world was spoiling for a fight it was in 1914. The lemmings, when they are mysteriously urged to their mass migrations, do not presumably anticipate the death at the end of it. A ferment, a fever, comes over them and they go. So the youth of Europe, in a wave of exalted enthusiasm, flocked to their countries' aid to die by the hundred thousand in the mud of the Flanders trenches.

Was there something so dreadful about the pre-1914 world that whole populations should have felt impelled to destroy it? In retrospect it seems a sort of paradise, but I am biased no doubt by the unique position that Britain held at that time. Yet it seems there were standards of honour, even in the squalors of battle, that have been steadily eroded ever since. In order to maintain any form of society certain basic principles must not be violated. When they are, the doors are wide open to anarchy and chaos.

The war fever that swept Great Britain certainly reached us at Oundle. Maynard and I were both sixteen. We were both at the top of the school and felt it had nothing more to offer. Compared with the immense challenge that headlined the papers and particularly as the start was going badly for us, as it always seems to do, school life grew petty and irrelevant. We must 'join up'.

But how? That was the problem. It was Maynard who solved it by seeing an announcement that the Royal Flying Corps would accept candidates for pilot training at the age of seventeen. In six months' time we should reach our seventeenth birthdays. Besides, for years both of us had followed everything to do with the air with avid enthusiasm. Our pocket money went in buying copies of *Flight* and *The Aero*. We knew all the types by heart. We could reel off the details of the machines in which the Wright brothers, Farman, Bleriot and Cody had made their hops. We argued the merits of Lathem's Antoinette against the Demoiselle. We understood, in theory, the way a machine was flown, how the 'aviator' manipulated elevator, rudder and ailerons to control its course. But that we could ever actively participate in such things, that we ourselves could be pilots, that seemed beyond the wildest possibility. Pilots! There was magic in the very word! And now here was the War Office actually asking for young men who wanted to be pilots! It may have been the patriotic thing to do, but for my part this patriotism was heavily overlaid with a thrilling desire to fly.

Anyhow, to cut a long story short, for I have described it in some detail elsewhere (*Sagittarius Rising*, Peter Davies Ltd, 1936), by the summer of 1915 we were accepted as civilian trainees; by Christmas I had learned to fly and been commissioned in the Royal Flying Corps. Three months later I put up my 'wings'. I celebrated my eighteenth birthday in France and a fortnight later was doing patrols over the front line. It was a six-month metamorphosis that could only have taken place under the urgent pressures of war.

The pressures indeed were great, for the Army had persistently scoffed at the value of the air. It was a new dimension, a new weapon, beyond their imagination and curriculum. But once they had woken up to its possibilities, they set an expansion rate for the RFC that was almost impossible. Aeroplanes were suddenly seen to be needed for reconnaissance, for photography, for directing the fire of guns – even, daringly, for dropping bombs. The RFC mushroomed at an incredible rate. In such circumstances much was sketchily conceived, hurriedly improvised, ill prepared.

My own pilot training, which took place at Brooklands on an old kite called the Maurice Farman Longhorn (a contraption you must go to a museum today to see), lasted for one hour and twenty minutes. At the end of this time I was judged fit to fly alone! Today, if it took ten times as long, the pilot would be considered outstanding. Of course, speeds were slower. Sixty miles an hour was then something you could only achieve 'all out'. This meant that reactions did not have to be so fast; but on the other hand, the controls were often ill proportioned and inefficient. Design was in its infancy. Everything was experimental. It was still a matter of wonder that anything which was heavier than air could fly in it. Aeroplanes were a marvel and the young men who piloted them no less marvellous.

I had only done twenty hours' flying when I reached the Front. I had had no training in map reading, formation flying, Morse code or indeed any of the techniques which were required to make a pilot 'operational'. So when the Squadron Commander was instructed to send a pilot back to base at St Omer for instruction on Moranes (supposed to be death-traps), he naturally chose the latest arrival, who was most useless to him, and sent me.

The Morane Parasol was a French high-wing monoplane which gave pilot and observer an uninterrupted view below and was perfect for ground observation. At St Omer my instructor flipped me round a few times – there was no dual control – and then turned me loose on the thing, which handled completely differently from any aeroplane I had previously flown. However, when I got used to my 'death-trap', I began to like it and now think back on the Parasol with genuine affection, for, despite its flimsy undercarriage and rudimentary controls, it turned out to be snug, lively and extremely reliable. So, a fortnight later, I was posted to No. 3 Squadron, then preparing for the great summer offensive, the Battle of the Somme.

———

A squadron of the RFC in those days consisted of twelve aeroplanes divided into three flights with four pilots and sufficient personnel to keep the machines flying. Each pilot had his own 'private' rigger and fitter, who looked after his 'mount' in a very personal way, cleaning it, polishing it, cosseting it with enormous pride. To each pair of mechanics it was their pilot, their machine, and they kept it on the top line as proudly as a personal possession.

The rigger of the First World War was a very special craftsman. He was responsible for 'trueing up' the aeroplane. Entirely made of flimsy wooden members, braced with piano wire and turn-buckles and covered with linen, it did not long remain in shape, especially if subjected to rough weather, evasive action or the attentions of 'Archie' – the off-hand pet name given to anti-aircraft fire. So, on returning from patrol, the machine had to be set up in flying position, while the rigger went over it with a gauge and level, carefully adjusting a score of turnbuckles in fuselage and wings to reset the angle of incidence, the dihedral, the longerons, exactly according to the maker's drawings, copies of which were kept in the flight office.

The fitter's sole responsibility was the engines. Our engines, on Moranes, were 'rotaries', that is to say the crankshaft remained stationary while seven cylinders set on it radially, complete with valves, tappets and the entire crankcase, whirled round it 1200 times a minute. So skilled were our fitters that they could tune up these engines to tick over like a car. The Le Rhone, as our engine was called, in spite of its topsy-turvey design, was a masterly example of engineering workmanship and balance. Moreover, it was extremely reliable. Throughout long months of daily patrols under exacting conditions, mine never broke down once – except one morning at 500 feet over the front line when a connecting rod snapped owing to metal fatigue, a very rare failure which could not be ascribed to faulty design.

In addition to riggers and fitters, each squadron carried its ancillary trades. There were armourers to service our Lewis guns, which held fifty rounds of ammunition in circular drums, the wireless officer with his squad of men to look after our primitive transmitters and Morse keys and also to check the hundred-foot wire aerial on its drum which the observer lowered – and sometimes wound up in a hurry if we happened to be attacked, since the lead weight at the end of it had a habit of winding itself round the fuselage. Then there was the photographic section who strapped the big mahogany cameras with their leather concertinas on the outside of the cockpit and in times of stress developed and printed hundreds of glass plates (yes, glass plates) every day. Add the transport section and the squadron was complete.

It was a simple set-up – no parachutes, no oxygen, no ground control, no crash or fire wagons. We pilots simply pulled on our fur-lined thigh boots, buckled up our leather coats, slipped on our gloves, fastened our helmets, swung up into our bucket seats – and we were off to 'dice with death', as we called it. Though, to us, that was a joke, it happened to be true: the active service life of a pilot in 1916 averaged three weeks. In addition the squadron was completely mobile. Canvas hangars and stores stacked into solid-tyred three-tonners, ground-crews packed into Crossley tenders, while the CO, with his adjutant and sometimes a doctor or a padre, travelled in the luxury of an open touring car.

Our work was with the infantry and before 1 July we spent long hours in the air perfecting a system of communications with the battalions who would spearhead the attack in our sector. We could signal down to them by operating a large klaxon horn attached to our undercarriage or by dropping messages in small weighted bags with long streamers. They could signal back with a sort of spring-operated venetian blind laid on the ground, which opened white and closed black. The men also carried small red flares, like the Bengal Fires of our childhood, which they lit on demand and with these we hoped to be able to pinpoint where they had got to when the advance was under way. To do all this we had to be continually circling and patrolling up and down the line at a very low altitude – 500 feet was the maximum from which any accurate observation could be carried out. This put us right in the trajectories of the smaller field guns, which in the final 'hurricane' stages of the bombardment before zero hour, numbered thousands.

It was, I suppose, a dangerous job, but of this we were strangely unaware. The roar of the engine almost blotted out the roar of the guns. All enemy machine-gun fire aimed at us was inaudible. The shells whizzing past us, when they were close, threw the machine this way and that, in the air eddies they made in passing. But by the time we felt these eddies they had gone by and the danger was over. If they should happen to hit us – as occasionally happened – we should be instantaneously atomised and never know anything about it. So we were able to carry on as calmly as if we were on manoeuvres.

The rudimentary nature of this liaison with the infantry will be obvious. In action it broke down almost completely. Under fire the cumbersome ground signalling sheets were lost or forgotten, so we didn't know where to drop our messages; the red flares which would tell us where the front line was gave the same information to the enemy and the men were understandably reluctant to light them. Had the attack gone according to plan, all might have been well, but it didn't. We often had no idea where our front line was and to mistake one of our own men for a German could have brought down a heavy barrage on the troops we were there to help.

NONETHELESS on 1 July hopes ran high. The hurricane bombardment of the previous two days had covered the entire Fricourt Salient with a rug of dirty snow – the falling shells. Nothing, we thought, could stand against the weight of that. The morning itself was cloudless. From 8000 feet, above the hot brown summer haze, I had been detailed to observe the explosion of two huge mines laid deep under a strongpoint at La Boiselle, designed to blow up and demoralize the enemy so completely at this point that our chaps would just stroll through. Watch synchronized, I circled tensely, waiting. Precisely on time, the earth below me heaved and a monstrous column of earth rose into the air. Up and up it came like the silhouette of some gigantic cypress tree, followed a second later by its mate. The two columns, which rose to over 4000 feet, hung there for a moment as monumental and unbelievable as the Pillars of Hercules. Then came a gigantic roar, drowning the sound of the engine and the thundering guns. My machine was flung over like a scrap of paper in a gale. I righted it and watched while the debris slowly fell away to reveal, far below, the two white eyes of the craters.

It was a magnificent overture to failure. For, as the days dragged by and the breakthrough stalled, we (from the air) could not fail to see, before the Army dared admit it, that the desperate stalemate of trench warfare had not been broken.

Extraordinary how the earth is flattened out by an aerial view even from quite a low altitude. A man lying flat needs hardly a foot to give him cover but all such fine detail is completely lost from above. We were puzzled, baffled, we could not understand what the hold-ups were – even though we had made many trips up to the line on the ground to try to take in the viewpoint and eyeline of those supremely brave men who would be making the attack, the poor bloody infantry as they were justly and compassionately called.

The conditions in which they lived and fought were as primitive as those of Neanderthal man, while we, on leaving the lines, returned to the peace and security of our mess where the earth-shaking bombardments that deafened them only reached us like the distant roll of summer thunder. It gave me a guilty feeling.

In dribs and drabs throughout the long hot summer, while the abortive offensive ground slowly on to its autumn halt such a host of impressions were forced on me that I could not at the time either really admit them or indeed see them clearly. My published account of those days was itself written twenty years after the event and the narrative remained as vivid as if it had taken place the week before; but the tragedy of it did not really touch me.

To sweep up, day after day, into the magnificence of summer skies and see below the immense disc of landscape, patterned with river, wood and field, receding mile after mile to a misty rim, 60, 70 miles away, all this had nothing to do with the war. The price of the privilege was a duty to further the destruction and defeat of the enemy. It was a price I paid willingly, without giving it much thought. Being so detached, so aloof, above it all, I could not grasp the horror, the waste of it. In our flimsy contraptions of spruce and linen we sailed around like umpires, noting an advance here, a hold-up there, and reported back dispassionately, without any idea of what the moves had cost.

Yet this literally superior position did not fail to develop (almost subconsciously) a growing sense of compassion for the mad futility that men were giving their lives for. How could a hundred yards of captured trenches thrill us, when we could see, beyond it, objective after objective receding to infinity? Were we to inch ourselves to victory at this snail's pace? The first whisperings of this monumental paradox stole into my mind then. There was something wrong with it all. With every ounce of ability and ingenuity they could bring to bear, the cleverest fools in the world had locked a million men into a bloody stalemate. Whatever the rights or wrongs of their ideals, as an exercise it was a total failure. There, a few hundred feet below us, was the proof of it.

Today I am convinced it is the invincible stupidity of men that puts the whole future of mankind in doubt. We have become so absorbed in the techniques of destruction that the last twinges of conscience have been eclipsed. The lunatic-genius never asks, 'Why am I doing it?' but only 'How can I destroy more thoroughly, completely and economically?' The part of us that realizes that the whole thing is useless and is leading a mad world faster and faster towards immolation on the altar of its own imbecility, is swamped, gagged, hypnotized. Is there any force so powerful as human stupidity? I do not pretend that I found any answers to all this as a boy of eighteen, but the seeds of doubt were sown and firmly pressed into the roots of my consciousness at that time. Only later did they grow into the challenge: 'Is there any hope for us all? Is there any way through?'

So July melted into August and, as the offensive stalled, more and more efforts were made to break the deadlock. In September the first abortive attack with tanks was launched (too few, too soon). After it had failed, desperately, day by day, we flew lower and lower. Machine-guns punctured my tanks, bullets came up through the floor and out over my shoulder, wings were half shot away, engine failure brought me down in the front line. But, by some miracle, I survived the holocaust for six months – and if that doesn't make a man believe in his luck, nothing ever will!

So at last I was sent home and went, with a few hundred others, to Buckingham Palace to have a medal pinned on my chest by a grateful Sovereign. Then, my tour of duty over, I found myself posted to Upavon to join the Testing Squadron.

———

IT would be difficult for any aircraft designer today to imagine the rudimentary state of the art in 1917. The Testing Squadron existed for the purpose of trying out any new design of flying machine submitted to it. On the strength of the tests, recommendations were made as to its suitability for use in service. The result was that the sheds, first at Upavon and later at Martlesham Heath, were cluttered up with a weird collection of aeroplanes. Merely to look at some of them, even in those days, gave us the willies. All these machines had to be put through their paces and for anyone who, like myself, loved flying for flying's sake it was a rare opportunity. Totting up the score from my logbook after the war, I found I had flown fifty-three different types of aeroplane.

Already the leading designers were beginning to evolve a style and character of their own. You could recognize anything from the Sopwith or de Havilland stable by a certain 'rightness' in proportion, a certain assurance in the way they sat on the ground and still more, of course, in the way they handled in the air. Any student of early aircraft design cannot fail to see that the Pup, the 1½ Strutter, the Triplane and the Camel are all by the same hand.

Throughout the winter of 1916–17 I was kept busy at this fascinating work and it was a wrench when, with the coming of spring, I was posted to a new 'scout' squadron then forming at London Colney.

Things had not gone well for the Allies that winter. During the Somme battle we had held superiority in the air. The enemy never ventured over our side of the line and it was almost unheard of for any of our infantry liaison patrols to be attacked. But now the position had been reversed. The Germans had got ahead of us with a new breed of offensive fighter which completely outclassed and outpaced anything we produced. Our slow clumsy reconnaissance machines were being shot down by the dozen. Our squadrons of fighter scouts, DH2s and Sopwith Pups were no match at all for the new German Albatrosses and Halberstadts. The air war had entered a new phase. We had to meet this challenge, match the enemy and re-establish our air superiority, now seen to be vital to the winning of the war.

The French answer came with the appearance of the Nieuport and the Spad, both sturdy fighter scouts. The British bid was the Sopwith Triplane and the SE5. In 1916 we had only attacked or defended ourselves if the enemy interfered with our reconnaissance duties. Now that the single-seater fighter had been evolved, whose only duty was the destruction of another single-seater fighter, the war in the air had begun.

———

No. 56 Squadron, to which I was posted, equipped with the new SE5, was expressly formed to meet the German challenge. Our job was to outfly and outfight Baron von Richthofen and his squadron of Red Albatrosses, which had become the bogey of the Western Front. The pilots had all been hand-picked, the Squadron Commander was a go-getter, and three weeks later I had the personal honour of leading this crack squadron over the Channel to France. There we spent some days hurriedly incorporating operational modifications to windscreens and gun-sights, practising formation flying, discussing our fighting tactics, a subject about which only Albert Ball, our recognized 'ace' knew anything – and he was a typical loner, as ignorant as we were of the techniques of mass attack.

At last the squadron was operational and thirsting for action. It was decided to send us all out together for the first big attack. I do not think I can do better than to describe that May evening – the world's first 'pitched' air battle – in the words I used when writing *Sagittarius Rising*.

The squadron sets out eleven strong on the evening patrol. Eleven chocolate-coloured, lean, noisy bullets; lifting, swaying, turning, rising into formation – two fours and a three – circling and climbing away steadily towards the lines. They are off to deal with Richthofen and his circus of Red Albatrosses.

The May evening is heavy with threatening masses of cumulous cloud, majestic skyscapes, solid looking as snow mountains, fraught with caves and valleys, rifts and ravines – strange secret pathways in the chartless continents of the sky. Below the land becomes an ordnance map, dim green and yellow, and across it go the lines, drawn anyhow, as a child might scrawl with a double pencil. The grim dividing lines! From the air robbed of all significance.

Steadily the body of scouts rises higher and higher, threading its way between the cloud precipices. Sometimes below, the streets of a village, the corner of a wood, a few dark figures moving, glides into view, like a slide into a lantern and then is hidden again.

But the fighting pilot's eyes are not on the ground, but roving endlessly through the lower and higher reaches of the sky, peering anxiously through fur-lined goggles to spot those black slow-moving specks against land or cloud which mean full throttle, tense muscles, held breath and the headlong plunge with screaming wires – a Hun in the sights and the tracers flashing.

A red light curls up from the leader's cockpit and falls away. Action! He alters direction slightly and the patrol, shifting rudder and throttle, keep close like a pack of hounds on the scent. He has seen, and they see soon, six scouts 3000 feet below. Black crosses! It seems interminable till the eleven come within diving distance. The pilots nurse their engines, hard-minded and set, test their guns and watch their indicators. At last the leader sways sideways, as a signal for attack – and suddenly drops.

Machines fall scattering, the earth races up, the enemy patrol, startled, wheels and breaks. Each his man! The chocolate thunderbolts take sights, steady their screaming planes and fire. A burst, fifty rounds; it is over. They have overshot; the enemy, hit or missed, is lost for the moment. The pilot steadies his stampeding mount, pulls her with a firm hand, twisting his head left and right, trying to follow his man, to sight another, to back up a friend in danger, to note another in flames.

But the squadron had not seen, far off, approaching from the east, the rescue flight of Red Albatrosses, patrolling above the formation on which they had dived, to guard their tails and second them in the battle. These, seeing the maze of wheeling machines, plunge down to join them. The British scouts, engaging and disengaging, like flies circling in a summer room, soon find the newcomers upon them. Then, as if attracted by some mysterious power, as vultures will draw to a corpse in the desert, other flights of machines swoop down from the peaks of the cloud mountains. More enemy scouts and, by good fortune, a flight of naval triplanes.

But nevertheless the enemy, more than double in number, greater in power and fighting with skill and courage, gradually overpower the British, whose machines scatter, driven down beneath the scarlet German fighters.

It would be impossible to describe the action of such a battle. A pilot, in the second between his own engagements, might see a Hun diving vertically, an SE5 on his tail, on the tail of the SE another Hun and above him another British scout. These four, plunging headlong at 200 mph, guns cracking, tracers streaming, suddenly break up. The lowest Hun plunges flaming to his death, if death has not taken him already. His victor seems to stagger, suddenly pulls out in a great leap, as a trout leaps on the end of a line, and then turning over on his belly, swoops, spins in a dizzy falling spiral, with the earth to end it. The third German zooms, veering and the last of the meteoric quartet follows, bursting ... But such a glimpse, lasting perhaps ten seconds, is broken by the sharp rattle of another attack. Two machines approach head-on at full throttle, firing at each other, tracers whistling through each other's planes, each slipping sideways on his rudder to trick the other's gunfire. Who will hold longest? Two hundred yards, 100 yards, 50, and then, neither hit, with one accord they fling their machines sideways, bank and circle, each striving to bring his gun on to the other's tail, each glaring through goggle eyes, calculating, straining, wheeling, grim; bent only on death or dying.

But from above this strange tormented circling is seen by another Hun. He drops. His gun speaks. The British machine, distracted by the sudden unseen enemy, pulls up, takes a burst through engine, tank and body and falls, bottom uppermost, down through the clouds and the deep unending desolation of the twilight sky.

The game of noughts and crosses, starting at 15,000 feet above the clouds, drops in altitude, engagement by engagement. Friends and foe are scattered. A last SE, pressed by two Huns plunges and wheels, gun jammed, like a snipe over marshes, darts lower, finds refuge in ground mist and disappears.

Now lowering clouds darken the evening. Below flashes of gunfire stab the veil of the gathering dusk. The fight is over! The battlefield shows no sign. In the pellucid sky, serene cloud mountains mass and move unceasingly. Here, where guns rattled and death plucked the spirits of the valiant, this thing is now as if it had never been! The sky is busy with night, passive, superb, unheeding.

―――――――

OUT of the eleven who had set out that evening, only five of us returned. I remember the quiet in the mess as we waited for possible news that others were safe this side of the lines. Our greatest loss was Ball, who was posthumously awarded the VC. All of us were shattered in various ways by the encounter. We had learned a lot. We saw that the SE5, splendid tough little fighter that it was, could only hold its own with the enemy by its ma-noeuvrability. It could not outclimb or outpace the Halberstadt or the Pfalz – and its fire power was less efficient.

From then on we altered our tactics, going out in pairs or in flights. Never did the squadron go into action again as a single unit. We dared not, until later that year, risk dogfights, which could only succeed when we had superior, or at least equal, num-bers. With no communication between pilots, no intelligence as to where the enemy might be or of his strength, there was an element of pure luck in every patrol. Only by craftiness, good handling and daring did we manage to keep our end up and, in fact, do quite well.

After a month of this gruelling work a piece of astonishing luck came out way. A formation of Gothas, twenty strong, had had the audacity to fly over London and drop quite a load of bombs on that comfortable metropolis. This was totally unexpected and a piece of infernal cheek – particularly as there wasn't a single aircraft in the whole of England that could get anywhere near the raiders! The resultant outcry in Parliament and the press resulted in emergency orders to bring back a crack squadron to save dear old England! That meant us! The men were rushed back to the Calais boat, while we took off in the highest spirits and that same night were operational at Bekesbourne, just outside Canterbury. But alas, when after ten days of parties and dances the Hun had not reappeared, we sadly reversed the process and returned to Estrée-Blanche.

With a jammed gun on the dawn patrol a few weeks later, I was jumped by a Hun at 15,000 feet. It was always the most dangerous time. The rising sun blinded me and I never saw him till his tracers came spinning through my wings. There was suddenly a red-hot iron laid across my back. In a flash I went into a spin and then looked up to see a Pfalz scout zoom away, thinking he had got me. I knew the SE was no match for that machine. I didn't know how badly I was hit, nor how much damage had been done to the machine (actually only one frayed elevator control wire remained). So I let the spin ride for a couple of thousand feet, then pulled out and came home. Tentatively I worked my shoulder. My shirt was sticky with blood, but it didn't seem to be much.

The doctor found a six-inch graze across the small of my back and showed it me in a hand mirror. 'You've got a cushy one,' he said. A lucky one would have been more like it. I had been leaning forward in the cockpit, crouched, struggling with the jammed gun (which was our bugbear with the Vickers). Had I been sitting upright that shot would have gone right through my heart. Well, a miss is as good as a mile ... A week later I was back in England.

That one summer daylight raid had panicked London. Quite complicated counter-measures for its defence were immediately set up. Home defence squadrons were moved in just outside the suburbs. Beyond them was a ring of kite balloons (quite useless) and beyond this again another ring of aircraft patrols. A rudimentary warning system of skywatches on the coast, out in the North Sea and (it was said) over in Holland, would give notice of any attack. A warm reception had been arranged for our friend the enemy – but the guest didn't turn up. It wasn't till August that he sneaked in – and then it was at night.

This, once again, caught us off guard. Stationed at Hainault Farm, just beyond Ilford, we were flying Camels – the latest light single-seater fighter – but nobody would have dared to dream of flying one at night. Night flying, in fact, was at that time almost unheard of. Practically nobody had done it; certainly nobody had been trained for it. The machines had no dashboard lights or luminous dials. The only method of landing was along a line of open tins, filled with rags and paraffin and lit — the flarepath, as it was called. It simply wasn't on but ... here were these bastards droning over Margate — one step ahead of us. As usual.

————

IT was a full August harvest moon that night. I happened to be on duty. Nobody, as far as I remember, told us to get into the air, for to HQ the thing was as unexpected as it was to us. But, after all, to be in the air was our job, no question. We had to decide at once. They certainly wouldn't hang about for us. We'd better have a go. But I felt pretty windy about it. I'd never flown at night. How could anybody know where they were when they couldn't see anything? However, scrounging a torch to flash on the instruments, I climbed into my Camel and taxied off down the flarepath nervously, full of questions. There would be no horizon, no landmarks, nothing to tell you if you were climbing or diving. How would you know what your speed was, your revs, your oil pressure, your course? It was just asking for it. I turned into wind with that strange fatalism pilots know, opened up and took off.

It was marvellous! A new magical world had opened beneath me. Every roof glinted in the moonlight. A few lights winked. The Thames estuary was a silver ribbon. The white plume of a railway engine floated over a wood. The thin pencils of searchlight beams were probing the sky. Keyed up to the limit of tension, I suddenly relaxed into this dream landscape. Far below I could see the river snaking into London. The flarepath sparkled like a golden brooch. Never shall I forget that wonder of that first night flight.

But finding the enemy — that was another matter. Not on this, nor on any other of the dozens of patrols I flew all through that winter and next spring, did I see an enemy aeroplane. But the pattern had changed overnight. From then on all home defence squadrons became night-flying units. It was not only London that began to be attacked. Night bombing soon spread to targets behind the lines in France. Enemy aircraft were already blowing up railway stations and fuel dumps and night-fighter squadrons were quickly formed to do what they could (and it wasn't much) to intercept them. It was, in fact, a pretty hopeless job and remained so, even when the technique of detection had been enormously refined. Even by the end of the Second World War, twenty-five years later, the problem of air-to-air detection had not been completely solved.

So, in October 1918, I went overseas for the third time, leading 152 Squadron on night-fighter Camels. We never really settled down to operations before the Armistice. No words can convey the release of spirit I felt then. The world was at peace again and I was twenty years old.

4

Back to the Middle Ages

WHILE the war lasted, it seemed it would never end. Then, suddenly, the mortal struggle which had completely filled my days was over. There before me, like a clean sheet of paper, lay my life. What would be written on it?

Within a fortnight of being demobilized, a lucky introduction placed me on the staff of Vickers Ltd. My work was to help to plan commercial air services in various parts of the world. Nobody had ever run such services and there were no aircraft suitable for them. So in 1919 this was plainly a non-starter. Then, with the help of two other pilots and three AVRO 504Ks adapted to take two passengers, we set up a small 'circus' and toured England offering the great British public joyrides at 10 shillings a time! As a piece of propaganda, to make people air-minded, it certainly helped; as a money-making venture it remained in the red.

But for me it had one enormous asset – I had an aeroplane for weekends. My destination was always one of two great country houses in the south of England, either Robert Mond's huge property near Sevenoaks or Melchett, the even more beautiful place belonging to Sir Alfred Mond, his brother.

The reason for these trips was not to interest the founders of ICI in the prospects of civil aviation; it was simply that for the first time in my life I had fallen deeply in love, and Mary, the second daughter of Sir Alfred, was the object of my affections.

Was there ever a year like 1919? For what seemed an eternity, our world had been bent solely on destruction. The nation had spent itself to the verge of bankruptcy. The casualties had run into millions. It was no time for rejoicing, yet, because at least it was over, a wave of light-hearted joy swept the country and we, the fortunate who came through, felt we had earned it.

Only this I think can explain the generosity and hospitality with which I was received into a world of wealth and luxury where I had no place at all. The life in these big houses, with their gold dinner services, the weekend house parties, the gaiety of many young people, the private performances of Russian ballet, the glorious summer, the music, the dancing on the moonlit turf, all this sparkling in the joy of youth, is something that can never come again. Into it all I swept down out of the skies to land in the nearest field. It was all wildly, impossibly romantic. But when at summer's end Mary allowed me to ask her parents for her hand they snapped me out of the idyll in a few sharp bitter minutes. I was made to feel I was just a penniless adventurer trying to marry money. (It was something that had never entered my head. I fully intended to make my own in life.) Violet, Lady Mond, made it quite clear that, while she was glad to entertain her children's friends and allow them to enjoy company of their own age, marriage was a different matter. She had no intention of letting her daughter trip up the aisle with a feckless young pilot. So the door of the big town house was firmly closed in my face and poor, sweet, lovely Mary, who never really had her feet on the ground, was later married off to a title. It proved disastrous. Finally free of that, she seemed somehow to have lost her bearings. A second adoring husband could not help; like some maimed bird, she trailed about forlorn to die before she was forty.

At twenty-one this was a tragedy for me. I felt my world had come to an end, but I was mercifully roused out of it by the prospect of an adventure so exciting, so wildly improbable, that it seemed the start of a new life. I was to go to Peking and teach the Chinese to fly!

———

IT is difficult for anyone today to think of China as the romantic place it seemed (and was) in 1920. Dragons, lacquer and jade, pale inscrutable faces, age-old palaces, the Forbidden City, the Temple of Heaven, the Mysterious East, this was the dream and it was very nearly true. No radio links and air services had exploded the mystery of faraway. Now you can reach the antipodes in the time it then took to travel to Venice by train. Tourism was a word that had not been invented. A few daring travellers, at the lowest called visitors, ventured into these remote parts. To go to live in China for a couple of years and to be paid for doing so, this was better than any fairy tale.

To me who had never been south of Amiens in my young life, sunset in Paris, the train journey through the Alps, the midnight arrival in Venice, the gondola through the black canals, this was only the first course in a feast of impressions. I was drunk with it. Even the heat of the Red Sea and the nine-day crossing of the Indian Ocean was rewarded, when we docked at Colombo, by the first sights and smells of the East, the rickshaws, the betel juice, the curry, the palms. Then it was the little country port of Penang, houses on stilts, the Malay jungle, rubber plantations and the first fireflies, sweaty Singapore and the basket trick performed on the pavement, Hong Kong bright with fairy lights for the arrival of the Prince of Wales, Shanghai with its teeming world of junks, dusty Tientsin, and finally, after six weeks, the great walls of the city of Peking towering into the night. Who could ask more of life?

Though we did not know it, while we were en route difficulties had arisen over some of the clauses in the Vickers contract with the Chinese government. The sixty AVRO 504Ks and the forty Vimy ten-seater passenger carriers (which were to inaugurate the Peking–Shanghai air service) were held up until these difficulties had been resolved. In effect, though we arrived in Peking in April 1920, no aircraft were delivered there till December. So we were at large in one of the most extraordinary capitals in the world, with nothing to do, for nine months!

———

SOME unknown Chinese, lost in the mists of legend, discovered that a piece of iron ore when suspended in a thread would always settle pointing in the same direction. It was an extraordinary and inexplicable mystery and must have some deep meaning. Even a caddy on the golf course would shout, when you had lost your ball, 'To the east! The east! A little to the north! Now a step to the west!' The compass became an integral part of Chinese life. Whole cities were laid out according to its command. Peking itself was set with its axis pointing precisely to the magnetic north and all its avenues, streets and lanes ran north/south or east/west as precisely as any grid city of today. They had, in addition, with the help of astronomers and astrologers, decided that one particular line of longitude was paramount and this became the north–south axis of their capital. With accurate precision they laid out the whole city, with its towering four square walls, its nine gates, its outer and inner courts and palaces, so that if all the openings on this axis were thrown wide, you could see, in one long uninterrupted vista, right through to the centre, where the Emperor on his lacquer throne sat like a god in the navel of the world.

But in addition to this, the capital was also laid out in obedience to a deeper symbol – that worlds lie within each other. Those nests of boxes, painted different colours, each opening to reveal another smaller one within, which had so intrigued me in childhood, were incorporated into the building of the capital. First there were the outer walls of the city itself. Then, within, were the walls of the Imperial City, where dwelt princes, courtiers, generals, administrators. Within these more private precincts lay the third and final enclosure, the Forbidden City, the dwelling of the Son of Heaven himself, aloof, supreme, unapproachable.

It was a rigid and symmetrical formula, but within it had arisen, through the centuries, the flowering of perhaps the most delicate and exquisite culture the world has ever seen. The palaces themselves, even the Throne Room of the Emperor, were, by Western standards, insignificant. But their architects knew how to use emptiness, the spacing and placing of gates and bridges, the subtle slight difference in height, so skilfully that they combined to give a sense of austere magnificence unequalled by any capital in the world. In comparison, our defiant castles and didactic cathedrals seemed the insistence of a civilization with a deep-seated inferiority complex. No need to shout about your strength or your faith when you know both to be supreme, unquestionable.

What an opportunity to be turned loose in all this with the greedy appetite of twenty-two! To be free to wander in a city still virtually in the Middle Ages, where the great fifty-foot gates were closed every evening at nine o'clock, where there was no public transport beyond millions of rickshaws, where the solid Peking carts with their mettlesome little Mongol ponies carried all loads that did not sway along on the backs of trains of dromedaries tied nose to tail. The broad avenues, the tiny *hutungs* (lanes) were teeming with life. Enormous wheelbarrows distributed water or coal. Peripatetic barbers shaved your hair (or plaited your pigtail) on your own doorstep. Even the wheeling flocks of pigeons made music with flutes tied to their backs.

Outside the gates lay the huge straw-matted theatres, the warren of lanes where the gold and copper beaters worked, where the lanterns and ornaments of kingfisher feathers were made, where the antiques worth pounds today could be bought for a few pence, where the endless fairs, markets, tea shops and temples jostled each other as closely as the thousands of cheerful laughing people, among whom the lacquered, high-born Manchu ladies with their tall head-dresses, impassive expressions on their rouged cheeks, walked stiffly and slowly, fingering their beads.

ONLY the foreign community stuffed into the walled enclave of the Legation Quarter seemed impervious to the magic of the last days of a civilization which in a few years would dissolve for ever. With their ridiculous petty protocol, their bridge and tennis parties, their polo and racecourse, their main preoccupation seemed to be a conspiracy to pretend that China did not exist. Small wonder if to the Chinese the Westerners were known as 'foreign devils'.

But among them, of course, were a few who had refused to put on such blinkers and with them I began an exploration of a civilization so utterly different from our own, so deeply rooted in its past, so rich in every way, that wherever you touched it – from carved bead to lacquer screen, from gold-tiled roof to painted scroll – the senses seemed always surprised, stimulated, and rested on everything with a sort of open-mouthed content.

There is no better way to get the 'taste' of a place than to set up house in it. I was too young to know this then, but some instinct prompted me to leave the comfortable hotel in which we stayed and find myself a small Chinese house, tucked away beyond the HaTaMen, in the eastern corner of the city. It was my first house and to it I owe the smattering of coolie Chinese I managed to acquire, but more, the delight of almost daily sorties into the rabbit warren of teeming *hutungs* which hung like a swarm of bees below the South Gate of the city.

In those days the old tradition of trades being compact communities (like guilds) had not died out, so you would find all the lantern makers in Lantern Street, all the cabinet makers in Furniture Street, the workers in jade, silver, embroidery or kingfisher feather all cheek by jowl in their respective quarters. So I haggled for blackwood chairs and tables, bargained for crockery and cooking pots, visited the market fairs, the night market, the flea market, the thieves' market, picking up all manner of things, from silk pictures to lumps of amber, from coromandel panels to Ming bowls, from bits of bronze to embroidered coats – and despising much that I would be proud to own today. Sometimes I did not even have to leave home. Jo, my 'boy', would introduce a smiling, bowing Chinese with a huge bundle over his shoulder, wrapped in blue cloth. Carefully kneeling on the ground, he would undo it, spreading out his wares for me to see and handing up those wonderful boxes (works of art in themselves) which, when I slid open the cover, disclosed a cloisonné bowl or a Kangshi cup, carefully embedded in a silk-lined cut-out specially designed to hold it. Then I would sit for an hour through the leisurely ceremony of admiring ostentatiously the things I did not want and at the last moment casually enquiring the price of the worthless bit I had set my heart on. It was a highly civilized ritual, both seller and buyer handling each curio with reverence and affection, turning them, holding them up to the light, sucking the teeth with pleasure, sighing at the thought of selling (or acquiring) them. At last the deal would be concluded, a great wrapping up of the bundle would begin and the smiling, inscrutable little man, for whom I had already begun to have an affection because he loved what he sold as much as I did, would withdraw. When at last all was done, I stood looking out over the tiny courtyard, hearing Jo, the coolie, the cook and the 'motorman' chattering cheerfully as they turned in to sleep together on the stone kang of the gatehouse – a very proud and contented householder, at the age of twenty-two.

I have been writing, of course, of the picturesque and romantic side of Chinese civilization as I saw it then. The tap-tap-tap of the nightwatchman's pieces of wood, which he struck together on his rounds, not to catch the thieves but to drive them away; the ceremonial procession, preceded by a brass band, of the fire brigade to a fire, which ensured that it would be well alight before they got there; the trotting convoy of open carts, each with a kneeling malefactor in it, hands bound behind his back, going, cheerful and laughing, to the public execution grounds to have his head struck off by a huge two-handed sword. There were, I am sure, widespread social injustices, poverty, corruption and cruelty, almost no hygiene or social services and practically no effective government, but it was, after all, the end of a splendid epoch, an epoch in which no idea of equality had ever existed, where the rich were rich and the poor were poor, where the lowest rung on the social ladder was occupied not by the beggar, but by the soldier. Now, half a century later, it remains an open question whether the revolt against inequality has produced a happier society. The Chinese 'man in the street' of 1920 seemed neither unhappy nor dissatisfied with his lot. His counterpart all over the world today seems to have his happiness eaten away by greed, envy and malice – as if life always owes him more. Neither our aims nor our methods in war or peace give the desired result. There is something very wrong somewhere.

The China that I knew, still half-buried in the Middle Ages, has disappeared today as if it had never been. In its place has emerged the greatest bid to change the structure and direction of society the world has ever seen. It appears to be succeeding and sends a shudder down the spine of the West because its aim of collective responsibility and collective effort are directly opposed to the personality cult and the worship of individual success which are the goals – and the cul-de-sac – of the West. China has millenia of civilized life behind her, splendid traditions and the most delicate, refined culture the world has ever seen, so when the excesses of violent effort required to effect such a radical change have slowed up and mellowed, there may well emerge a new mould for the shape of life to come. After all, a highly sophisticated, refined society had existed in China for centuries when Russia was no more than a barbaric horde of nomadic tribes. Half a century of scientific modernization cannot replace that.

Had I to choose to be overrun by one or the other, I would choose China every time. Wise, orderly government is deep-seated in the national character, part of their heredity, of their genes. I need hardly add that all these sombre reflections didn't bother me in the marvellous carefree days when I lived there. But the material for these reflections had been given. Some saner approach, some better solution than the carnage of the war from which I had just emerged, must exist – if only men could find it.

———

ALTHOUGH Peking itself was an endless treasure house for exploration and delight, there were other wonders, harder to reach, which called us out beyond its walls. The city itself stands on a flat alluvial plain, but on the horizon lie the Western Hills, distant only a score of miles from the capital, but (in those days) inaccessible except to a carefully planned expedition. Here, during the last renaissance of Chinese civilization in the early eighteenth century, the Emperors Chien Lung and Kang'hsi had encouraged the building of temples and monasteries, so that the folds of hills were richly studded with these innumerable jewels (there were said to be over four thousand of them), places for retreat, refuge and contemplation.

Very few people, either Chinese or foreign, bothered to visit these sanctuaries, but hearing of one temple, said to be the last where the Buddhist monastic way of life was still fully observed, I eagerly accepted an invitation to join a party arranged to pay it a visit. To try to give some of the flavour of those halcyon days, I will describe that weekend in some detail.

There were six of us. Two other men, Chinese-speaking members of the British Legation, had rustled up three nice hygienic nurses from the American Hospital and the six of us left, with our 'boys' and baggage, in an open coal truck on the railway line which dumped us literally in the middle of nowhere, five hours on foot from the temple.

As soon as they saw us, the local members of the Transport and General Workers' Union, in the form of the 'donkey boys', descended on us volubly and violently demanded our custom. It took half an hour to sort out the jostling mêlée and get our caravan loaded. This was because we travelled, as was then the custom, in style. Style meant that not only our beds and bedding and personal clothes had to be loaded, but food, linen, glass, silver and a wood-burning stove complete with oven. Finally twenty-five minute donkeys were festooned with all this, while six large mokes were mounts for us. So we set off in a long file, bells on the donkeys' delicate hooves jingling at every step, the 'donkey boys' calling to their beasts, 'Prrr-up, prrr-up', up the first slope of the uplands towards the hills.

It was a glorious autumn afternoon. Now, after the summer rains were over, the country had reverted to its tawny emptiness. The scale was vast. Over the plain, the gatehouses of Peking looked insignificant on the horizon. Before us the folds of the hills rose cool, mysterious and inviting. The track wound upwards towards a distant landmark, a group of tombs beneath a grove of white pines whose dark foliage stood out clearly in the immense dry landscape.

Here, after two hours, we stopped, sweating and glad to rest. We had walked most of the distance, the donkey saddles having played hell with our backsides. As if by magic the servants produced tiny cups of boiling green tea – the coolest of all drinks, they said, for hot weather. We sat down in the shade of the trees.

What a place it was! The head of some family, centuries ago, had planted the trees and built the enclosing wall. There stood his tomb, like a large stone port decanter, dominating all the others. The site was perfect, lonely and peaceful, looking out over the plain. Under the enormous trees the groups of blue-coated 'donkey boys' squatted with their patient little beasts. Everything seemd extraordinarily still. Nobody would ever molest or move these tombs. Respect for ancestors was axiomatic in Chinese custom and had been for thousands of years. Didn't we know? Our attempt to enlarge our future aerodrome had been thwarted by a group of tombs in the centre of it. 'You must move the aerodrome, not the tombs.'

Soon we were on our way again. The path now entered a deep ravine. Great boulders lay along the dry river-bed, huts clung to almost precipitous slopes, gnarled trees twisted out of crevices, exactly like the silken scrolls of Chinese landscapes I had so often seen and never believed to be true. Now the going got steeper and rougher. The path left the valley and began to mount. A stone *pailou* (a sort of ceremonial archway) marked the entrance to a tiny hamlet. Cobbled, smelly and very poor, the inhabitants looked at us with their impassive eyes, without a trace of interest. Beyond this it was a scramble, 'boys' calling to their beasts, all of us breathing heavily, clambering up and up, towards some goal, felt to be close above now, but still quite unseen. The boom of a deep bell rang out above our heads, the path turned to steps, and then suddenly, in the dusk, we were there on the small level place before the entrance gate of the temple. It looked out over mile after mile of interlocked hills. An enormous bronze bell suspended under its *tingah*, four columns and curling roof, was rung by swinging a tree-trunk, hung on chains, against it. While the servants unloaded the gear – for no beast must defile the sanctuary – we sounded the bell and stood listening to the echoes. We had arrived at Che Tai Ssu – the Temple of the Terrace of Ordainment.

———

ALTHOUGH it is more than seventy years since I stepped through that gateway, I still retain a living impression of the aura of the place. Words cannot convey the subtle amalgam of such experiences. So I will simply say it was evening after a hot day and the cool air carried long draughts of resin from the pines. The place was not just a temple, but a complex of many temples, set one above the other, studding the steep hillside. We walked, silent with wonder, through twilight courtyards, up flights of steps where carved white marble balustrades glowed luminous in the dying light. Overhead there was always the shadow of trees, and the stooping eaves of temple roofs listened, attentive to our passing. At last we emerged on to the main terrace.

How do places become 'holy'? It does not just lie in what we call the beauty of their setting, nor in those constructions that men erect in which to observe certain rituals sacred to them. Rather it would seem as if each pilgrim carried, almost unbeknown to himself, an emanation of devotion and love that he leaves, like a fine patina embedded into the very surface of the place and that this strange encrustation of longing and hope, clinging to wall and column and stone, reflects some subtle vibration calling to those who follow. Thus, over the years, through countless acts of piety, a sort of spiritual perfume grows and pervades the air. Like bees we bring our honey to be ripened in the hive and the scent of it calls the latest comer home.

Every Buddhist temple has quarters set aside for travellers and guests. Here it was a spacious courtyard adjacent to the central shrine where a towering Buddha, smiling and contemplative beneath the painted rafters, sat on his lotus seat. On every petal tip a minute reflected image of himself smiled back to him above. But these and other treasures we would save till morning. With speed and dexterity the servants unpacked. The girls took one room, we another, and within an hour we dined by candlelight. From some shrine lower down, the strange rhythms of beating drums carried to us on waves of sound, rising and falling on the still evening air. Said Jo, my 'boy', when I asked him what it was, 'Master, they are driving the devils out of the temple.'

But later, as we sat relaxed and drugged by the magic of the place, we saw a number of shadows moving towards the terrace that fronted the main building. In the centre of this stood a bronze vessel, low, square, as big as a bath. A priest appeared in an orange robe and started scattering gold and white discs, paper prayers, into the bronze. Two other assistants seemed to be tying something to the trees. These three carried lighted tapers, flickering as they moved, and lit the faces of what we now saw to be a simple family come to offer prayers for their departed father. They were ranged before the cauldron into which the priest now dipped his light, setting fire to the paper prayers. At the same moment the other two put their tapers to the trees. Suddenly the peace of the place was shattered by a train of sputtering explosions. The skeins of crackers tied to the trees were going off like machine guns. The prayers rose flaming into the air, the family fell before them prostrating themselves. The temple eaves glowed vermilion and green. Blue smoke curled up into the trees, the deafening explosions calling the attention of the Lord Buddha to the fact that prayers were coming up. Impossible that the Master of the Universe could sleep through that racket! No further need to worry! The whole ceremony, so dramatic, simple and festive, lit the gloom like a burning jewel. Then darkness again and the shadowy figures filing away into the night.

I cannot end this chapter without speaking of two other scenes which perhaps will never be seen on earth again. It was next morning when the *Hoshang* (Abbot) visited us. An old man, very tall, in an orange robe reaching to his feet, he greeted us with elaborate politeness, offering his gift, a small tin of lychees made in Japan. With him came a tiny smiling bearded man in a deep green robe. Looking down on his bald cranium I saw on it nine little scars arranged in a square. How, I asked, had he come by them? His eyes twinkled. 'Ah!' he said, 'It is a penance, a severe penance, which it was necessary to undergo. . .' and he seemed to reflect for a moment. 'Nine small cones of sulphur are affixed to the head. Then they are lit. They smoulder for a long time. It is ten days before they are quite burned out. It is a powerful reminder . . .'

The Temple of the Terrace of Ordainment was an accurate description of the function of the Che Tai Ssu. Here it was that the novices completed their training and devotions before being permitted to wear the yellow robe of full priesthood. About a hundred of them were doing so when we were there.

We realized this next morning when the scent of incense and the sound of many voices chanting a short mantra reached us from a courtyard below. We went down to see a crocodile of grey-robed figures emerging from the building and winding slowly forward as they traversed the stone terrace before the temple, from side to side. The short phrase of the prayer stabbed the sunlight and the faces looked pale, trance-like. We were witnessing a scene of mass hypnosis. A bowl of watery soup with balls of dough in it had been their diet and four hours' sleep their rest for six weeks. The 'thickness' of their bodily appetites had been thinned down to transparency under their will, so that another part of them, hidden, difficult to find, might peer through.

Having reached the front of the terrace, the file turned back on itself, still chanting the monotonous phrase, and at last the whole company re-entered the temple. Suddenly the voices stopped. A high-pitched bell rang three times. Then a strange sound – the rustle and thud of a hundred bodies falling flat on their faces before the Buddha. Three times this prostration was repeated. Then it was over. Totally withdrawn, with mask-like faces, hands crossed, hidden in their sleeves, they filed away. Not a word was spoken.

At the time I remember feelings of repugnance and perplexity that these men and women (for there were women among them indistinguishable in face and clothing from the men) should submit themselves to such an austere discipline. Was this the way to 'find God?' It was certainly not my way. But now I see it a little more clearly.

There is always a price to be paid. Something has to be given up, suffered, accepted, before there can be any freedom from the tyranny of appetite. If such freedom (the only freedom) is the goal, then each may choose the way to it that suits him best. But there are no short cuts. You cannot have something for nothing.

We stayed in the temple three days. Aesthetically it was a treasure house. Every building, every courtyard, every altar, every bronze, seemed to be so perfectly set in its function or its frame that the whole achieved a chord of harmony which rings clear for me, even today. If you could match this outer repose and peace with such an inner state you would have learned all there is to be learned. Nothing demanded or insisted, but everything called or pointed, clinging to the wayfarer, begging him to remember: there is something to be learned here. Enquire within.

5

Straight and Level

O NE early morning on the voyage out to China there was a
tap on the wall above my head. It came from the cabin next
door occupied by a young woman on her way to join her husband
in Japan. She had been complaining of headaches for some days;
but when I went in to see if I could be of any help, it transpired
that the seat of her trouble was not in the head, but more, as one
might say, fundamental. For this, fortunately, I had a remedy on
me which afforded instant relief; but it did not last. She had almost
daily relapses and it turned out to be necessary to continue the
treatment for the rest of the voyage – which, of course, I was only
too glad to do.

In Peking there were not half a dozen unattached young
women in the whole foreign contingent, but one or two charitable
matrons, overcome with pity for what may be described as a hard
case, took the considerable risk of paying me occasional visits. The
palliative became an irritant, for at twenty-two I had a healthy
appetite. In a word sex had become – and continued for the next
forty years to be – a problem.

In those days I had, I suppose, a passable imitation of good
looks. Imitation because, feature by feature, it was nothing to
write home about; but the whole, set off by my height and my
exuberant high spirits and vitality, conspired to make the façade
appear a good deal better than it really was.

It was the vitality that saved me – then and later. A wide range
of interests and the acquisition of many different skills have
always been an irresistible magnet to me. The obverse of this –
superficiality and a great difficulty in getting to the bottom of
anything – goes with it. Sex, mercifully, has always remained on
the margins. If these at times threatened the main text, some sort

of inbuilt brake corrected the danger. The margins were necessary to the balance of the page; but finally they were no more than a place left open for private arabesques and embroidery, certainly not matters to parade or boast of, like Don Juan with his farcical '*mille tre*'.

AFTER I had been in Peking six months I was introduced to a remarkable Russian family, who had recently arrived there. The father, General Horvath, had been at the time of the Revolution (only four years previously), Plenipotentiary for the Tsar throughout the Far East and Director of the Chinese Eastern Railway.

In addition, in his own right, he had vast estates in Yalta in Central Russia and Harbin. Between these, the family travelled everywhere in their own private train and maintained a large retinue of bailiffs, servants and bodyguards. Shorn of his position and all his wealth and property by the Bolsheviks, the General had retreated first to Harbin and then, when his life and family were threatened, escaped over the border to China – just in time! The patriarchal family, with its attendant relatives and hangers-on, settled in the Austrian legation (then vacant as a result of the war), having still sufficient resources to live, for the moment, on the scale to which they had been accustomed.

The six children, three daughters, aged nineteen, eighteen and seventeen, and three sons, aged sixteen, fifteen and fourteen, were devoted to their mother, who came of the Benois family and had inherited a pleasant amateur talent for the piano and for painting in watercolours. While the General looked like Moses, with his white beard and imposing presence, his wife was really the inspiration of the family and managed to hold it together through the shattering experiences they had undergone.

It happened that before leaving England I had studied singing as a pupil of Vladimir Rosing, a dramatic tenor, whose interpretation of Russian music was unique. I have never heard a singer quite like him and he and his circle introduced me to the world of Russian music, then comparatively new on the London scene. The vibrant 'glare' of Rimsky-Korsakov, the nostalgia of Moussorgsky and Borodin, the excitement and the shock of Stravinsky, all this came out of a culture that made music quite different from any I had every heard. I liked it very much, so at once felt in sympathy with my new Russian friends. There was always music in their house, somebody was always trying over a song, or learning an accompaniment, and, while none of the children or their mother could give a performance, their love of music, the informality of their life, with the samovar centring the table and never less than twenty people at any meal, all epitomized to me the Russian 'soul' and I became a daily visitor.

MEANWHILE the Vickers contract with the Peking government had never really got off the ground. There had been nine months' delay before the first machines arrived, and when they did and our team of air-mechanics (all hand-picked from the best men with me in the war) had erected them, great obstacles arose in the the training programme.

What sort of selection board the Chinese had set up to pick our first batch of pupils I never knew. When I first saw them dressed in long black silk robes that reached down to the ground, small black satin hats with red buttons at the crown on their heads, their clasped hands quite hidden in their sleeves, I could hardly believe my eyes. They bowed to us and smiled. They smiled and bowed again. They were exceedingly respectful, they had beautiful manners; but somehow I couldn't see them doing aerobatics. However, perhaps I was wrong. We should have to wait to feel their touch on the controls.

The art of flying is basically to acquire an innate sense of three-dimensional balance in space. The pupil has to learn to feel, almost without knowing it, the attitude of his aeroplane to the horizon. Often this sense can be developed; but if it cannot that man will never make a pilot. Judgement and experience is, of course, required to put a machine down and take it off; but, given the basic endowment of balance, all this can be acquired. The instructor's job is to demonstrate this correct balance, first by flying 'straight and level', later in turns and more delicate manoeuvres. Though a good instructor and his pupil don't need to say much to each other, what they do say is essential; training cannot proceed without it. Imagine then the predicament of an instructor aloft with a pupil with whom he cannot communicate at all! After a couple of circuits to let the chap get the feel of the machine and having, of course, thoroughly primed him beforehand through an interpreter of exactly what I was going to do, I would tentatively begin to take my hand off the stick to see if he was 'with me'. A moment later the nose would shoot up, the wing would drop and the panicky pupil, terrified at what was happening, would 'freeze' on to the controls, jamming his feet on the rudder. The more I shouted at him '*Dung-y-dun*', which literally translated means 'Wait one wait', or, more colloquially, 'For Christ's sake, man, let go, can't you?', the tighter his grip would become. Then a sort of tug-of-war would ensue, after which, if I could win it – and that often seemed doubtful – I would return to terra firma as quickly as I could, call the interpreter and give him my comments on the pupil in somewhat short-tempered phrases. As the interpreter himself had no idea about flying and as the words he had to use were, until then, non-existent in the Chinese language, heaven knows what the wretched pupil was told. Finally the interpreter would smile apologetically and sum up. 'He is very sorry, sir, and next time he will try to do better.'

'If he does any better than that, we shall both be dead!'

Training was a slow business. Out of our first batch, only one, little Mr Ma, emerged as a natural pilot. He was going to be very good; but alas, sent up by some local war lord a year later on a machine he had never flown (a Handley Page), he crashed and was burnt to death.

The whole object of all this training was, of course, to produce Chinese pilots to inaugurate the first air service from Peking to Shanghai. Vickers had supplied Vimys for this service in the spring, but we did not take it seriously, first because there were no trained Chinese pilots, no aerodromes, no ground staff, no refuelling arrangements, in fact no organization whatever, and finally because the distance was 800 miles, far beyond the range of the Vimy's tanks.

However, right in the middle of the summer, when the temperature was sitting at 105 °F, and just a week before the rains – which in north China can be predicted with astonishng accuracy – some shift in the political chess-board, some pressure, some threat – we never knew what – resulted in an order to start the service immediately. After banquets and speeches and festooning the aerodrome with flags, posing as a Chinese pilot, I took off with two mechanics as passengers and half a pound of mail. With this heavy load, I got as far as Tsinanfou, 200 miles away. That night the rains came — and when it rains in north China, it rains. Next day the machine was down to its axles in mud and the whole project was summarily abandoned. But it had been started, that was the thing. Nobody would enquire whether it had continued.

———

I cannot leave those far-off days without a backward glance over the great city of Peking as it looked then to the very few of us fortunate enough to see it from the air. In the flat, tawny landscape it stood within its great walls — 60 feet high and broad enough for twenty men to walk abreast — cut out of the surrounding emptiness as sharply as a seal or some jewelled monogram lying in the dust. The nine great gatehouses that topped the walls, three to a flank, with their emerald roofs, decorated the outline. Within a filigree of streets separated them from the rectangle of the Imperial City, a green-enamelled patchwork of palaces; within this lay the core, the golden-roofed complex of the Forbidden City with its great white courtyards and marble pediments, the Throne Room towering at the centre, the matrix of it all.

Raising the eyes, the country beyond the walls was empty, bare till you spotted the broad approaches to the Tombs of the Ming Emperors. The broad processional way, flanked by colossal statues of gods and elephants, brought, even from the air, a sense of amazement at the scale of it all. Beyond, on the horizon, stood the Great Wall of China, one of the wonders of the world, snaking endlessly through the mountains, like some sleeping dragon, always on guard. Then, sweeping west, back over the hills, there lay the Summer Palace, no less impressive in scale. On the slopes of an artificial hill, made from excavating a huge lake, the Empress Dowager had laid out a gilded retreat. Marble houseboats were moored to marble wharfs, pavilions were linked by walks shaded under painted eaves, courtyards were punctuated with monstrous bronze dragons. The Summer Palace had caused a scandal when it was built because the old termagant had filched a million-pound foreign loan intended to modernize China's fleet and built herself this extravangaza instead. But what a legacy it was! Better by far than some old iron ships that would anyhow have been broken up by today . . .

Then, as we swung south over the city, in the maze of twisted lanes that clustered outside the walls, there stood the scaffolds where the lengths of blue cotton cloth, fresh from the dyers, swung high like pennants in the wind, there lay the huge, square, mat-walled theatres, squat as empty cardboard boxes, there at last, south of it all, the glorious pagoda of the Temple of Heaven, the triple roofs, dark blue as lapis lazuli, looking down through the ample park towards the cream disc of the Altar of Heaven, shining like a pendant pearl. All this is a medieval high perspective of old China which nobody will ever see again and I count myself most fortunate to be able to set it down.

Throughout that summer my relations with the Horvath family had ripened. They were the only cultivated, artistic family in Peking. So I suppose it was inevitable that in the autumn of 1921 a double marriage was arranged. Mimi, the eldest daughter, married a Russian count and the second daughter, Eudoxia, or Douska as she was always called, married me. Being yellow with jaundice and so weak I had to be supported by the first of my six best men during the Russian Orthodox ceremony, I appreciated neither the beauty of my wife nor the great feast that was held afterwards.

Some weeks before the wedding I had been forced to consider whether it would be wise to remain in China or not. The original contract with the Chinese was running out. In spite of the glamour of the East and the easy, attractive way of life, I came to the conclusion that in China the European would always be an out-sider. So I decided not to renew the contract. Some instinct insisted I must return home – though I had no profession, no job and nothing whatever to return to.

It was a romantic celebration of our marriage to spend our honeymoon in a Chinese temple. But this time, my 'boy', the faithful Jo, insisted that it would not be fitting for us to travel on foot. So where the climb into the mountains began we found two large Chinese chairs awaiting us. Each was slung between a pair of long wooden saplings and when, rather gingerly, we sat on them we suddenly found ourselves hoisted into the air, as four coolies, each taking one end of the two poles, started the long climb into the hills.

The days of the sedan chair had long been over and I did not like the idea of being carried, but once used to it, we found the saplings long and supple and our chairs beautifully sprung, so to speak. The coolies set a sharp pace, breaking into short bursts of song from time to time to keep their spirits up. Looking back at my bride at turns in the path, I shall never forget the sight of her, like a princess, floating, swinging high in the air and laughing, never quite sure, on the steep bits, if she could keep her place. These were magical moments to be remembered in hard days ahead.

Three weeks later, after our honeymoon in a temple in the Western Hills, my bride and I left Peking and set off on the thirty-six-hour rail journey to Shanghai where we had booked our tickets for the voyage home. It was only looking back many years later that I began to realize the trust the family placed in me and the devotion of my wife. The parents had only known me a few months. None of the family spoke a word of English and my French (in which all conversation had been carried on) was sketchy. Yet they confidently placed their most beautiful daughter in my hands, to take her 10,000 miles away to a strange country, whose language was unknown to her, where she had not a single friend and where the sort of life she would have to live in a big city on limited means was utterly different from the princely surroundings of her childhood and upbringing. It was a pretty heavy gamble for a girl of eighteen to take, but she never looked back and, I should add, seventy years later, in spite of all vicissitudes, continues even today to face what has in fact been no easy life with constant stoicism, courage and success.

Back in London, my mother took us in and I began to cast round for something to do. I had no money, no training in anything except flying, no equipment whatever for life beyond youth and a certain unfocused, undirected ability. Then luck intervened in a quite unusual way.

While in Peking I had been indisposed for some weeks with a mild rheumatic fever. A member of the Metropolitan Vickers staff, out in Peking to sell trams to the Government, hearing that a colleague was sick, had spent some of his leisure hours by my bed and we had become quite good friends. While my wife and I had returned home by Suez, he had gone the other way and come back across the United States.

One morning the telephone rang. It was the kindly sympathetic voice of Richards, my Peking friend. 'You know, Lewis', he said, 'I think broadcasting's the thing for you.'

I had never heard the word. 'Broadcasting?' I said. 'What on earth's that?'

6

Broadcasting?
What's That?

WHILE stationed at Rochford in 1918, I was surprised one day to find that a wireless officer had been posted to my flight. The squadron was engaged in the night defence of London. We were flying Camels, single-seater fighters. We were not equipped with wireless and we had no need of it – so what was the fellow going to do?

It transpired that he had some new secret equipment – a small black box which he would stick in the locker behind my seat and a somewhat similar one which he would keep on the ground himself. When he spoke into a sort of telephone mouthpiece he claimed that I should be able to hear him, even 5000 feet up and a couple of miles away. When I switched on I would be able to tell him if I had heard him and so we should have, as it were, a 'wireless' conversation.

It was a new and amusing idea, but it didn't work very well. I heard him, he couldn't hear me; he heard me, I couldn't hear him – and so on. Then he disappeared to make improvements and I thought no more about it.

The tremendous implications of that little test passed right over my head. If he could speak to me, he could speak to anyone within range of his transmitter. He was broadcasting and when I replied to him, so was I. But if I did not grasp the possibilities, others did, and within three years of the end of the war, America, with its extraordinary flair for applied technology, had set up broadcasting stations right across the continent. The novelty had become the rage and the rest of the world came stumbling along behind, wondering if they could not do the same thing.

That telephone call from Richards changed the direction of my life and confirmed a pattern which was to recur again and again,

so that one might say it was a part of my fate. I should always have
the opportunity to be in at the start of new things, never lead them
and never remain with them long enough to draw any real profit
from all the effort I put in.

It transpired that many of the big electrical firms in England
were actively engaged in the preliminary stages of obtaining
government permission to set up broadcasting in the UK. The
Marconi Company was first in the field. They owned most of the
useful patents and had already established an experimental station
at Writtle. Their rivals were a consortium of several companies,
including General Electric, Metropolitan Vickers, British Thom-
son Houston and others. The revenues required to defray the costs
of the service would be borne partly out of profits on the sale of
receiving sets, partly on an extra percentage, a sort of sales tax,
added to the price. While the Marconi Company had already
begun to prepare rudimentary programming arrangements, the
consortium had not. They were in fact looking for a likely chap
in this absolutely unknown field to do it for them. Richards remembered me. I was, he thought, 'artistic' and this was vaguely
what was required. So I was interviewed and engaged as the Programme Manager of the consortium at £400 per annum.

———

BEHIND the scenes a good deal of bickering was going on as to the
form the broadcasting service should take. The questions of pool-
ing patents, potential profits, royalties, licence fees, all these and a
good deal more were being thrashed out between the companies·
and the Postmaster General. Although there was much public
criticism of the delays, the issues involved were seen to be vital.
The American system was set up purely to make money. They sold
time to anyone who would buy it. This had already resulted in a
cheapening of the service to the public (it still does), each sponsor
vying with the next to produce the most popular ear-catching
programme. Kellaway, the British Postmaster General of the day,
profiting by their mistakes and feeling a certain sense of public
responsibility for broadcasting as an educative medium, came up
with an entirely different approach, and the House of Commons,
after deliberating on the matter at some length, ratified the decision to set up a single broadcasting service under the Post Office,

responsible not only for the technical transmission, but for the programming as well. To meet the considerable costs of running such a service, the public would be required to pay a licence fee of 12s 6d for the right to own a receiving set, part of which would go to the broadcasting company and part to the Post Office itself. On 18 October 1922 the British Broadcasting Company, with a capital of £100,000 was licensed by the Post Office to establish a national broadcasting service.

Anyone with the interest can read about all this in Asa Briggs' well-documented compendium on the details of those days (*The Birth of Broadcasting*, Vol. 1. Asa Briggs), but at the same time it must be said that you get no more of the thrill of starting up the service from his account than you would experience the excitement of flying a Phantom from a studying the blueprints.

Advertisements were placed in the leading morning papers for candidates to fill the main posts. It will give some idea of how little the possibilities of broadcasting were realized if I say that for the job of Director of Programmes only five replies were received. Two of them came from Arthur Burrows and myself. He, the Marconi nominee, was appointed Director and I his Deputy. Stanton Jefferies filled the post of Musical Director, while the man chosen to be General Manager of the new company was a certain J. C. W. Reith.

My first recollection of him is still vivid. We were standing on the pavement at the bottom of Kingsway opposite Bush House. I stood 6 feet 4 inches; Reith was even taller. A sort of lofty detachment surrounded him. The gash on his cheek from a war wound added a certain severity to his mien. He had a pronounced Scottish accent, a neatly rolled umbrella and very fine hands. Those were my first superficial impressions of a man of whom in the early days I often grew intolerant and impatient for his lack of appreciation and understanding of the nature of programme building and the qualities of artists. He seemed to have no interest in or liking for any of the arts and often appeared to look on programmes as a necessary evil, produced by persons of strange character and dubious morals, utterly foreign to his strict religious background and high principles. He admitted at the outset that he had no idea what it was all about; but he had one great virtue: he left us alone to get on with it. Indeed he had no option, for in those early days he faced problems basic to the whole structure and future of the

broadcasting medium. He overcame them brilliantly and successfully, but it left him little time for anything else. He was in every
sense a big man, just and generous in his relations with his staff.
He had the ability to grow with the job – and that meant growing
very quickly indeed – and long before he retired acquired a
legendary status and a peerage. I must add that in later years, long
after both of us had left the BBC, my admiration and respect for
him steadily increased and grew into a genuine affection.

———

So, on the second floor of the General Electric Building in Kingsway, we started work in one big room, in a corner of which was a
small cubicle set aside for our General Manager. In the middle of
the room was a large table which, as the days went by, was piled
deeper and deeper in fan mail, mostly from children, for the
Children's Hour was certainly the BBC's greatest success. Besides
Reith there were three of us: Arthur Burrows, Stanton Jefferies
and me. Soon we were joined by Peter Eckersley, Chief Engineer,
and Rex Palmer, Manager of the London Station.

It was a non-stop scramble from nine till five. Then the entire
programme staff – Burrows, Jeff, Rex Palmer and myself –
clapped on our hats and ran off down the road to Marconi House
and rushed up to the studio, a small attic on the top floor of the old
Gaiety Theatre. Here we opened the evening's broadcasting by
improvising entertainment for the children. The studio was about
20 feet square and was hung with several black vulcanite telephone mouthpieces on strings, each carefully tilted to face the
instruments of our five-piece 'orchestra'. The technical refinements
were in the charge of a small tubby man, Chief Engineer of the
Marconi Company, aptly called Round, and the day he produced
a sort of iron jam-jar lying on its side in a sling of sorbo rubber,
and announced (to our astonishment) that it was a new microphone and would pick up anything in the room, was the first step
forward and released us from the telephone operator's technique,
which glued us to a mouthpiece.

In those early days some doubts were expressed as to whether
broadcasting would succeed. Perhaps the public would rebel at
wearing earphones (for the loudspeaker did not then exist) and
get tired of tinkering with the 'cat's whiskers' of their primitive

receivers. But we knew from the mail that something new had entered the social life of England. We had no doubts and gave all the energy and enthusiasm of dedicated young men to the growth of the new medium.

For absolutely new it was. It is impossible for anyone today to imagine a time when radio (and later TV) did not exist. The press was the only means of distributing news. It was the only, all-powerful voice of public opinion. In every field editors directed attention where it suited them. The public judged a politician, an artist or a social question on the say-so of a small bunch of journalists who had only too often the most superficial knowledge of their subject – and whose comments were frequently slanted to please their bosses. If you wanted to see a play, a conductor, a fashion parade or a football match, you had to go yourself. You had to make a personal effort.

Now, almost overnight, the centuries-old pattern changed. The public could participate. They need accept nobody else's opinion of a public speaker or an artist; they could hear him for themselves. Opponents on political or social questions could present their own case. In times of emergency the whole country could be inspired (as anyone who heard Churchill will never forget) to a single purpose.

Producing daily programme material with such a scale and range had never been dreamed of. At first in 1922 we did not really grasp it ourselves. The world's ear was our oyster. Into it we could pour anything and everything that could possibly interest it. The entire range of the daily news, the wide gamut of music, the stimulus of debate, the drama of playwrights and poets, the wealth of education, the consolations of religion, all human endeavour was there, to be fined down to the point of the microphone and then amplified out wider and wider to the ends of the earth.

———

IT was an extraordinary and unprecedented situation – an opportunity and a challenge, not only to us, but to many others who very soon saw in this new scientific octopus a dangerous monster that could strangle their livelihood. The press feared for their monopoly, the concert halls for their audiences, the sports arenas for their crowds, the churches for their congregations. On every side we were creating new problems and at the same time offering new possibilities. It took many years for all this to stabilize itself. In a few years broadcasting completely revolutionized the public's attitude to its own life, widening horizons, posing questions, bringing a ferment which even today is far from subsiding and on which some of the more dubious values of the medium still rely.

Of all this the world was made free. It came to them without their making the least effort. The phrase 'an armchair critic' took on a new dimension. Everybody had views on everything. If governments or dictators took charge of the medium and slanted it for their own ends a fanatical mass bigotry could be created in a decade. How much of the frenzied hysteria in which we flounder today is due to mass media? Those oh-so-reasonable 'personalities', the rumour-mongers, the scare-mongers, the prophets, the pundits, all of them know that to succeed they must exaggerate. Hertz and Marconi, unwittingly, have a lot to answer for. But they, like all scientists, were only interested in the how and the why of the world around them. The excitement of finding out and developing overshadowed any question of whether what they found out and developed would be of value to society. Rutherford did not foresee Hiroshima. Men of great vision and impartiality would have to be given the trust and confidence of the entire world before any new set of values could evolve. What hope was there of that! The pros and cons that beset us on every side lead only to bewilderment and frustration. We give up. There seems to be no longer any yardstick. But yardstick there must be, if the world is not to immolate itself on the altar of its own stupidity.

Of course we, the young band of pioneers at the start of broadcasting, did not think of ourselves as scientists. Yet scientists we were, scientists in a new 'discipline' of titillation and persuasion. Naturally such an idea never occurred to us and we should have repudiated it as ludicrous. We were simply lucky enough to be doing a marvellous new job and utterly wrapped up in the best way to do it. I still remember vividly the sudden widening of our programme horizon when the Post Office suggested that they put a microphone into Covent Garden. The first outside broadcast! Programmes need not come to the studio, to us. We could go to them. This meant an endless new vista of possibilities and we seized on it avidly. A few weeks later we broadcast a Communist meeting from the Kingsway Hall which ended with the singing of 'The Red Flag'. Then Stanton Jefferies got together with the London Symphony Orchestra and we organized a series of concerts in Westminster Hall which he himself conducted. I arranged a season of Shakespeare plays directed by Nigel Playfair and personally handed a cheque for £1000 to Chaliapin for our first celebrity recital. So it went. Everything was new. Everything was being done for the first time. All day we planned the programmes, every evening we went down to the studio and announced them. We were working up to eighteen hours a day and thrived on it.

For me it was not only a musical education to listen to studio performers of every kind, but it opened the way to meeting everyone in the artistic life of London. From Noel Coward to Paul Robeson, from Sir Gerald du Maurier to George Robey, from Gertie Lawrence to Sybil Thorndike, they were all, if not friends, at least interested enough in the possibilities that broadcasting could offer to admit a young ambassador of the latest novelty to their circle.

By this time we had moved the offices down to Savoy Hill, where we had several studios. Broadcasting had caught on and was mushrooming with a vengeance. Staff was doubled, trebled, quadrupled. Other stations were being opened at Birmingham, Manchester, Glasgow, Cardiff. Techniques somehow or other kept pace with the growth. In the background Reith was battling with the Post Office, who were dragging their feet in collecting the licence fees on which our income depended. We were in the full flood of development and nothing at that time had crystallized into the dreadful arterial sclerosis which sooner or later reduces all big organizations to bureaucracy and satisfaction with the second rate. I personally was greatly excited by the possibilities of radio drama and with the help of the engineers set up what was then called the multi-studio technique, the original mixing panel by which sound from different studios could be brought in and blended, music, artists, sound effects, into a single transmission. It is the commonplace of today: then it was an exciting innovation and I wrote a play to demonstrate its effectiveness.

This is not a history of broadcasting but simply an attempt to recreate the sense of riding the tiger of a big adventure in my youth. Reminiscence can be a dreadful bore. All the same, I will add one more sharp memory of those days.

———

IT was a great occasion, the first time all the stations in the UK would be linked together to receive the nine o'clock news. This was what we then called simultaneous broadcasting and it marked such a step forward that it was thought necessary to give it special emphasis. This emphasis was to take the form of a 'few well-chosen words' from the Earl of Birkenhead. I was deputed to go across the road to the Savoy where his Lordship was presiding at a private dinner in the Pinafore Room. I knew nothing then of his weakness, but on entering the room I saw at once that the noble Earl was drunk. I was filled with consternation. In ten minutes he had to be on the air. England was waiting and how the devil was I going to get this man across the road and up into the studio in time? A secretary went and whispered to him. He seemed to recollect that he had made the appointment, lurched to his feet and came across to me and allowed me to conduct him through the corridors and out into the street, ungraciously shaking off my arm when I attempted to guide him. I hoped the fresh air might sober him up, but it evidently did not, for he positively reeled into our lift and without saying a word to me entered the studio. I was convinced we were in for a disaster and saw the scandal of it echoing around the country. But it was too late to stop anything now. I whispered to Reith, 'He's high as a kite', but Reith, if he heard, retained his composure. The red light came on. The ears of the whole country were connected to our microphone. Reith made a brief announcement introducing the great man and stepped back to allow him to speak.

It was then the miracle happened. Swaying backwards and forwards on his feet with a glazed expression, Birkenhead delivered, absolutely impromptu, without a note or a single slur or stumble, a brilliant comment on the occasion, perfectly phrased, clearly articulated, absolutely to the point. Reith, as he conducted our great guest out of the studio, caught my eye and gave me the ghost of a smile.

———

IF Reith was a man of high moral principles determined to raise
the BBC to a position where it could command the respect of the
country – and later of the world – he succeeded beyond any
doubt. But his principles and his integrity inevitably resulted in a
certain stiffness and inflexibility in the face of a period of history
when values were very rapidly changing. Considerable pressure
was put on him from many quarters to relax the guidelines he
had laid down, to be more accommodating here, to be more
broadminded there. He made enemies by refusing to give way,
foreseeing with more vision than the opportunists that once the
gates were opened there would be no end to the cheapening of the
service, to the lowering of standards.

I too had standards, though of a different kind. I believed in
quality. I knew that quantity was its bitterest enemy and saw, as
time went by, the inevitable encroachment of the mediocre, the
second-rate. First our daily programme lasted for three hours only,
then four, then five, then six. I remember Reith sending for me to
arrange an early-morning programme for people coming off night
shift. I protested. How could we maintain any semblance of quality if
we spread ourselves like this? He shrugged. We were a public
service and must serve the public.

Of course, it was true, but somehow it took the heart out of my
effort. Bureaucracy was creeping in. I became entangled in endless
committees. Committees on religion, on education, on technical
balance, on pretty well every aspect of programme building. It was
a sort of paralysis. If the time so spent had gone into the programmes themselves, we could have maintained the quality of the
service. Of course, I was very young, enthusiastic, impatient,
impulsive, and with all that went an inevitable conceit, intolerance
and lack of judgement. The idea of keeping my job, time-serving,
playing safe, all the slogans of mediocrity were anathema to me.
I was concerned with a personal view of excellence, and the
individualist, however high his motive, is always a bit of a
nuisance in the machine.

One morning, when some particularly stupid, time-wasting
committee had been set up, I rebelled. I lifted the receiver and
called the Managing Director. 'I want to resign,' I said.

'Come and have dinner and let's talk it out,' Reith replied.

That evening I opted out of a certain career, a steady income
and a good pension, of all that security for which people are ready

to sacrifice themselves and put up with a lifetime of frustrations and buried hopes. I was still under thirty. I believed intensely in a do-it-yourself life. It may have been foolish, but, inevitably, we all do what we must. Besides, my self-confidence was complete. It never occurred to me that with my abilities I could fail. So I launched out, without any misgivings, to live by my wits. I have done so every since.

7

Truth and Beauty

W E are all from birth (and perhaps before) the slaves of influences. We think, act and react, whether we know it or not, almost entirely according to precepts that have been impressed on us by parents, relatives, nurses and so on. The soft wax of childhood and early youth, moulded by those around us, gradually hardens and the man finally emerges with a character largely carved out from everything that has been suggested to him as right or wrong, good or bad, desirable or worthless during the years when, as it is said, he was 'too young to think for himself'. Youth is a crucial time, for, once the mould has set, it is next to impossible to change it.

There have been three important influences in my life. Two of them belong to my youth. The first of these was what may be called an artistic influence. It came in the form of a man, later a close friend, whom I met even before I went to China. He was the painter Charles Ricketts, RA.

There are people who have the ability to discern the importance of things in relation to past and future, while they are still happening. They have a sort of 'historical' sense. Churchill is the most obvious example. In a hundred utterances during those stirring years of the Second World War he was able to see our defeats and victories of the moment and relate them to the long perspective of our national traditions and aspirations. It is an inspiring gift in the grand manner and I have not got it at all.

Not till many years after it is all over can I begin to discern a clear picture of how past things have been and put them into focus. But to give some idea of the influence of Ricketts on my youth, I must step out of the mere chronology of years and anticipate, bringing together, as far as I can, a host of associated memories, to create some sort of portrait of my friend.

There are flowers in the Easter fields and a dapple of clouds in the blue sky and we are motoring down to Cambridge to see some friends. The place looks scrubbed, groomed, fresh gilt and crimson in the arms over the college doors, the lawns like velvet, the Backs sliding in enamelled stillness. My companions are carefree, carefree and sentimental. Cambridge means their youth, their years of ardent study, their betrothal, their marriage; their roots are here. To me Cambridge is no more than a name, a chance lost for ever – 1914–18. . .

We stroll about the town, pass a building with a columned portico, a thread of Greek among the Gothic, the Fitzwilliam Museum. The Fitzwilliam! The word taps gently on the dusty wicket of my mind. Do I not remember a phrase, spoken sometime, somewhere, at random, 'We're leaving most of our treasure to the Fitzwilliam'? We go in. There, sure enough, is the sign 'To the Ricketts and Shannon Rooms'. Now the past comes crowding and I hurry down the corridor. There they all are, the things I have known for years! The noble Greek vases, the flying Tanagras, the bronze men (handles of an urn) arched back like swallow divers, the wooden duck with sliding wings (rouge for an Egyptian queen), the ivory monkey, minus one leg, smaller than my finger. I can see it lying in the palm of his small hand – 'Look, my dear boy, every hair!' Then the drawings: the Watteaus, the Fragonards, that superhuman Rubens head, that angel by Tiepolo, the Rembrandt cartoon. . .

Suddenly I don't want to look any more. These works of art brought together from every epoch with an eclectic and impeccable taste, displayed in the cool serenity of a musem; it is like going to a cemetery, gazing at a mummy in a crystal coffin; the presence that once informed it all, the daily life which flowered among these things, the flow of conversation, of laughter, the sense of being in the intimate company of great art collected by a zealot, himself a genius, all that is gone, gone. . .

It would be wrong to think that I held any special place. Ricketts had Shannon for a lifelong friend and many other intimates besides. I did not meet him until just after the First World War. He had turned fifty; I was twenty-one. I was learning to sing. Vladimir Rosing, my teacher, the 'dear beast' as Ricketts affectionately used to call him, occasionally held small parties at his Baker Street flat. There was that Chekovian informality that is part of the Russian

soul. The tenor fancied himself as much as a chef as he did as a
vocalist and wandered between guests and sink, singing to either
impartially and sucking the fruit juice off his fingers. The music
lay in torn untidy heaps, pages were always missing; there was
always a dearth of spoons and glasses; the maid had always
given notice; the place was always in an impossible muddle – but
there remained the glorious music. In the numerous interludes we
guests chattered among ourselves. But that evening we listened to
Ricketts.

He was a small man with a slight stoop, carelessly dressed in
blue serge. A cigarette was usually in his mouth (and its ash on his
waistcoat), his hair grew round but no longer over his head, he
had a moustache, a goatee beard and very talkative hands. Inade-
quate description with perhaps a touch of the grotesque: there was
none in reality. The face, high forehead and chiselled nose, was all
intelligence. He listened acutely, with a curious inner concentra-
tion, like a setter pointing, but he never listened for long. Vitality,
gaiety, exuberance bubbled out of him. Almost any remark would
set him off. He would link up your banality to his mind, flatter
your intelligence by reading some fragment of truth into it, and
then he was off. His conversation was a monologue, but in it there
was nothing pedantic. His extraordinary erudition, the catholicity
of his knowledge, was all leavened with a faeric imagination and a
French nimbleness of mind. Constant verbal surprises kept you
alert ('deer like moths or mushrooms', 'pansies with delicious
depraved faces'), and he would lead on from one subject to
another, evoking from flower or phrase whole centuries of thought
and civilization. 'Time does not exist: I could have told Einstein
that years ago.' Each epoch lived, its people were alive, he knew
their circumstance and felt their life as if it were his own; and,
while he talked, you did so too. Not for nothing had Oscar Wilde
remarked, 'I am going to take you to the one house in London
where you will never be bored.'

I was young then, proud in the ignorant vanity of youth. It did
not occur to me that Ricketts was unique. He was immensely
intelligent, of course; he had charm, humour; he was an artist;
but the world, for all I knew, contained many such men. Why
not? In youth everything seems possible. It was only with the
steady passage of years, faced more and more with the ignorance,
opacity and folly of the world at large, that I began to make

comparisons. It is only now that he has been dead for many years that I can begin to assess the richness of the life he shared with me.

———

To this callow youth, then, fresh from the war, as enthusiastic as he was ignorant about art, Ricketts offered friendship; it endured till the day of his death. He opened the doors of the aesthetic world to me, gave me a sense of belonging, long before there was the least justification, to that curiously inchoate body of men, 'the artists', those who in every age have created things that endure the longest. He apprenticed me to this world, inspired themes, subjects, situations; midwifed my earliest efforts, advised, criticized; and when the work was presented to the public and failed miserably, saw always something in it that made me think I was right and the world wrong, that I had not failed, after all. But then, like all artists, he knew about failure. . .

After his death Shaw remarked that Ricketts lived *en grand seigneur*. Like most of his comments it was extremely acute. Ricketts himself said: 'I live like a grandee.' And when I did not see the point he explained how grandees used to live. Their reception rooms would be rich and luxurious, filled with noble and beautiful things, fit places in which to dispense hospitality and receive their peers; but the rooms in which they habitually passed their days would be almost poverty-stricken, puritan in their simplicity. The studio in which Ricketts worked and lived was such a room. He had no sense of comfort. The 'easy' chair in which you 'relax' was anathema to him. His 'easy' chairs cost (at the time) 35 shillings and were almost devoid of padding. His sofa was as uncomfortable as a waiting-room seat at a railway station. All were covered with blue cotton cloth at a shilling a yard, the stuff out of which butchers used to make their aprons. His ashtrays were saucers, his palette an old plate, his warmth a square black-leaded stove. Partly this was poverty. All his life he had skimped and saved on daily expense in order to amass his magnificent collection. When I knew him it was worth a fortune and had a ready market value, but the habit remained. Friends could not understand this. If you had Old Master drawings worth £50,000, then surely you could afford a car? But you could not. You walked or went by bus; and it was by doing this for a lifetime that you had what you had.

But if the studio was spartan, the reception rooms were princely. On the first floor of Townsend House (now pulled down) was a small museum. Egyptian antiquities, Greek vases and Tanagras lived in glass cases. Below were drawers holding beads, gems or Chinese hair ornaments (kingfisher-feather butterflies trembling on little springs, presents sometimes to selected lady visitors); there were Adam sofas and chairs, Italian side tables, a marble torso, a bas-relief, a picture of Don Juan by Ricketts, a portrait of Mrs Pat by Shannon... But this room was never lived in. Days would pass when it was not visited. It was open only when friends who cared to see, and would understand its rarity, were shown around. Yet it was not, like a museum, cold and detached. It was a set piece, true; but it was none the less a room, arranged in perfect taste.

The dining room, the bridge from work to entertainment, was unique. Ricketts had the sort of antennae which enabled him to distinguish an object of merit whatever its period or use. You would not think that Old Master drawings would be at home with a Chinese birdcage, red and green marble-topped tables could not live in amity, Empire chairs might swear with Morris chintzes, French knives could not harmonize with Georgian silver, a modern blue glass bowl could never stand at the feet of a Grecian statuette; the whole certainly could not be lit hard with clear bulbs hanging from plain porcelain shades. Yet in fact all combined to give a sense of luxury and elegance that was incomparable. Each object, being in itself perfect, added its lustre to the whole, so that the room, which was besides, winter and summer, filled with flowers, glowed with a radiant and compelling beauty.

———

OF all this I was made free for many years, a constant visitor, welcome morning, afternoon or night. It would have been, it was, enough; but there was more. A stream of gifts: a Chardin still-life, a Japanese screen, theatre drawings, rare books, prints, a portrait bust, his only one ('I'm having you cast in plaster, you fraud, you're not worth casting in bronze.'). All was given with a spontaneous gaiety that enhanced the gift. Yet when he did not wish to give there was more. 'I'm not giving you that book, you beastly rotter. Mind you bring it back. Here give it me now.' And he would take it and write on the flyleaf: 'This belongs to C. Ricketts.' Yet, after he died, inside the bronze mask of his head done in his youth was stuck a strip of paper: 'This belongs to C. Lewis.'

At the time of his life when he was most successful he always maintained he was dead. 'My dear boy, I died during the war, I have been dead for years.' He had a sense of utter failure at a period when he might have been basking in the recognition of his talents. He did not give way to self-pity or ennui ('Superior people are never bored') but a sudden staccato rage would fill him when he found something he had done had been passed over and a lesser thing acclaimed. 'Let's go out and get drunk. What do you say? You're only bearable when you're drunk.' So, often, we set out with bacchic intentions. We always returned sober.

What could I, what did I, give in return for all this? I have always wondered and I wonder still. A prodigal generosity flowed from him, enriching each in the particular direction he needed it most; to one money, to another advice, to a third sympathy, to a fourth encouragement. Many do this, I know. He differed only in the quality of what he did and the manner in which he did it; he differed only because he did it, among others, to me. Yet he received from wiser men, it seems, some return: appreciation and a maturity to match his own. In spite of it, something eluded him, some fulfilment which an affectionate nature craved. He did not ask from me what he was well aware I could not give. Sometimes, to strike a fairer balance, I have wished my nature had been otherwise . . .

To cap it all, there was the Rupi – my villa in Italy. I had found the village near to which it stands two years before and come across a bit of land bordering the lake, which the owner was willing to sell for some £300 – a sum then far beyond my means. Returning to London after a spell of work, I talked with all the enthusiasm of a discoverer about this secret corner of northern Italy, unspoiled, untouched by time and progress. Here, I said, I doubled my vitality and output, here was the only place to work, here was the loveliest spot in Europe, only eighteen hours (as it was then) from London.

Next day, just before lunch, Ricketts came trotting into the dining room, holding a piece of paper in his hand. 'My dear, now listen to me. I've just sold some Persian drawings for a fabulous sum. What good is it to me? I'm an old man. I shall only buy more art. I'm tired of art – no, really. From now on I intend to live only for food. Now here's a cheque. Take it and buy that piece of ground. I've allowed an extra fifty to cover lawyers, deeds and things. . .' I protested volubly and emphatically that I couldn't dream of accepting such a gift. 'My dear boy, don't be foolish. Take it, take it! After all' – and he looked up at me affectionately – 'don't let's be sentimental; but it will be something to remember me by.'

———

It was two years later. I had been all summer in Italy. The Rupi, as we called the place because of the precipices under which it stood, was beginning to take shape. Paths had been cut through the woods, vines and peaches planted along the old terraces, steps twisted down to a bathing pool among the rocks. Constantly I wrote to him about it all; for he never saw, never would come and see, the gift he had made me. He was staging a play for Matheson Lang, but most unusually for him, would not go near the theatre, leaving all the arrangements to others. Shannon's accident and stroke had unnerved him. To live in the same house with a life-long friend, to have that friend still moving in the house, apparently healthy and normal but quite gone, a fine painter sunk to a gentle imbecile, his sensitive nature was torn to shreds by it. Perhaps, most of all, the fact that his friend did not recognize him, or if he sometimes did, viewed him with hostility, numbed him like a mortal wound. Yet there was nothing to be done. With astonishing courage he hoped on, selling treasures to meet the terrible expense, making sudden trips abroad out of a desire to forget, reading, working, maintaining all his interests; but with a feverish and unnatural energy – even for him.

He had not been well, I knew. Some casual phrase in a letter had alarmed me, but the doctor said it was nothing and was treating him for indigestion. I got back to London in the late afternoon and rang the house. Ricketts, so the faithful Nicolls said, was not too well. He was going to bed early, but would I come round and see him next morning? It was quite early when the telephone rang. 'I don't know if it's much good your coming round, sir. Mr. Ricketts is dead . . . Yes, sir. Somewhere between six and ten, sir. He was all right when I took up his morning medicine at six. Yes, sir; he must have died in his sleep . . .'

His ashes were to be scattered to the four winds, so the will said; but none was awake that morning as we walked into Richmond Park. It was still and misty under a pale sky. A deer, with a green bracken frond in his horns, watched from a nearby coppice. Bengy Lowinsky was holding the box. It was a plain red shoe-box, tied with a piece of string, full to the brim with sharp grey ashes. The five of us dipped into it and scattered. The ashes fell on to the searing grass. We went on scattering, solemnly at first, as befitted the occasion, but soon in a sort of frenzy. Suddenly I had an almost uncontrollable desire to laugh. There was something eternal, after all, in scattering the dust of a dear friend back into earth. Yet I could hear the imp of his laughter choking and gurgling in my head. We had been scattering it seemed for hours, and still the box was half full . . . It was then that Bengy had an inspiration. 'Wouldn't you like to scatter the rest on your ground in Italy?' The situation was saved.

I hollowed a niche out of the living rock of the precipice. In it I set up his mask in bronze, facing the mountains and the setting sun, with tablet duly inscribed, and then one winter morning, with a light snow falling on black water, quite alone in the breathless stillness, I completed the rite.

Well, there it is. All that is sixty years ago. Others, more instructed than I, may appraise or criticize his work. With that balance I am not concerned. The work remains. His love of art, and his devotion to every side of it, glow in the life of all who knew him. For me he had spoken his own epitaph many years before.

It is lunchtime in the dining room again. My memory makes it now. We celebrate my thirtieth birthday and lying in the bowl of the dessertspoon at my place is a superb intaglio ring, cut by a master 500 years before the birth of Christ. The conversation turns to poetry, to the sonnet form, and Ricketts, in some prescient mood, hurries from the room and comes back with a volume of Christina Rossetti in his hand. He never read aloud but on this one occasion; and I see him there across the marble table with the Rembrandt behind, hunched in his chair, holding the book high, a cigarette trembling in his other hand, speaking in a timid hesitant voice, surcharged with his emotion at the words:

Remember me when I am gone away,
Gone far away into the silent land;
When you can no more hold me by the hand,
Nor I half turn to go, yet turning stay.

Remember me when no more day by day
You tell me of our future that you planned:
Only remember me: you understand
It will be late to counsel then or pray.

Yet if you should forget me for a while
And afterwards remember, do not grieve:
For if the darkness and corruption leave
a vestige of the thoughts that once I had
Better by far you should forget and smile
Than that you should remember and be sad.

8

My Eminent Friend

THE second influence of my youth, second only because it started a few years later, was that of an even more elderly man, who already held an international place in the world of letters. His influence and that of Ricketts ran concurrently. The two men had quite different points of view about almost everything, yet they were friends and each held the other in high esteem. While Ricketts was emotional and impulsive, his counterpart had an Olympian detachment, an outstanding intellect and a remedy for all the world's ills – socialism. He was, of course, George Bernard Shaw.

Although I knew little of his work when I started BBC programme planning at Savoy Hill, he was obviously the sort of celebrity that anyone would try to bring to the microphone. So without more ado I wrote boldly off to Adelphi Terrace to invite him to come along and introduce our first series of Shakespeare plays that Nigel Playfair was producing. Rather to my surprise, I got a prompt answer on one of the famous postcards. 'No!' it read. 'Shakespeare by himself is all right and so am I. But the mixture would be a bore and a failure.'

Nothing daunted, I had another go, telling him that broadcasting was the new art form of the times and he ought not, could not, afford to leave it out of his calculations. Wouldn't he come and have a look round, wouldn't he read one of his plays himself, or perhaps write one for us? To this I received another postcard saying perhaps he might drop in some time. I made a note to nudge him in about a month's time.

But when the next week, one afternoon, the house phone rang and the commissionaire announced laconically, 'Mr Bernard Shaw to see you, sir', I jumped out of my chair and rushed down to the waiting room at a run to find him sitting quietly among the children and their parents who were taking part in the Children's Hour that day.

It was a real case of hero-worship. I led him off round the studios, talking nineteen to the dozen about all we were doing and planned to do, with breathless exuberance, while my Olympian visitor put in occasional succinct questions. What did we pay? How large was our audience? Had we a scale of royalties? I told him we were at the beginning still, we could promise him an audience of 50,000–100,000, but we weren't very rich. Would he perhaps read a short play and accept a fee of a £100! It stopped him dead in his tracks.

'A hundred pounds!'

From his tone of voice it was evidently an insult. I stammered something about it being all we could afford and ... But he was not listening, absorbed in mental arithmetic. 'An audience of 100,000 people at, say 5 shillings a head, £25,000. Assuming that I take 20 per cent royalty, that works out at £5000. Can you afford that?'

I replied emphatically that we could not. This wasn't the theatre. There was nothing to see. It was quite different ... 'And besides,' he went on, 'you will be the ruin of me. Who will ever come to see my plays once they have heard them? A hundred thousand people would fill a theatre for six, nine months.'

I told him more people would come to his plays. People who had never heard them would learn how wonderful they were and flock to the theatre.

'It's perfectly obvious you can't possibly afford to pay me,' he cut in, 'so' – and he paused for dramatic effect – 'I will do it for nothing.'

To say that I was delighted would not convey at all that I felt. I saw something, in that moment, quite wonderful and new to me – the extraordinary effect of one of the rarest of human qualities, magnanimity. It placed him, for me, quite outside the ordinary run of men. Of course he was wealthy, he could well afford to make the gesture, but wealthy men, in general, are wealthy for the very reason that they are not and never have been generous.

A few weeks later G. B. S. came to the studio to read his *O'Flaherty, VC* with impeccable verve and artistry. Not one of the staff took the trouble to be there to welcome one of the greatest men of our time. Reith would never have dreamed of missing a peer or a politician, but of what account was Shaw? That didn't worry me. I had him all to myself and when it was over we walked back together towards Adelphi Terrace and dropped in at the Tivoli to see *Warning Shadows*.

———

FROM that day on he allowed me a certain intimacy. I could not really say I was a friend (as I could of Ricketts) because I do not think Shaw had any 'friends' as the term is generally understood. He was, it seems to me now, a lonely man. In fact I remember a phrase in a speech he made when Einstein visited this country, paying tribute to the prophet of scientific relativity: 'From us, in our little loneliness, to him in his great loneliness.' But, at the same time, he knew everybody. First at Adelphi Terrace and later at Whitehall Court, I was invited to lunch almost every week for many years. These lunches were works of art in themselves. The guests were never more than four in number and lunch was always formally served. Shaw presided at the head of the table, Mrs Shaw at the foot. The four guests were surprising in their variety. There you might meet H. G. Wells, Lawrence of Arabia, Elgar, Gene Tunney, Aldous Huxley, the Webbs, besides every star in the theatrical profession and many who aspired to be so. Also (because there was an impish circus strain in him) there was sometimes a smattering of very odd fish, young women with judo black belts, weird psychotherapists, harpsichord makers. The conversation was almost entirely a monologue of comment and reminiscence by Shaw and I never heard him repeat himself. Asked on one occasion if his characters were all invented, he replied that sometimes they were taken from life. Captain Shotover, in *Heartbreak House*, for instance, was moulded on Gordon Craig's father who, on his death-bed, had refused to eat the bread of extreme unction unless he could have some cheese with it.

When I first met G. B. S. he was seventy, I was twenty-four. He was tall and thin, stood erect and still wore a Norfolk jacket and trousers fastened just below the knee. The fashion for these suitings had gone out with the turn of the century, but Shaw went on wearing what was actually 'fancy dress' until the day of his death. His head was squarely carried on the shoulders, his chin drawn in, and this gave an impression of lofty detachment from all around him. The back of his head was curious: the neck had no nape. Broad lobes ran down from the crown right into the shoulders. He attributed his remarkable intelligence to this extra cervical capacity. A lifelong vegetarian ('I have not eaten meat for twenty-seven years: the results are before the public'), it was clear he enjoyed, even in extreme old age, quite exceptional health. The skin was clear, pink and fresh; the eyes (one fiery, one philosophical) bright and sprightly; the white hair and beard always groomed and fine in texture. In repose the face was composed and thoughtful, as if contemplating some problem. In animation his lively wit, exploding like fireworks, was accompanied by a high abrupt laugh and sudden jerky movements of hands and arms as he made his points. These were usually extremely acute and paradoxical comments on the topic of conversation. 'What the world calls genius,' he said, 'is only an accustomed way of tickling it.'

He was the unique combination of a fine perceptive mind allied to a gorgeous sense of fun. He went straight to the heart of a problem and exposed it as a joke. What you had followed with serious attention was suddenly capped with truth, a truth that always seemed hilariously funny. But behind the wit, the anecdote and the magic of his plays, the clarity and style of the beautiful English, the insight into character and situation, lay a wealth of practical common sense about any problem that came his way. He would settle your private affairs, the education of your children or your future career over a cup of detoxicated coffee. When I sent him my plays to read he would reply with devastating postcards: 'Your literary age I take to be about seven. You dress yourself like an acrobat and expect people to be amused by antics that any street arab could throw. Now, if you were to dress yourself like the Governor of the Bank of England, you could probably produce an astonishing effect by turning cartwheels in Threadneedle St.'

He was well aware of the value of these postcards, now sale-room rareties. Some years later when I had amassed quite a number, at a moment when he knew me to be struggling, he enlivened the day and came to the rescue with a hurried note: 'There is a lunatic at present at large in London who is willing to buy my letters for exaggerated sums of money. I advise you to unload without delay' – and was delighted to hear I had done so.

But the postcard I treasured most was one I received after

inviting him to come to the Arts Theatre to see *The Unknown Warrior*, my translation of Paul Raynal's masterpiece *Le Tombeau sous l'Arc de Triomphe*. It read: 'Yes. I will come to the Thursday matinée. In my *Unknown Warrior* there arises a great need in a future war to discuss what happened in 14/18. Nobody can be found. So the Archbishop of Canterbury and the Dean of Westminster, the Prime Minister and the Foreign Secretary decide to assemble in the Abbey at midnight to raise the Unknown Warrior from his tomb by Black Magic. They enter and find Christ seated on the Tomb. He agrees to grant their request. The Unknown Warrior rises from the Tomb and asks them what they want – in German. Yours faithfully, G. B. S.'

IT is not difficult to imagine what it meant to me, a youngster in my twenties, to be close to a man for whom I soon conceived such an admiration and affection. It started me off writing plays – in the Shavian manner, of course. But they were no good and it didn't take me long to realize that his manner was inimitable. But more than this his work kept bringing me back to ponder on the chaos into which the world seemed to be floundering deeper and deeper. For Shaw's plays were not just bright ideas, good stories or dramatic situations, they arose from quite another source, a desire to show up the false values, inequalities and stupidities of the age in which he lived. The sense of situation, the taut dialogue and the fun were all merely technical aids to this aim. But it happened that his theatrical genius was such that plays took on a life of their own and will last long after the windmills at which he tilted cease to be social issues. It is hard to imagine the violent controversy that his early work aroused. Theatres refused to allow his plays to be performed, newspapers would not carry advertisements for them. When his first play, *Widowers' Houses*, was presented by a Sunday society for one performance, Shaw took a curtain call. Among the enthusiastic applause was one loud, long 'Boo!' from the gallery. But Shaw was equal to the occasion: 'I quite agree with you, sir. But what are we two among so many?'

But it was not the fireworks, it was the ideas which attracted me. He had something to say and said it with consummate skill, calculating every scene for maximum originality and effect. Even the laughter was calculated. 'Human nature, such as it is,' he used to say, 'can stand serious conversation for about twenty minutes. It is then necessary to relieve the tension and make them laugh.' This was his technique at public meetings where he always made a joke during the first minute, not to get a laugh, but to listen where the laugh came from. If it came from the back of the gallery, he was being heard all over the hall and it was that that mattered.

For many years he watched over my career with paternal care and I grew to idolize him, for, in those days, when I was part of the spearhead of the exploding mass medium which was changing the whole shape of society and in touch with many of the leading figures of the day, he was the only man among them who appeared to have any social conscience or any practical suggestions to offer to combat the dragon's teeth which I felt were everywhere being sown among us. With each play that appeared – *The Apple-cart, Too True to be Good, On the Rocks* – I expected some sort of revelation that would wake the world up to its situation. Nothing of the kind happened, of course, and later a sort of disillusion began to overtake me. It was many years before I understood that all social reforms are superficial and simply, so to speak, shift the weight on to the other shoulder. For the world to find a way through we have to dig much deeper than that.

———

TODAY I don't set much store by those political views that made Shaw such a controversial figure in his early years. What I remember is the splendid vitality of his bearing, his magnanimity, his greatness of style. I never saw him slumped, he was always erect. I never saw him depressed or bored or touched by self-pity. He was a living example of the Parable of the Talents, broadening and deepening his work so that at seventy (when I first knew him) he had just completed his masterpiece, *St Joan.* He confirmed in me the desire to emulate the way he lived, fully and generously, to leave the world richer for having been in it. All the socialism was just the theory of his work. Put into the mouths of living men and women, it was forced into the background. Only prejudiced people argued that all Shaw's characters just spouted Shaw – as if the broad humanity of *Candida,* the wit of *You Never Can Tell* or the compassion of *St Joan* did not exist! Ask Sybil Thorndike, Edith Evans, or any other actor or actress who has played his plays: you will not find that point of view.

The admiration and veneration that was heaped upon him in later years might have turned the head of a lesser man, but he remained steady throughout it all, praising his contemporaries in memorable phrases. Asked on one occasion what he thought would remain of his work a thousand years hence, he replied that in the encyclopedias of the time would appear an entry: 'Shaw, George Bernard. Subject of a bust by Rodin'.

───

Now in old age myself, I think of him as one of the great influences of my life, for he set standards of conscience, integrity and professional craftsmanship I have never met elsewhere. His life was cast in a large mould and he thought and acted with a natural magnanimity that made other men seem petty and vain. There was a severity approaching Olympian grandeur about his later years, but it was always tempered by his mischievous and rapier-like humour. I remember sitting in his study one morning when Maurice Chevalier was announced. Then at the height of his career, charming and debonair, this great professional, then a young and extremely attractive man, sat at his ease, chatting of this and that. Came a pause in the conversation, and Shaw leaned forward in the most engaging way, 'Tell me, Mr Chevalier,' he said enquiringly, 'you act, don't you?'

Great writers are always surrounded by swarms of critics and commentators, praising or denigrating their work. But I cannot bring much critical faculty to the man who, in my early youth, gave me the largesse of his company, the benefit of his wisdom, the hilarity of his wit and the encouragement and tolerance of a father at the outset of my rather mercurial career. Trips to Hollywood, the South Seas, the Second World War and South Africa separated me from him for many years. But three months before his death at ninety-four I returned to visit him at Ayot. He greeted me as if I had not been away a week. His mind was as clear as ever, but he was not much interested in the world around him. He was past writing, he said, but was spending the days meticulously putting in order a complete edition of his works with all the alterations and additions that had accrued over the years. Alone now in the modest house, for Charlotte was dead, his faithful housekeeper served the usual impeccable lunch. Still walking erect with the aid of a stick, he waved my car away down the lane when I left him, never to see him again.

9

Drama in New York

I N the early days at Savoy Hill, when we were all working under considerable pressure, Reith thought it would be a good idea if heads of departments broke off their work about four o'clock and everyone got together for tea. In this way we would be able to keep in touch with each other's problems. Informal discussions were better than committees and we should all get to know each other better. After I had resigned from the BBC, Reith told me I could come in to these teas whenever I liked and for a few months I often did so.

One afternoon a stranger was there. Reith introduced him as a Mr Aylesworth, and it turned out he was the President of the National Broadcasting Corporation of America. A few days later I received a letter from him saying he had heard I was an expert in radio drama and that in the States this aspect of broadcasting had not been developed at all; would I care to come over to New York and teach the NBC how to do it? I would have a completely free hand to produce, say, three plays, in a period of three months, passages would be paid and the fee £600. I owed this, of course, to Reith's recommendation and promptly accepted the windfall before Aylesworth could change his mind!

It was true that I had been much attracted to the possibilities of radio drama. In that first series of Shakespeare plays I had seen at once how readily they adapted themselves to the new medium. I had evolved the technique of putting the various ingredients of a play – voices, music, effects – into separate studios to have control of the volume of each through the mixing panel. I had encouraged playwrights to try their hand at writing radio plays and moved on myself into the adaptation of novels. Stories from Dickens, Conrad, D. H. Lawrence and others came alive in quite a new way through the microphone. The development had been rapid. Soon we had quite a library of special music and sound effects recorded on disc, much simplifying and improving our techniques. So, with all this know-how at my finger-tips, I packed a suitcase of sound effects, lent by the BBC, and embarked on the *Bremen* for New York.

'Get those damn discs out of here, Mr Lewis, and make it snappy, see!' It was the first of many shocks I received when I reached the NBC studios. The broadcasting and gramophone companies were locked in a fierce struggle. No discs of any kind were allowed to enter NBC offices and if mine were found heaven knows how many million dollars' compensation would have to be paid. Broadcasting in America, as I quickly found out, was something absolutely different from anything I knew. It was esentially a commercial enterprise. The NBC, in effect, merely provided studios and a microphone to anyone who could pay for them and depended on this sale of studio time for its revenue.

It was a thriving business. Everyone who had anything to sell or promote rushed to this new ubiquitous method of advertising. Rates soared. The NBC in 1930 had a 'licence to print money' and had lost no time in getting on with it. Programme staff as we understood it did not exist. The programme was the business of the man who bought the time. There were a number of 'runners' who spent their days selling the idea of radio advertising to anyone who wasn't already converted, and their success (and salary) was measured by the sponsors they pulled in. Studios – and there were many of them – were booked from morning till night, weeks ahead. There was no 'sustaining' time in which the broadcasting company carried the cost of the programmes themselves in order to put out something that nobody would sponsor. I was, I suppose, one of the first people to face them with this problem. Here I was over from England with a mandate from this President to put on radio plays. They had to do what they could, but they had no idea what a radio play was and in any case saw no reason for such an innovation when they hadn't a free studio from 6 am till midnight.

When I politely announced that I should require three studios for a production, their chins dropped with a clang to their navels. 'Three studios!' It was madness. It meant the loss of thousands of dollars. 'And, of course, three three-hour periods for rehearsal,' I added.

'Rehearsal!' they were nonplussed. 'What d'ye want to rehoise?'

'Well, the actors, you know, and balance – music, sound effects and so on. . .'

The President had landed them with a nut, that was evident. But they were very polite. They explained that at the NBC no studio was connected to any other. Each had a line direct to the transmitter. Technically it was impossible to link one studio with another, to control volume or anything like that. It was my turn to think them mad. And how could I put on a production?

It took literally weeks of patient explaining for them to begin to see what I was after. There was no studio control panel, no way of listening in to what was going out, no talk-back between the producer and players – and, of course, no gramophone turntables. Nothing. But, much more important, they were not interested. I hadn't the knack of selling the idea which was essential to get their co-operation. There are people from Europe who know how to adapt themselves to America and thrive there. People, often quite unknown, suddenly acquire a fame and fortune they have never known at home when they reach the States. I have had three shots at making my way in America. They have all been failures.

My last production for NBC was the famous play by Carel Capek, *R.U.R.* I had managed to get two studios – after midnight when the station was closed down! I don't suppose a thousand people heard the play. Western Electric had lashed up a mixing box on a chair at which I and the engineer were stationed with earphones. This stood in the studio where the actors performed. The music and effects were in another. As far as effects were concerned, we were back to nineteenth-century props. Hand-turned drums with canvas stretched over them made wind, lead shot rolled on a tray did for the sea, half-coconuts were horses' hooves and so on. The whole thing had an absolutely 'amateur theatricals' air, but strangely enough everyone concerned enjoyed it. Even one or two of the staff allowed 'Maybe you got something there, Mr Lewis.' But it was too soon. America was not ready. They didn't need this sort of programme. When they did they got to it in quite another way – soap opera.

But I had other irons in the American fire. My dramatic efforts were not confined to radio. I had written three plays, starting off with an ambitious blank-verse drama on the death of Montezuma, which nobody wanted (but for which Ricketts executed a superb set of dress and set designs now in the National Arts Collection). I had followed this with a modern comedy, *Jazz Patterns*, produced at the Everyman, a perfect flop which earned me £5 in royalties. Now I had with me another play, *Iron Flowers*, produced by a Sunday society, in which a New York producer was interested. It got so near production that I was fired with ambition to write another comedy which would finally succeed in New York.

10

Dreams in Italy

I T was now 1924. So, writing ahead to Douska (my wife) to take the two children, we had acquired (Ivor, aged 4, and Celia, aged 3) to the Lago Maggiore, I followed a fortnight later. For the past two summers we had taken our annual holiday as guests of the conductor Albert Coates, in his villa at Cerro, a small village on the then unknown bank of the lake opposite Stresa. Somewhere near there I hoped we could find a little place for the summer. We found it at a village called Arolo, five miles south of Cerro, a tiny house right on the lake rocks, six rooms and a rent of £18 a year. As we could then live comfortably there on £3 a week, we could manage for the summer on what I had earned in America, so we settled in and I started to write. The new play was finished in a month. Despatched to New York, it sold right away with an advance of £100, for autumn production. I was elated – prematurely, as it turned out – for the six months' option expired, and though it was renewed for another £100, the play was never produced. It disappeared – and I have even forgotten its title!

Life on the lake was idyllic. We were always in or on the water. My son and daughter soon learned to chatter fluently in the Milanese dialect. We got an outboard for our dinghy and explored the lake.

One day near the village I noticed a deserted stretch of lake front, backed by a precipice about 500 feet high. There seemed to be a strip of woodland about 50 feet above the rocks that dropped sheer into the water. This strip ran along the coast for about a quarter of a mile. Next day we found our way along the cobbled lane that led to it and, struggling through the brambles, scrambled all over it. The place was magical. Half of it was overgrown with chestnut, hornbeam and lime, the other half had at one time been vine terraces, now fallen into disuse. The views across the lake were immense. The sun set over the water behind the snow-capped Alps. It was far bigger than appeared from the water. There were places where steps could be made to lead down to a port for a boat and for bathing. In the village it was known as the *runco* or wasteland, because the earth was too poor to grow much. So it was going cheap. Nobody, in those days, thought there was any value in beauty.

It was this ground which, as I have previously described, Ricketts gave me as a present. I think of all presents it was the most satisfying ever given to me. This was partly because it was a challenge – a totally unexpected possibility to develop talents (if I had any) for transforming this strip of wild woodland into a garden and siting somewhere in it a secret hideout to write in. Fame as a writer was all I cared about then.

As soon as I became the legal owner, we started work – and here, quite simply and unobtrusively, enters Adolfo. My Italian was non-existent, but there was a rascal in the village with a wooden leg who spoke a few words of English. So, *faute de mieux*, I engaged him for a couple of weeks to start clearing the ground. I soon saw that he did practically no work, while the young peasant he had brought along to help him never stopped. I noted how strong and accurate he was with a pick, how he talked and joked good-humouredly, but never paused, how he seemed quite oblivious of the way his one-legged mate found any excuse to stop to gossip, how he went steadily on, hour after hour, and seemed as fresh at the end of it as at the beginning. This was Adolfo and from that moment a relationship started to grow between us which never looked back. Wooden Leg soon faded out and in his place came another strong young villager, Onorate.

These two, Adolfo and Onorate, formed a partnership that continued unbroken over the next ten years, right through until the outbreak of war in 1939. I soon found out Adolfo was far more than just a peasant labourer. He was a qualified *capo maestro*, with a licence to use dynamite. He had worked all over Italy, building tunnels in the Alps and aqueducts in Calabria. He was an expert in reinforced concrete, but equally at home building a dry wall. But over and above all his abilities he was a shrewd, humorous, practical man who had the knack of making everything seem easy. He was never at a loss when faced with a new problem. He could read a drawing, even my rough sketches, and I found I could leave a long programme of work in his hands to find that he had somehow grasped the essence of the idea. 'You are the hand of my head,' I said to him once. 'More of your heart,' was his reply.

In addition to all this Adolfo had another quality of the robust Italian of the north – he was absolutely and naturally honest. He would work for months at a time without pay, when I was absent for some reason, trusting me completely to turn up some time with money to bring him up to date and meet the bills he had incurred – of which he kept an accurate and thrifty account. I am glad to say I never let him down. So a warm bond of affection and respect grew up between us. In this he never once overstepped the limits of what he considered to be our relationship. He was the living embodiment of Shaw's adage: 'Keeping your distance is the secret of good manners.' But he brought a homely warmth to everything he did that was irresistible and attached himself to me and my children and to everything we wanted to do with unflagging enthusiasm and discernment.

So we began turning this rocky wilderness into what the locals called a *paradiso*. For, soon after we had bought it, they woke up to the fact that it was a wonderful place. 'We had to wait for the Englishman to show us the beauty of our own village,' they said. Below us, as we worked, stretched the shining levels of the lake. Four miles across on the opposite shore ran the main road from Simplon to Milan, but here we were in untouched country. Sometimes we could distantly hear the hum of cars as they came up through Arona, Belgirate, Stresa and Baveno, to snake off through the defiles north to Domodossola. Above that road the mountains rose steeply into the spine of the Alps and behind this majestic backdrop of interlocking peaks the sun set every evening, leaving a bland twilight of content that seemed to roll over the village like a mist.

Along the ledge, about 50 feet above the water, we began to make paths, build walls and steps under pergolas leading down through shady tunnels of hornbeam to the water, a tiny port for boats, a sandpit for sunbathing. In some places the ledge was wide enough to get in a tennis court and the little house that came later, but sometimes it shrank to a few feet and the rocky crags rose almost sheer for 500 feet. It was from this that we hit on the villa's name – the Rupi, the villa of the crags. At the southern end of the ground the precipices eased off into steep terraces. Here we replanted the vines that had once been cultivated and set in fruit trees. But most of the place was overgrown with a scrub wood of oak, lime, hornbeam and acacia, cut to the ground every six years for firewood. These thickets we began to tame and thin out, cutting the ten or fifteen sapling trunks to five or six and the next year to two or three, so that a canopy of shade began to spread above large trunks, to disclose new vistas of lapping water.

———

So it went, slowly and steadily over the years. Often I was impatient at not having the sort of money that would have enabled me to finish it in a year or two; but now, looking back, I see how much better it was for growing slowly. Adolfo and Onorate worked all the year round for eight years. In that time they built about half a mile of paths, a dozen flights of steps, a tennis court, a port, a house, to say nothing of miles of walls and projects such as bringing electricity, piping the whole ground for water and installing an electric pump to lift it to a reservoir at the top of the terraces.

The little house itself – a big living room, one bedroom, kitchen and bathroom – Adolfo only just managed to squeeze on to the ledge. The precipice at the back rose so shear that a stone dislodged from the summit could fall right through the roof. Sometimes during winter storms quite large rocks did so and more than once we were flooded out, swilling the water out with brooms while Adolfo, in the pouring rain, plugged the roof with the spare tiles we kept to hand.

As it all matured and the trees grew up, the place gradually mellowed into an idyllic retreat, a marvellous secret refuge from a world rocketing towards self-destruction. All through those years I was battling to make a living, to educate my children, to paddle my own canoe in a world where it was growing increasingly difficult to do so. I was away across Europe, over to New York and California, on to the South Seas and back. But always, behind it all, lay the call of the Rupi, and through all those active exciting years this background existed. A filigree of thought would slip in at all sorts of unexpected moments: the rocky wilderness above which the eagles wheeled, the trusses of blossom that stood full to the pacific skies; how the camellia and magnolia followed the forsythia, the wisteria turning from a grey mist to a mauve torrent, and then the nightingales, the roses. . . Wherever I was it was still there, waiting to restore me to sanity and peace.

When war seemed inevitable I remained there till the very last moment. What would happen to it all? England and Italy were going to be 'enemies'. Would it all be blown up, or commandeered? 'Do not worry; I shall be here,' said Adolfo. Six years later, when I returned, scrounging a jeep and driving into the little piazza one evening, a fortnight after the Armistice, there were shouts of joy and recognition. The whole village turned out. After the excitement of kissings and greetings and the pleasure of seeing them all again had somewhat died, 'How is the Rupi?' I asked.

'All right. It is all right. It was let to an engineer. He took good care of it. Then, well, the *brigante neri* tried to. . . but we took care of that . . .'

'Could I move in? I've got a week.'

'Yes. Why not? It's easy.'

Adolfo always made everything easy.

Next day I was to learn that the village had taken all the furniture, linen, pictures, crockery, silver, and salted it away in bottom drawers and cellars to save it from the *brigante neri*, those so-called police who, after the capitulation of Italy, were robbing everywhere. Now they brought it all out and a strange procession trooped down to the Rupi carrying everything on their heads.

That evening it was all back in place. Rina was there – just the same – to cook one of her famous risottos, as she had done for ten years before the war. Adolfo and I dined together and toasted the peace in wine he had trodden with his own feet. After six years of war, in one day, everything at the Rupi was back as it had always been: not a spoon was missing.

11

Elstree to Hollywood Jungles

I F I were to go on from episode to episode, presenting myself as a man who has led a successful, varied, interesting career, free from worry, free from trouble, it would be very far from the truth. In fact, from the moment I left the BBC to 'paddle my own canoe', it was a struggle to keep afloat. I had not, in fact, sufficient talent to succeed even when opportunity offered; but worse, when I achieved some success I found I lost interest, threw away the possibility, and moved on to something new. To make a profit in life it is a dreadful handicap to be jack of all trades and master of none. How curious that when, later in life, I saw this handicap clearly and was on guard against it, fatally the same pattern returned again and again. We do not realize the power of the negative forces in life, the forces that keep us where we are.

But in the early days the idea of failure never entered my head. I was full, overfull, of self-confidence and bursting with vitality. I became the official programme critic to the BBC, writing weekly reports (which nobody ever read). I did a radio column for the *Observer*. I translated and adapted plays for the theatre. I joined HMV as an expert when the 'talkies' were just coming in and they hoped to supply the sound know-how that the film industry did not possess. I obtained a contract from the BBC to write or adapt nine plays a year for the medium and produce them. In short, I was running here and there, struggling to make money to keep my family and educate my children. But I did not see it like that. Money was, I considered, a secondary consideration. I was look-ing for a new career.

It opened in the form of a mandate from G. B. S. to transfer one of his plays to the screen. He saw the arrival of the talking picture as an opportunity to give his work a wider audience and he allowed me the privilege of being the first to try to do it. British International Pictures jumped at the chance of screening a Shaw play, nobody having so far persuaded the great man to have anything to do with films. They were willing to pay the price – not to cut or alter the play in any way and to accept an absolutely unknown, untried man as director (me). It was a heavy gamble.

Shaw was curious enough to start me off with a one-act play: *How He Lied to Her Husband*. It had three characters, one set, and was as much like a movie as a cow is like a pianola. Somehow or other I had picked up the technique of laying out a shooting script. BIP showed me every consideration, putting a studio at my disposal for a month and giving me their best cameraman. They were convinced, of course, that, knowing nothing about it, I should be pretty slow and make a lot of mistakes. In fact, I rehearsed the cast (Vera Lenox, Edmund Gwenn and Robert Harris) in town till they were word and action perfect, worked out every camera angle before we went on the floor and completed the picture in four days! This staggered BIP. They imagined me to be a genius – an opinion of which I did not disabuse them, having the same idea myself! Shaw was delighted with the result. The picture (now a collectors' rarity) was the antithesis of a movie – since it did not move. The critics scorned it. It didn't lose money because it had cost so little to make (£5000), but it resulted in my being offered a two-year contract as a film director. I was off on a new career.

———

M y first assignment was the opera *Carmen*. It was a pretty ambitious subject for a novice, especially on the shoe-string budget of BIP. The main difficulty (as on the stage) is finding a lady to play the title role who weighs under 16 stone. We found one (Namara) who weighed only nine; but, unfortunately, when Malcom Sargent got her into rehearsal with the London Symphony Orchestra, she sang flat. The next problem was how to manage the crowds and the bullfight at the end of the story without paying for a bullfight or a crowd. BIP solved that by purchasing the complete bullfight sequence from a silent picture on the subject made by the great French director Duvivier some years before. 'Just cut your principals into it,' they said.

At first this seemed an impossibility; but somehow or other, on a brief location at Ronda in Spain, we managed to find the exact spot where Duvivier had set up his camera ten years before. In Seville, to get some close-ups, we hired a bull which a young bullfighter induced to charge him, and when we got home purchased from Express Dairies one of the full-sized stuffed Friesian cows which in those days decorated windows to sell their milk. This cow, painted black and ornamented with a pair of authentic horns, looked real enough to face our operatic bullfighter waving his red flag, provided we used only short flashes. (Our cow, incidentally, was a good enough fake to scare the daylights out of a couple of chippies, who came on it in a gloomy corner one evening in a passage outside the studio, thought it was real, dropped their tools and ran!)

If you want to prove that hard work never hurt anyone, you have only to turn to the sort of hours film units worked in 1931. For the period when the picture was actually being shot we were up at 6.30 every morning to get to Elstree and see the rushes of the day before at eight o'clock. Then on to the floor where we would work right through till nine or ten o'clock at night. BIP did not allow a director the luxury of a producer to look after all the hundred and one queries that arise in the making of any picture. All this I handled myself with the assistant director in the intervals between shots. In addition we had a seventy-piece orchestra to accommodate in the studio. All the music was recorded live. The playback technique had not been invented. To maintain the action over long musical sequences we had to employ three cameras (which ruined the lighting). Considering all the difficulties and the technical problems raised in this, the first opera ever recorded on film, I still consider it a bit of a triumph to have completed a ninety-minute feature in thirty shooting days for the sum of £17,000. Today if it cost £1,700,000 it would be cheap. Of course, the work was hard, but an enormous enthusiasm and goodwill prevailed. The unions had not then begun to strangle the goose that laid the golden eggs. The picture gave BIP a certain prestige, but financially it was a flop.

People who lose money are usually willing to gamble more in the hope of recouping what they have already lost, so now BIP accepted a light comedy I had written. It concerned a young man who fell in love with a wax model in a shop window and spent the rest of the picture finding the original. For this I not only wrote story and script but music and lyrics as well. I also directed and cut the picture. I don't suppose anyone else has ever been fool enough to do the whole thing just for the director's fee – supplying story, script, music and lyrics free! It was a blatant piece of exhibitionism. With enough sense to gather a first-class team around me I might have brought it off, but I was far too cocksure of myself for that. The picture, though it didn't actually lose money, was a worse-than-average second feature.

Nothing daunted, I finally committed cinematic suicide by attempting the first Shaw 'feature' – a film of *Arms and the Man*. The same adamant conditions – not a word was to be cut – obtained. All the wit and sparkle of the stage play evaporated as mere verbosity on film. BIP had had enough. *Arms and the Man* lost real money. Shaw had brought me in and Shaw saw me out. Blessed be the name of Shaw! The door was closed in my face. I was not wanted.

For the first time in my life others had tired of me before I tired of them. It had a disastrous effect on me. I got the first glimpse of how superficial my abilities were – and quickly looked away. At the same time I was far too proud to go round to other studios asking for work. In fact I had now acquired quite a lot of the technical knowledge required to make pictures; but a film director has to have more than this, a certain prima-donna quality of self-confidence, of behaving as if there was nobody in the world like him. Now I had lost all this, I was absolutely deflated. Moreover, from the handsome salary of a film director, I was suddenly without any visible means of support. My marriage had run down. My wife had returned to China. My children were being taken care of abroad. I was alone with my failure. The young women who at that time flocked to my bed did not console me. I could see no way ahead. At thirty-four it felt as if I was finished. Shaw had once described me as a 'mercurial antelope'. Well, now the creature had no jump.

FOR two years I lived with this sense of failure. Then Peter Davies Ltd decided to publish the manuscript of my flying days in the First World War, eighteen years after the event. I had been tinkering with it for some time. Now I rapidly completed it and when it came out under the title *Sagittarius Rising* and got rave notices, including a whole-page eulogy from G. B. S. in the *New Statesman*, I was exceedingly surprised.

Hardly had this occurred when the BBC decided to open the first television service in the world and took me on as Director of Outside Broadcasts. The start of TV has been too well documented for me to add much to it. The beginning of things is always exciting. It is only when people begin to slip back to repeating what they have done before that boredom and bureaucracy move in. How right the Red Queen was to observe to Alice that you have to run faster and faster to stay in the same place! In that dreary moribund pile called Alexandra Palace we battled with all the early problems, worked the long hours, got the kick that comes from all pioneering, but I never really settled into it, for when *Sagittarius* appeared in America and *Time* got enthusiastic a telegram arrived from Paramount Pictures inviting me over to Hollywood to collaborate in the writing of a script on the history of aviation. As the salary (£200 per week) would earn me in a month about as much as I would earn in a year with the BBC, I quickly signed, packed my bags and left on the *Rex* from Genoa.

———

So in a period of six months I was swept up from the trough to the crest of a new wave to revel in a brief period during which (for the only time in my life) I had more money than I could spend.

It was the twilight of the great period of American movies, though the industry did not know it. In three years the Second World War was to come and 'pictures' would begin to fight their losing battle against rising prices and TV. But then it was rolling along on an extravagant scale that you could not credit till you got there. Studios vied with each other to sign up every writer, director or actor in the world that might conceivably be valuable to them. Idle stars ate out their hearts at huge salaries and promises of work that never came off. Well-known writers found they were not even wanted in the studios that paid them. Successful producers were shocked to find their salaries continued long after the contracts had ended and when they offered to return the money were told it would upset the accounts if they did. The famous director Eddie

Goulding, who was a great improviser of stories, told one, in his cups, to Louis B. Mayer who promptly bought it; but when Eddie had been paid and asked to deliver, he could not remember what the story was! So it went. There was so much money, everybody took it for granted and, far from being the dreadful 'immoral' place I expected, I found the Hollywood stars and their satellites friendly, hospitable and not at all ostentatious of their wealth. In the glorious climate, floodlit tennis courts and private pools provided an evening's relaxation and exercise. Open-air barbecues and an early bed were the rule for hard-working people who had to be on the set, made up, by nine o'clock in the morning. The industry was candidly commercial and made no bones about it and I rather liked their no-artistic-nonsense attitude to any long-haired propositions. At least you knew where you were.

However, my contract, which was for five years breakable every six months, luckily turned out not to be of the do-nothing variety. I was assigned an office, a desk and a lot of sharp pencils and settled straight down to work with my collaborator, Philip MacDonald. Our assignment was to find a story which would bridge past and present, exploiting the romance of the birth of aviation in 1902 and moving on to 1937, a period of thirty-five years – just too long to allow one star to carry the picture. During the ensuing six months we wrote five scripts, none of which began to look like getting off the ground. The Scenario Editor of Paramount, Jeff Lazarus, was a rough but pleasant Coney Island Jew and his knack of reducing the writer's work to its essentials still remains vividly in my mind. 'Boys, if you can't tell the story in two lines, you haven't got a story. Take Romeo and Juliet. Now in two lines, what's the story of Romeo and Juliet? I'll tell ya: boy loves girl and her old man don't like him.'

We were never able to tell our story in twenty lines, let alone two, but we were bound to recognize the precept as valid. So we battled on, day after day, just as if we were in any other office job, and failed to come up with anything that was not politely consigned to the waste-paper basket. I soon discovered there were outer and inner circles among Paramount scriptwriters. Those who were firmly 'in' wrote script after script that went straight to the floor for Bing Crosby or Bob Hope. Outside were others fighting to get in, writers with one successful picture to their credit or perhaps an outstanding stage success. Outside them again were the people, like me, who had been brought over for a one-off assignment 'on spec'. Our chances were pretty slim.

They were in fact, for us, slimmer than that. For soon the grapevine told us that Bill Wellman, then an established director, had already been engaged to direct 'our' picture. Everyone knew that Bill Wellman carried his own writer and would accept nothing that he hadn't written. So what were we writing scripts for? Why had we been engaged? The whole operation was a point-less waste of money. There would be no future in it. It was just as mad as all the other extravagances. But at least we were working and the cheques came rolling in. I had a pretty house in Coldwater Canyon and if the Californian scene was pretty nutty in the movie world, it was even more wildly improbable outside it.

Amy Semple MacPherson went on trial on a charge of fraud and embezzlement brought by her sister. The evidence was enough to have damned any minister of God in the Old World for good, but not in the New. Amy rallied the faithful, passed bed-sheets round the congregation in her huge 'temple' to which people pinned fifty- and hundred-dollar notes to pay the costs of the trial (from which she emerged as innocent). Her chorines (on bicycles) opened the 'service' with a chorus 'Peddling away to Jesus' and when He came on stage for an interview with Amy, He bowed Himself out, walking backwards.

'Religion' was, in fact, good business and a whole street in Hollywood housed, in queer-shaped buildings, the headquarters of dozens of strange sects, all vying with each other for public support. For if, as Amy had proved, you can once get public confidence, the money rolls in. Some would say that all religion was a confidence trick, based on the promise of some future life which, obviously, can never be guaranteed. In any case, the soil of California seemed peculiarly adapted to breed a population of naïve, credulous simpletons all too willing to be conned into any plausible rigmarole an orator could invent.

But the extravagant improbabilities did not end there. It is, after all, improbable to find active oil wells in the middle of busy streets with the traffic whirling past them. It is improbable too, when introduced to the Captain of the Homicide Squad of the Los Angeles Police, to be invited to take shares in the oil well yourself.

It was after an all-night session with the squad at their station on the twenty-second floor of a downtown skyscraper that the suggestion came up. I had gone along there with a fellow script-writer on the chance of catching a murder call. Some time past midnight it came and five of us leapt for the elevator which hurled us downward to the basement to fall into an open police car which, headlights and sirens on, shot out into the crowded street and took off at seventy through all the traffic lights to find on a slum pavement a young Negro lying in a pool of blood, his shin-bone sticking through his trousers. He had jumped (or been pushed) from a seventh-floor window. The whole thing was grim and macabre, but the boys went about their work in a very professional way. Names, addresses, witnesses, they got it all buttoned up and had the poor chap away to hospital in twenty minutes.

When we got back to HQ they began to talk about their well. It was situated right in the middle of two other areas that were already bearing heavily. For $100 a fortune was in sight. I paid up willingly.

Some nights later we made up a party in two cars, complete with wives and girls, and went off to visit the well. Once out of town, California is a barren land. We stopped for an open-air barbecue supper in the yard of a ghost town. People had once lived here mining for gold and, when the vein gave out, had abandoned the whole place. In the brilliant moonlight the deserted houses, white paint peeling, did indeed look ghostly. The doors creaked to and fro on the night breeze. The noisy gaiety of our party seemed somehow an offence in this eerie place, which echoed to the only nostalgic sound I heard in America – the wail of the sirens of the great steam trains bound north for San Francisco.

At last we came to the well. It stood on a rise among dry rolling downs. The were the sounds of heavy engines, spurts of steam and, in the ditch round the derrick, the oil and water pumped from the well was burning. Oil! In the flickering light the drillers looked huge. Wearing heavy helmets and enormous gloves, they man-handled sixty-foot lengths of three-inch pipe, screwing them deftly into other lengths already half-sunk into the ground and turning, turning slowly as the drill sank lower in the grip of a heavy chuck. There was something heroic about the scene. It was easy to be caught by such a gamble. Any minute the drill might burst through into the subterranean lake and wealth come pouring up through the pipe. They were down 5000 feet. Any moment now! It was sure to happen when we were there. We waited and waited. Slowly the grinding pipes sank lower. The moonlight lit a primeval scene of man wresting his plunder from the earth. We drank coffee and waited some more. At last we went home. But later, at 6000 feet, the rig was abandoned. The well never came in.

THOUGH we never let up on our efforts to find a solution to our script problem, as the months went by it became clearer and clearer that we were getting nowhere and the day arrived when I was politely told that my contract would not be renewed. The six months were up. It was curtains. Although the Hollywood scene had an almost hypnotic fascination about it and to fail there seemed total failure, it was plainly useless to hang about on the prospect of work which might never materialize.

Then, just as I was packing my bags, Gaby Pascal turned up. I had met him when lunching with G. B. S. before coming over to Hollywood. I remembered how he had talked then in terms of great epic pictures about India and I had mentally classed him as one of those engaging charlatans who occasionally used to show up at Shaw's luncheon table. For him to get the backing to make any of those epics would be a confidence trick (since he freely admitted he hadn't a bean) that I felt was most unlikely to come off. But he had one quality I did not suspect at the time, a quality I shared with him, a genuine affection and admiration for G.B.S. But beyond this, as it turned out, he had a flair for raising money and, more important, that prima-donna quality I have referred to earlier of getting people to believe in him by behaving in the grand manner like the movie moguls of the time. He might indeed have proved to be one, had he not accepted the serious handicap of trying to establish himself on Shavian subjects. These were finally to prove the ruin of him, as they had done, on a much smaller scale, with me.

However, here he was, enquiring if I would consent to make a script of *Pygmalion*. I do not think he would ever have done so had not Shaw himself suggested it and had he not been, at that time, willing to fall in with anything the great man wished. There were, of course, the usual built-in snags. Not a word was to be cut

or altered; but Gaby was brimming over with confidence. I agreed
to have a go.

The central theme of *Pygmalion*, as everyone knows, is a bet to
pass off a flower girl as a duchess. But in the original version of the
play Shaw bilks the issue; the scene where the bet is won is side-
stepped and so the effective climax to which the play is building
never comes. This was a glaring dramatic fault and I wrote to
Shaw pointing it out to him. He might as well, I said, have written
St Joan and omitted the trial scene. Then the sparks began to fly. It
soon became very clear that Shaw thought this of no importance
whatever. Eliza's metamorphosis and Higgins' precious phonetic
alphabet were the two pillars of the play and it took all Gaby's
Herculean blarney (later on) to pull them down. To begin with
G.B.S. would have none of it. So I settled down to the sad task of
breaking up the dialogue into endless shots, knowing that, as it
stood, the film would be bound to suffer the same fate as *Arms and
the Man*. Pointing out this central defect to Gaby – which he
caught on to in a flash – was, I supppose, my only real contribution to the script (for which in some mysterious way, together with
three other writers, I got an Oscar). I finished it, handed it over to
Gaby and left for the South Seas.

12

Dusky Paradise

M ORE than a year before I came to California I had done
some research into the history of the Pacific and the enigma
of its population by races which could not be indigenous to the
area. Reading about the early navigators – Roggwein, Wallace,
Bougainville, Cook – and their explorations in these unknown
seas, a desire had begun to take shape to go there and see for
myself if anything at all remained of that idyllic way of life which
seemed to have seduced everyone who had ever been there. If I was
to go at all, now seemed a good moment, since I was halfway there
already. All I had to do was to catch a coaster down to Panama
and pick up the monthly French packet plying between Marseilles
and the New Hebrides. This would call at Tahiti, and it was
Tahiti, the Queen of the South Seas, which embodied for me the
tragedy of a murdered civilization.

It seemed that our own civilization was well on the way to being
murdered also. The screams of that neurotic house painter from
Munich were already becoming piercing and the pattern of
double-crossing threats and lies with which the world was soon to
become embroiled was already taking shape.

My memories of the First World War had not left me. In fact,
though they had remained underground most of the time, I found
they had developed in me a tendency to look for anything which
might promise even a slim chance of a better way of life. I could
not then have defined exactly what I meant by this, but I felt that
the world's growing appetite for material things was evidently
coarsening its texture. As the years went by it seemed to me to be
getting more and more out of balance. It was this that had led me
to value art, for artists – in whatever branch they practised –
seemed to be moved by quite a different set of standards. They

were influenced in some mysterious way by a desire to struggle to
give expression to 'something' essentially their own and to persist
in the face of poverty and difficulty, whether the world recognized
or acclaimed them or not. They had to do it. They were, so to
speak, under orders. Taken all together the world of art repre-
sented a massive counterbalancing force to the material side of life.
It alone seemed to hold some hope for the future.

Tahiti, from what I had read, had evolved a form of society
quite different from anything to be found elsewhere. For a
thousand years the island had remained free from all outside
influences, a unique dot in the vast emptiness of the Pacific. Its
people's communal way of life, their humane attitude to their
neighbours, even to war, seemed to be another attempt to evolve a
society harmonious, tolerant and sane. Apart from the romance of
the coral reefs and the lagoons, the large-hearted *vahinés* and the
simple life, I wondered if anything at all remained of the idyll that
the early navigators and then the missionaries, whalers, and slave
traders so effectually destroyed. So I set out from Panama, on the
Ville d'Amiens, paquebot mixte, on the fourteen-day crossing of
the Pacific.

The dream of Utopia must be one of the oldest dreams of man.
The reformers that overthrow dynasties, from Akhnaton to Lenin,
are all motivated by a longing to make the world a better place to
live in. Bougainville, who followed Wallace to Tahiti (bringing
syphilis with him), returned to give latitude and longitude to
Rousseau's dream of a perfect society and the French Revolution,
at least in part, grew out of it.

What was it that they found which left such an indelible impression on the Western world, so indelible that even now, after
200 years, the mere mention of the threadbare phrases 'South Sea
island' and 'blue lagoon', bring a misty look to people's eyes and a
longing for some rare perfection not to be found this side of
paradise. It was the innocence and purity of a people who in a
thousand years had evolved a simple society perfectly adapted to
their island life. Because they were free from fear, they did not
cringe or hoard; because there was enough for all, they did not
give a thought for tomorrow, living openly and candidly in the
moment. They had no written language and therefore no prece-
dents or archives. There was practically no crime, no prisons, no
disease and, best of all, no money. The only valuable thing on the

island was a red feather. They helped each other in all communal enterprises, building, fishing and feasting. In their rare tribal wars, when one man killed another the family of the dead man received the killer into their home and thereafter treated him as a son. They gave away their first-born children to near relations, fearing to spoil them by too much love. The only art they had brought to perfection was that of dance and mime.

Add to all this a balmy climate, never under 70 °F, never over 80°, constant breezes, abundances of fish and fruit, no pests, no diseases, no more dangerous animals than pigs, rats and hens; all this crowned by the love of beautiful women who, naked to the waist did not even have to be asked. Well, it is not hard to imagine the effect of it all on weary, lusty sailors who had been cooped up on board a small ship for months.

> There never was a paradise to equal this. Days that were languid and kind, nights that were garlanded with stars, girls that were perfumed with the scent of flowers, dancing and singing to make glad the heart, love at the door of sleep . . .
>
> In return for these inestimable gifts the men who came there gave the islands syphilis, gonorrhoea, cholera, smallpox, tuberculosis, alcohol and Christianity – all unknown before their arrival. Within a century their sum total had the effect of practically wiping out the population and utterly destroying a gracious civilisation.
>
> *The Trumpet is Mine*, Cecil Lewis, Peter Davies Ltd, 1938

Browsing through all this history, a terrible indictment of our way of life, with a mixture of remorse and anticipation, we passed the perfect days talking interminably with the dozen fellow passengers about it all, wondering what we should find there now. The cuisine on the *Ville d'Amiens* was excellent, the captain and crew friendly and, as the old tramp nodded her way through the Trades, one had the feeling of leaving the world behind. The dreadful crisis that was brewing in Europe receded into the background. No papers, no radio, reminded us of it. It seemed indeed like 'outward bound' – a voyage into another dimension.

———

THE morning on which we were due to sight the island dawned overcast. Heavy squalls formed in the sky ahead of us, throwing a black pall over the place where the land should be. Then, as the sun rose, its rays, striking the curtains of falling water, formed a perfect rainbow. Scudding before the wind a little island schooner, white sails glistening, completed the setting. Then while we looked it seemed as if the further rain curtains parted. Framed in the rainbow arch, the outline of the mountain peaks of Tahiti appeared, ghostlike, as if etched on heavy sky. A moment later the squalls blew over, the rainbow dissolved and Tahiti lay before us in all its incomparable beauty. It was the sort of arrival one might wait a century to see, and all that morning, running along the northern shore, we were glued to the rail watching the panorama unfold. The peaks were still wreathed in clouds, but down their flanks, cut into deep ravines and densely wooded, the white threads of waterfalls plunged, to be lost where the foaming rollers broke against the reef. Finally we came through the pass to anchor by the wharf of Papeete.

After three days at Rivnacs – a famous thatched-hut hotel – I followed the course I had learned in China, found a house and moved in. It stood on the edge of the lagoon in a coconut grove and was made entirely of bamboo, roofed with pandanus palm. For windows it had hanging shutters propped up on sticks. A bedroom was raised a foot off the ground to allow the air to circulate beneath. There was a tiny kitchen and a shower, a narrow place to sit and watch the rollers thundering in – and that was all. It was the most engaging house I have ever lived in, nothing more than a light cage of air – and the rent was £1 a month.

Of course, we had to have a house-warming party and that meant roasting a pig and inviting the local chief, musicians, girls and dancers. Most of them turned up in the afternoon. The boys began to dig a pit in the sand, the girls to thread garlands of frangipani and tiare tahiti which they gathered from trees nearby. When the pit was finished a big fire was lit in it, which died down to leave the lava cobbles, taken from the beach, almost red-hot. Quickly covering them with banana fronds, they laid the pig on top, with half-coconut shells holding the entrails laid along its flanks. More banana fronds covered all this. Then more fronds, sacks and sand until it was all hidden up to ground level and you could walk over it, unsuspecting (except for the marvellous aroma of roasting pork) that it was there.

The girls sat on the ground and, tying a cotton to their big toes, threaded on the blossoms through a needle. By dusk there was a mound of garlands waiting for the guests. Driving stakes into the sand, the boys laid rough planks on top, making a low table which, when you sat on the ground, was just high enough to get your legs under it. On this more banana fronds were laid, making a green cloth on which they strewed more flowers. The chief had now arrived with his ceremonial dish. It was a wooden bowl on pillars, all carved from one piece of wood, and into it (the pit having been dug out) the girls piled the meat. So perfectly roasted was the pig that its flesh came clean off the bones and soon the huge bowl was overfull. By this time the guests had arrived and we crowned them with the garlands and threw them about their necks, making them half-drunk with the heavy perfume, before we broached the demijohns of wine.

The sun had set over Moorea in great glory, the moon was up, the stars were out and the Milky Way fell like a glittering cascade straight into the sea. So we sat to supper. Four hollow bamboos, filled with coconut oil, stood at the corners of the long table. Now they were lit.

I have never in my life made part of such a feast as this, so simple, so improvised, so gay. The happy people chattering in English, French and Tahitian, the girls beautiful with their garlands (which strangely somehow even became the men), the laughter that grew out of the proper technique for eating with your fingers, using only the first two and your thumb and keeping the others quite clean, the excitement of eating raw fish with a salt-water sauce and then dipping into the great bowl, pressing succulent morsels on neighbours, passing the sharp red wine, all this combined with the magical moonlit setting, the feeling of being far away from the world, liberated from all sadness and care, fused those hours into a moment of joy which can never come again.

So when the feast was over, half-drunk with it all, we rolled up the fronds with the remains of the meal and threw them in the sea, the table disappeared as if by magic, the guitars set to in earnest and the singing and dancing began. There was nothing, to my surprise, dreamy or lethargic about it, none of that sentimental scooping of Hawaiian songs, but a fast vigorous rhythm which, when we tried it, footing the fine sand, soon had us gasping for breath. But it was glorious. The girls, sure of their beauty and allure, advanced towards the men, fixing their eyes on theirs and, keeping their shoulders still, rotated their smooth bellies provokingly nearer and nearer till they gently rubbed their partners who, with a like motion, rubbed them back. It was an invitation to aroused desire which was no sooner given than they retired again, eyes daring eyes, soon to come back eager for more.

Later, much later, I was sitting, leaning against the house, side by side with Mama, the wife of my landlord, Teraitua. She must have weighed sixteen stone and now she, also quite drunk, whispered to me. 'My man and I have been thinking. You must have a wife. It is necessary for a man to have a wife. You understand. Now that girl, the little one, there' – and she pointed – 'she will make you a good wife. She would like to stay ...'

'Tonight?'

'Of course, tonight.'

'Well ...'

I got up and approached Marama, for so she was called.

'All evening I have been dancing, for you, only for you.'

It was a manifest fib, but that didn't seem important.

'Shall we go in?'

The guests had melted away, the guitars, still humming, receded through the palms. Suddenly there was no sound but the surf on the reef.

'Under my hair is the knot of my *pareu*.'

It fell to the floor and moonlight, coming silver through the slats of bamboo, striped the dark young lady.

'Your bed, is it strong enough for love? Sometimes I have gone through.'

'Let us try.'

Marama sat on it and bounced up and down. 'It seems solid,' she said.

Early before dawn, I woke to find the bed empty and heard the water splashing in the shower. Marama came back dripping, wrapped her *pareu* round her and combed her long black hair.

'You are going?'

'I must go. I will send you mangoes and a pawpaw. Come and see me. My house has a blue gate – not far. You have been so good to me ...'

She was gone. My 'wife' had come and gone quicker than any wife I ever had.

IN the days that followed I explored much of the island. Here was the bay where Wallis had first anchored, here was the long curving beach where Cook had come upon a fleet of double canoes, 160 strong, pulled up along the shore. Manned for action with paddles and warriors, dressed in their robes, breastplates and towering helmets, they presented 'a grand and noble appearance such as we had never before seen in this sea'.*

At night the fishing canoes would pass, the torchlit men standing erect in the bows, with their long-pronged spears, making a heroic frieze against the reef. It was the reef and the endless rhythmic thunder of the surf which dominated the whole life of the island. Crossing the calm lagoon, only as you approached did you realize the size and power of the waves which curled ten or more feet high, seemed to hang for a moment and then thundered down on the coral, the boiling foam flooding over into the lagoon. How could tiny creatures have withstood such fury? Yet they had, slowly building a rampart wide as an arterial road, protecting the beaches within.

Sometimes the reef stood almost a mile offshore, sometimes not a hundred yards, but the lagoon itself was a maritime museum. Coral clumps grew up to the surface, sometimes in flat fronds like a cedar tree, sometimes in spheres 5 or 6 feet across with velvety antlers like the horns of baby deer. All this 'furniture', in soft greens and pinks, lay sunlit on the white sand floor, making the metropolis of a million fish.

> The fish! The jewels of the still lagoon. The tiny blue ones, chips of a midday sky; their friends in jade, the dandies, sunning themselves above the coral fans, proud of their crimson eyes; the goldfish with violet spectacles; the black and silver squarefish, aldermen, never in haste; the parrot fish, vicious with long beak, dressed in a peacock's tail; the pipefish, still as an old twig; the lemon man-in-the-street fish, drifting in crowds; fish ruled in straight lines or criss-crossed like squared paper; the pickle fish, lime green and mustard; blue fish barred with white and white fish barred with blue; fish busy feeding, idling away the day, loafing to see the world; frightened fish flashing to shelter and, rare, the mottled bag fish, swelling in fear; the deadly Nohu with its poisoned spines hidden in sand; the gaudy mullet coming out at dusk to paint the town red.
>
> *The Trumpet is Mine*, Cecil Lewis

* There is a picture of this scene, painted at the time, in the Greenwich Maritime Museum.

It was towards the end of those perfect days that we heard there was to be a feast on Bora Bora. A new Methodist church was to be opened and all the population of the Leeward Islands was invited. The *Potii Raiatea*, a *goellette* – that is a schooner with an auxiliary engine – was dreadfully overcrowded and we lay in rows on the hard deck to sleep. But there are not many places left in the world where you can make an ocean voyage under sail and our two-day trip, calling in at Moorea and Raiatea, brought us finally to our destination on the evening of the second day. Bora Bora is a magnificent extinct volcano embroidered with low islands and a lagoon big enough to berth a fleet. As we skirted the reef in the sunset, rolling slowly with the swell, the entire crowded shipload of people and their music engulfed us in a wave of sadness, softened only by the setting sun which turned us all to gold. Then, as the night came down, the moon emerged from behind the peak above a wreath of cloud and the schooner nosed in through the reef to moor at the wharf. It seemed like the world's end.

———

THE problem for Bora Bora with a population of under a thousand was how to feed and sleep over 3000 guests for a week. Somehow or other they had done it. It was a real example of the old ways: give mutual aid in all communal enterprises. Everything had been organized and prepared over months. Pigs had been fattened, extra crops of taro and sweet potatoes had been grown, trees had been cut, palm fronds collected, and in all this, some giving food and some labour, not a penny had changed hands. Along the foreshore they had built shelters, long thatched roofs on light poles under which stood tables and benches for meals. During these a Tahitian parson, clad in a tail-coat, pin-stripe trousers and an open shirt, harangued the company with an endless account of the history and traditions of the island. It was an incongruous sight and I could not take my eyes off his feet – he had terrible elephantiasis.

The long shelters, at which 4000 people sat to the midday feasts, served as sleeping quarters for all those who could not be put up in the houses that stood along the shore. Marama was a friend of the local policeman, who had made over his upper room to guests. It contained two double and five single beds, so we slept in company and woke to bathe cautiously in the lagoon, keeping a sharp look-out for sharks.

It is impossible to convey the lightness and gaiety that pervaded everything. The girls, all in white, had somehow transformed their clumsy bundles of luggage into ironed frocks and big hats for the church ceremony. The greater part of the company stood in the hot sun outside the church, which could not hold a tenth of their number. Along the shore groups of people constantly passed to and fro, singing, calling to each other, strumming guitars, stopping to meet friends from other islands. Out on an islet on the reef thousands of fish had been penned in the shallows. A murderous young shark caught in the nets had died trying to get at them.

But for me the climax came in the evening when the choirs from four islands sat grouped on the ground beneath the spread of one huge flame-of-the-forest tree, whose blossom, thick and heavy, stood out crimson in the garish light of a big pressure lamp. Against the trunk was a rostrum where the clergy from the islands briefly exhorted the assembled company. Then, as they cried '*Himeme*!', one or other of the choirs would burst into song. They took the key from a long-drawn-out note sung by one voice and then the rest crashed in over it like surf on the reef. There was nothing sentimental about the music. It had professional precision, complex rhythm and harmony and was delivered at a crisp vigorous pace. Hymn followed hymn. The men crouching at the back of their choirs cupped their hands and sang into them to make a diapason groundwork to the music. Back of the choir again stood the rest of us, 3000 people listening in the moonlit Pacific night. Above towered the mountain; below, almost as if in a cave, was this listening congregation, spellbound by the music. I have never heard or seen anything in my life remotely like it, and one beautiful tune, pure and compelling – gone now, though then so powerful I thought it would stay with me for ever – put me to sleep and wakened me again at dawn. The *Himene* had lasted through the night.

BUT, alas! like all things, those perfect days came to an end. I have never parted from a place with so much sadness. The whole of Papeete came down to see the old ship leave. The invisible threads that bound us to them stretched and snapped as she slowly pulled away from the wharf. It was almost unbearably poignant, for, although we had sworn to return, I for one knew that I should never, never, never come back. We had escaped from another world, a terrible world now preparing once more for an orgy of mass murder on a global scale, and like dogs must return to our vomit.

The extraordinary contrast between man's possibilities and the depravity of his actual behaviour tormented me. It went round and round in my head. The West had brought a plague of serpents into this island Eden. Not one thing had been of benefit to them. Like a man with a contagious disease, everything we touched sickened and went rotten. Our sophistication was a complex set of improvisations just able to keep our own way of life turning over. Even this was failing, in ever-growing complexities and frustrations. Why was it that purity, goodness and peace seemed always to be overwhelmed and drowned in these tidal waves of evil? Was there any kind of winding-up process which could effectively counteract the running down? Man, the so-called crown of creation, was proliferating like a cancer. The 'lower' animals whom he despised (except when he could eat them) were far above him, clean and sane in comparison. Not for nothing was Jesus born among them. The inn of our daily life was certainly no place for Him.

All these unanswerable questions croaked in my head like ravens. I went straight down to my cabin and began to write an account of those days in Tahiti (*The Trumpet is Mine*, from which I have quoted earlier). Under the stress of too much emotion it was overwritten; but in spite of all the sugar and cream, it posed a question that any thinking man could usefully contemplate.

13

Mother Love

B Y now my youth should have been over. I was rising forty. But my vitality and zest for living seemed unimpaired. After a brief stop-over in Hollywood to stay with my good friend Eric Maschwitz, I took a refrigerated fruit ship home from San Diego. Crossing the two oceans I finished my Tahitian travelogue and retired to Italy to write a novel (*Challenge to the Night*). It concerned an escape to the South Seas and, as in 1938 such escapism was far from people's thoughts, it claimed little attention. But the story was highly dramatic and stood me in good stead four years later.

Most of my Hollywood earnings had evaporated. But in Italy, before the war, I could live at the Rupi for £2 a week including wine and cigarettes. In the nine years since Ricketts had given me the place, it had matured wonderfully. Trees and shrubs had grown, and paths, pergolas, walls, a little port for boats and bathing, a tennis court and a tiny house had been built. Adolfo had done all this, as I have said, mostly in my absence, and now it was finished, a perfect retreat for writing.

It was, as a matter of fact, completed before I left for Hollywood and now Adolfo had moved on to build a villa for close friends who had purchased a lakeside property adjacent to mine. I had designed it and throughout my year's absence Adolfo had been blasting away the blue granite to make cellars below the terrace on which it was to stand. He said he had many times longed to give it up, for it seemed endless and for a whole year nobody had come to see his work and encourage him. But he had doggedly persevered and now huge piles of stone stood round the hole sufficient to build the walls of the entire house. My return cheered him and we set to work.

Every morning from eight to one I worked steadily at the novel. Then I would hear Rina's steps coming along the path to set my lunch. The rest of the day was spent with the builders. There were many plans to draw, modifications and alterations, besides all the details: ironwork for staircases and verandas, the furniture, light fittings, fireplaces, carpets, cupboards, colour schemes. Even the crockery (down to the ashtrays) were specially made in the *ceramica* at Laveno.

I suppose it is any designer's dream to have a client who gives him an absolutely free hand, never interferes, never comes near the place and trusts his taste implicitly. It was my good fortune to have such an opportunity and I put it to the best use I could. Everything was made in the house, the furniture, the fitments, the stuffing of the mattresses, the easy chairs. From Valtellina we ordered carpets to my own design. From Milan we procured salami marble for tables. When at last it was finished and we stood on the big terrace looking over the lake, Adolfo, proud, as well he might be, of his work, slapped the wall affectionately, 'And if we come back in a thousand years,' he said, 'you'll still be here.'

So now we sent the owners a wire and they came out to find a new home waiting for them and lunch steaming on the table. It was quite a moment and their dazed impressions as they wandered repeatedly from room to room, slowly taking in all the work he had done, amply repaid our effort. For me it had been a labour of affection, unpaid, except in gratitude, which was more than sufficient for me.

But the clouds were gathering. The Nazi war machine had moved into top gear and the lies, the propaganda, the perfidious treachery of ruthless men, shocked and horrified the world. Yet a curious optimistic lethargy prevailed. England was certainly unready for what was patently to come and did not want to face it. If we looked away, perhaps, the nightmare would disappear. But it didn't. Munich came and went and in the summer of 1939 I returned once more to Italy. I was working on a memorial to Charles Ricketts, editing all his letters and journals, sifting through a lifetime of correspondence (now in the British Museum) to select what I hoped would present a portrait of this remarkable man, my patron and dear friend (*Self-Portrait: Journals and Letters of Charles Ricketts*, RA, edited by Cecil Lewis, Peter Davies Ltd, 1938).

In the middle of this came a month, so strange and unsought, I suppose I should include it as a sort of tailpiece to my youth, closing those ampler days which the war was to bury for ever.

Sagittarius had appeared in a German translation and one day I received a letter from Bonn. When a friend translated (for I do not speak German), it was just another fan letter, interesting to me only because it was written by a girl glider pilot, aged twenty-one. I replied (as I always do) thanking the writer and thought no more about it.

Returning to Italy I was surprised, a few weeks later, to receive another letter, this time in English, from the same source. The young woman who wrote it raised many philosophical questions. She was evidently no friend of Hitler's and deplored what was happening in Europe. She felt crushed by the regime and wanted to know what any individual could do to combat it. Because my book contained certain general observations about such things, she seemd to imagine I had found some solution (which was far from the truth). She added that she and her mother were thinking of taking a holiday in Italy and if they passed my way, would I consent to meet them? The letter was somehow sad and touching and I replied saying I would be pleased to do so.

Shortly after this another letter arrived, this time from the girl's mother. It was, I think, the strangest letter I have ever had in my life. It described at some length how the writer had lost her husband in the First World War, how she had devoted her life to her two children and never remarried. Now after all these years, all the care and love she had lavished on them was being trampled upon by a political set-up which cared nothing for the ideals and standards by which she had lived herself and which she had passed on to her son (now a doctor) and her daughter. She begged me to believe that not all Germans were Nazis. Now life was being smashed to pieces on her head. For her this did not so much matter, her life was over; but her daughter, though physically fearless, was bewildered and frightened. It was clear, she said, that I was a man of ideals and noble character (!). Her daughter had never known a father. Because she was desperate (and there was perhaps little time), she would like to send her daughter to me. If I could help her to lose the 'death-wish' which obsessed her and teach her how to face life in the bitter years that were certainly coming it would be the most precious thing one human being could do for another. Of course, by worldly standards it was the most immoral thing a mother could do, to send her only daughter to an unknown man; but I, she was sure, was not that sort of man. I understood her need and her daughter's need and would help her.

This letter, unusual to say the least of it, quite unnerved me. The honesty and pathos of it touched me. The trust that I could help flattered me. I felt I could not, should not, refuse. On the other hand, honestly, what help could I possibly give and what was I letting myself in for? The girl might be bandy-legged and cross-eyed, be suffering from acne and halitosis and I should be saddled with this monstrosity for how long? 'She is very quiet. She will not trouble you, but if she troubles, send her away,' the letter said. It might be easier said than done, unhappy women have a habit of clinging . . .

I replied cautiously. I was very busy. I lived alone and had gargantuan sexual appetites. Besides, I had had a motor accident and had a wooden leg and a glass eye. If, in spite of all this, her daughter still wanted to come, I would arrange a room for her in the village and could see her from time to time.

I thought this might put her off. The answer was a wire giving me the date and time of the girl's arrival.

When the day came Adolfo and I set off in the old car twenty miles up the lake to Luino. The villa I had built for my friends stood empty. I had asked their help in allowing me to open up a room for my guest. It had a glorious prospect over the lake, and was about ten minutes' walk from my place. It would keep the visitor at arm's length.

I was on tenterhooks as we drove along. I was an absolute fool to let myself in for this, to allow the peace of the place to be broken by this unknown intruder, to get myself involved in a blind date of such proportions. It was stupid, it was mad – and I was busy. And help! How could I possibly help anyone! I could not even help myself. On the other hand, I was alone. If she was pleasant, a little society would be welcome in the evenings. But suppose she was just a pushover! Mothers never knew what their daughters were like. I had had erotic fan mail before. They were the only letters to which I did not reply. But there had been nothing erotic about all this. So the thoughts turned and turned in my head. What on earth would the woman be like? The train chuffed into the station.

IT is difficult not to see the past through pink (or grey) spectacles, but I do not think I exaggerate if I describe the girl that stepped from the train as one of the most beautiful I have ever met. She swung down her suitcase like an athlete. She gave me her hand and looked me straight in the eye, so candidly yet so demurely I felt at once perfectly at ease. As we drove along, she spoke in her correct, halting English of her journey, brought her mother's regards and betrayed no signs of the neurotic I had feared. Hating Hitler and all he stood for, she was, I suppose, nevertheless his ideal of German youth – blue eyes, clear skin, golden hair, trim, strong, self-possessed. It sounds like a catalogue of the characteristics of a Wagnerian heroine. But the reality, the health, the warmth, the gentleness, the trust, all this belied the spartan amazon at which I had always scoffed. Already the beauty of the lake, the glorious afternoon, seemed to have relaxed her. From time to time, threading the twisty road, I stole glances at her. She must have done the same. 'Tell me,' she ventured, 'please, but which is your glass eye?'

When we stood on the balcony of the villa and I had shown her the room she was to have and pointed out the precipice along the lake beneath which my place lay hidden, she looked at it and for a moment said nothing. Then ... 'But it is a long way and I should come here alone at night. . .'

'In my place there is only one bed, I'm afraid.'

'But I can sleep on the floor. It does not bother me. I came to be with you.'

'Very well then, if you wish.'

'I will not trouble you. You will see.'

Adolfo, with one of his knowing smiles, shouldered the suitcase and we went down to the Rupi.

Some years when spring comes late and sudden on the lake the alpine snows melt so quickly that the water rises eight to ten feet overnight. Overbrimming with ice-cold water, it floods out into the meadows, washes the boats off the shores and in three days carries away all the debris of the year. That night we took the boat after supper out into the misty moonlight. Not far away a stream, usually a trickle, had now been so swelled that all the pollarded mulberries on its banks were submerged so that their heads lay on the water like huge thistledowns. Up the stream, guided by these beacons, we paddled till the trees met overhead. Here the still water was swathed in drifts of pussy willow, glistening like snow.

The lake is always a pretty romantic place. Now, as if to show off, it surpassed itself. Perfect day succeeded perfect day and the Rupi framed them to perfection. The little house, perched between the precipice and the water below, had only one bedroom, joined by an archway to the big living room, but it was not true that there was only one bed. A small alcove beyond the fireplace held another and here my guest slept. Her simple clothes, her ridiculous little sponge bag and toothbrush, seemed somehow to make her innocent like a child or a nun. Very early in the morning, before I was up, she had showered and I would see her miles away over the water, rowing the little boat. She would row ten miles before lunch and when my morning's work was over I would go down to bathe to see her pulling steadily towards the port. Then a leisurely swim to cool off and a healthy appetite for the risotto or tagliatelle Rina had prepared.

It was true, as she had said, 'I will not trouble you.' Yet trouble me she did and I could not really explain why.

Perhaps it was the secret wonder of the place (for it bewitched all who saw it), perhaps it was the peace, the possibility of forgetting for a brief time the ruthless regime bent on death and destruction from which she had so daringly come to be rescued, had made her – and I do not say this boastingly – fall deeply in love with me. I do not know what it was or how it happened but it was evident and it seemed to her perfectly natural and complete.

That I was strongly attracted and aroused goes without saying. No normal man has a beauty walking naked in his house without being very well aware of it. Besides, she had quickly abandoned her little bed in favour of mine. Yet I did not 'love' her, as she did me, and told her so quite clearly and openly.

'But I do not ask anything of you. You have given me everything.'

When kissing and touching had roused us both to flash point, she would lie open and whisper, 'Oh my darling, take me. Take me – if you want...'

What curious perversity or reluctance held me back I have never been able to discover, but somehow I could not bring myself to soil her purity with something which for me was mere eroticism. It was not that I feared to commit myself, more that it would somehow have committed her perhaps to some hope in the future, at a time when the future looked pretty hopeless.

Anyway, after a month, when it was clear we were on the eve of war, she left for home, still an intact virgin. She wrote: 'If I have changed, it's your love that changed me.' But it was her love she meant. Her mother wrote: 'I bore my child but you have made her living.'

When after the war, she wrote: 'I am alive. Are you?', my second wife – for I had remarried by then – tore up the letter in a fury. It was, I suppose, the best thing to do.

14

A Fight for Life

I F wars have to be fought at all it seems to me there was a good deal more justification for fighting the Second World War than the First. In the First, the ordinary Tommy had (as I remember it) only an amorphous feeling that it was his duty to destroy a sort of phantom called the enemy. But all the exhortation and propaganda never really convinced me that the Jerry who was trying to get his sights on me was any less of a man than I was. He was trying to kill me, of course, and I was trying to kill him; but that was only the technique of the situation. There was no malice in it – and from the stories of fraternization that took place in the front-line trenches, it is clear that many others, on both sides, had the same sort of feeling.

In 1914 the Western world was spoiling for a fight with little idea of the long stalemate and ghastly carnage it was getting itself into. In 1914 everybody wanted to fight: in 1939 nobody wanted to. It was a very different situation.

In all recorded history there can hardly ever have been a creature who could boast such an inventory of vices as Hitler. Paranoia, hysteria, neuroticism, sadism, genocide, he combined them all and spewed them out with a vitriolic oratory that terrified his victims and sent a shudder through all who heard him. In 1939 there was no doubt that the world had an enemy – and it was plain to everyone what sort of society would ensue under the thumb of men entirely devoid of conscience. That 'evil man', as Churchill called him, had to be confined if the lethal epidemics he spawned were not to infect the whole world.

It is common to condone the actions of figureheads by saying they are only the spearhead of a general symptom – if X had not appeared to lead it, then somebody else would have turned up. But would the course of history have been the same if Alexander, Julius Caesar or Napoleon had not existed? We forget, it seems to me, the all pervading power of influences, the insidious hypnosis of suggestion. People's attitudes, their morals, ideas of right and wrong, habits, styles of daily behaviour, all depend to an extent we can neither realize nor admit, on the persuasion (as we rightly call it) of those to whom we are prepared to listen. It is extremely hard to stand against such tides of exhortation. In 1939 the Western world, to its credit, did so stand and thus staved off, for a few years at least, the creeping paralysis of anarchy which now gains on us all.

I remember feeling sick in the stomach at the prospect of fighting another war and particularly one where the odds seemed loaded against us to the point where we could not possibly win. However, with a sort of fatalism, after Munich, I rejoined the RAF reserve of officers and, shortly after war was declared, was posted to Thorney Island to become a controller, responsible for the briefing and debriefing of the Anson crews who were flying patrols over the Channel and along the French coasts. During the 'phoney war' period of 1939 the country might still have been at peace and it was not until the Nazi tanks began to sweep west like a tornado that we realized we were in for a life-and-death struggle. Even then in the mess at Thorney the boys remained quite unflappable. I remember one wing commander standing at the fireplace sipping his sherry before dinner on a day when the news had been particularly bad and French troops had been totally incapable of standing up to the enemy. 'After all, sir,' he remarked to the CO, 'what can you expect? They're all niggers south of the Channel.'

Early in 1940 I was moved to the Air Ministry to join the RAF publicity staff, concerned with the daily communiqués put out from Whitehall on the progress of the war. During the Battle of Britain this was exciting work. Down in the War Room in the bowels of the building it was sometimes impossible to believe the news of the daily victories. A wave of pride and gratitude for the gallantry of the men who saved England swept through the country.

But when the summer was over and the nightmare of night bombing began, the position grew far more serious. It was a calculated policy of attrition to sap the centres of industry of their power and their morale. Here, although our radar screen could

With Mother, 1898

Showing off, 1903

Cricket in 1905

Leading 56 Squadron to
France, 1917

After a visit to the Palace
for my M.C., 1917

My hut on the beach, Tahiti, 1932

Ah! Tahiti!

Publishing *Sagittarius Rising*, 1936

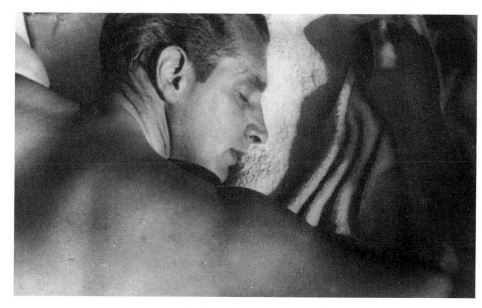

Sunbathing at the Rupi, 1938

Just demobbed, 1945

Making T.V. feature, *Never Look Back*, 1977

View of Albania from Pantocrator, 1985

With Marmaduke Hussey, Chairman of the BBC, 1990

With Fanny on our terrace, Corfu, 1991

give detailed information as to the number of raiders coming in, their height, course and probable objective, the system was not accurate enough to make anti-aircraft fire effective, nor could it direct night fighters close enough to the enemy. It was the last 100 feet in height, and perhaps 200 yards in range, that the night-fighter pilots found it impossible to bridge. They would be right up there among an enemy formation, unable to see them.

———

I was fortunate enough to join Air Vice-Marshall Sir Philip Joubert during this period as his staff Wing Commander. His assignment was to explore every possible means of detecting and foiling the enemy's bombing attacks. It was, of course, highly secret work, particularly in the radio area where attempts at 'bending the beam' soon began to have successful results. I was not told (nor should I have understood) the technique by which this was done; but its principle lay in the skilful mimicry of signals being sent out to the raiding aircraft from their bases in Germany. These false signals caused the pilots slightly to amend their courses and, as they were usually flying above the overcast, unable to see the ground, resulted in their bombs being dropped wide of the mark, often in open country miles from their objective.

So desperate was the situation that all sorts of other methods were tried to intercept the raiders, some so primitive as to be almost medieval. I flew one day in a Wellington, equipped with a heavy winch and five solid iron cannon balls attached to it by lengths of steel cables. These were dropped through the hatch one by one as the winch unwound. Trailing behind and below the aircraft, they made a sort of curtain. By skilful direction from the ground, it was hoped that this curtain would intercept the course of the incoming bombers and so destroy them. As we rolled out the balls, the terrible drag of their weight and the hundreds of feet of wire so crippled the speed of the Wellington that it almost stalled. It struggled up to 12,000 feet and above, and the experiment was abandoned.

Another method of the same kind, but more ingenious, was developed (I believe) through the gramophone companies. A large set of racks were fitted in the aircraft, divided into over a hundred sections. Each section contained a 'charge' and when set in action the sections opened one after another at intervals of about ten seconds, each dropping their 'charge' in turn.

The charge was ingenious. It consisted of a small parachute, 100 feet of string, at the end of which was a hand-grenade, and below this another smaller parachute. As it floated down under the bigger parachute, the wing of the enemy might be caught by the string. Both parachutes would keep it taut, but the bigger one would pull the grenade upwards till it burst on contact with the leading edge of the wing. I was present at a demonstration made before Churchill of this device. The parachutes opened one after another making a line of floating white dots as they slowly drifted down. But it proved extremely difficult to direct the aircraft at right angles to the oncoming bombers and tell them exactly when to deploy their curtain, and this method was also abandoned.

A third method, more ingenious still, consisted in fitting out a Baltimore with a full-sized searchlight. When the belly of the aircraft was filled with a ton of twelve-volt batteries, wired in series, this provided sufficient current to activate the searchlight for about forty seconds. At a range of some 400 yards it proved almost impossible for the enemy to escape from the beam, since at that range the most violent evasive action entailed only small deflections of the light. Two Spitfires flew with the searchlight aircraft, in formation on its wing-tips. Ground radar had no difficulty in directing the attackers within a 400 yard range and as soon as the enemy was held in the light the Spitfires went into the attack. Forty seconds does not sound long, but at 300 miles per hour things happen quickly and it proved quite sufficient. Two squadrons, I believe, were equipped with this device, but it did not come into action till the worst of the bombing was over. Meanwhile of course, the real answer, air-to-air radar, was being developed, but it did not come into general use until the war was over.

———

EARLY in 1941 a notice appeared in the *RAF Gazette* which changed the course of the war for me. First World War pilots, the order said, who wished to return to active flying duties and could pass the necessary medical examination would be accepted for retraining. Though by then I held the rank of Wing Commander and had an extra £200 per annum Air Ministry allowance, the longing to get back into the air outweighed all other considerations. I applied, passed the tests, was accepted, reverted to Flying Officer and went to Reading to see if I could still fly. Flying is, in fact, rather like riding a bicycle, a question of balance which, once acquired, is there for good. In 1915 it had taken me one hour and twenty minutes to go solo. Twenty-five years later it took me one hour and twenty-five minutes. I completed my elementary training on a Magister and went on to Upavon to take an instructor's course.

I completed the course and was posted to Booker as an elementary flying training instructor, given command of a flight, promoted Flight Lieutenant and turned loose, with a dozen pilots, to teach boys who had never been off the ground how to fly the de Havilland Moth. In the First World War I had been accounted a first-class fighter pilot, expert in aerobatics; but there is nothing like instructing to teach you accurate flying. By the time I had been at it three months, I was flying far more skilfully than I had ever flown before. This was because an instructor, giving his patter to the pupil over the intercom, must, if he is any good, suit the action to the word, the word to the action. Useless to say, 'Slowly ease the stick back towards the stomach – so – now bring it right back, and the aircraft ... lands ... on three points' if, while you are saying it, you are still floating 6 feet above the ground!

Pupils were graded by the time it took them to go solo. Any who managed this with nine hours' instruction were destined for fighters, nine to twelve went to bombers, twelve to fourteen to transport aircraft. Those who could not make it by fourteen hours would have to be content with other jobs in aircrew.

In this work I put in over a thousand hours' flying and, with my pilots, trained hundreds of young men to fly. Among them was my own son, whom I was proud to get solo in seven hours and twenty-five minutes. I believe it is the only instance in the RAF of father teaching son to fly. I was now forty-four and thought I had found a useful job which would last me through the war. I had re-married, and lived in a cottage near the airfield. In my spare time I had written a novel (*Pathfinders*) and was busy on plans for an ocean cruiser (having, as a result of my trip to Tahiti, conceived a desire to sail round the world and taught myself to design yachts). So it was a shock to have this comparative 'peace' shattered by an overseas posting. I was to command a staging post in Transport Command under Air Commodore Witney Straight, whose group was strung out from Bahrain to Casablanca. I joined a convoy at Liverpool and from Algiers flew in to Cairo. (For a fuller account of this overseas posting, see *Sagittarius Surviving*, Leo Cooper, 1991.)

———

CURIOUS how climate and a change of scene affects a man. In England I had assumed I was really only a hangover from the First World War, incapable of flying aircraft of greater power and complexity than Moths. Masters and Harvards, Hurricanes and Spitfires all intimidated me – they were too fast, too complicated, and I had no wish to break my neck in them. But I had not been in Cairo a week before I asked Witney if I could convert to Spitfires. He sent me to Bulbeis, where I put in four hours on a Harvard. Then my instructor showed me the tapes on a Spitfire and left me to it. I was pretty nervous about taking off in an aircraft which was then the fastest and most advanced in service, but my year's experience as an instructor came to my aid. I followed the drill as carefully as any pupil before first solo and found, of course, that the Spit handled perfectly and was, because of the reserve power, easier to fly than any other aircraft I had ever taken off the ground.

My son had left Booker long before my overseas posting. I did not know where he had gone, but rumour whispered that many pilots completed their training in Africa. Could he, by a stroke of luck, be in Egypt?

It was worth a try. I contacted Training Command. Yes! He had been to Rhodesia, moved back to Palestine and now was doing his final course on Hurricanes at Ismailia in the Delta, not 50 miles away.

I thought it would be fun to surprise him, since, for all he knew, I was still at Booker, so I flew over and got down just as he was coming in to land. He made one of those landings of which the ninth is the best, gambolling down the runway like an inebriated buffalo. As he slid back the canopy and took off his helmet, I remarked laconically, 'That was a pretty ropey landing!'

His incredulous stare of astonishment changed to a shout of pleasure 'Dad!' and I went off arm in arm with my Sergeant Pilot son to lunch. The following week we celebrated his twenty-first birthday by dining at the Mena House Hotel and seeing the Great Pyramid (both of us for the first time) by the glare of an arc-light moon.

———

BUT now work began. I was posted to command the staging post at Catania in Sicily. The boys had come right up through the desert campaign. After that everything was anticlimax and the morale was very low. It took some time to steady it up, moving the men out to the beach, rebuilding the airfield offices (which the Huns had blown up) and getting our transit hotel into something like order. It was my first command and called for quite a variety of effort.

Staging posts were, as the name implies, units whose job it was to look after the miscellaneous aircraft of all kinds that flew in, *en route* to the UK or the Middle East, or to coddle visiting VIPs but, most important of all, to care for the ferry pilots whose job it was to take new aircraft up to the front (by then half-way up Italy) or bring down those that had done their time. Ferry pilots, supposed to be resting after their tours of ops, were often flying anywhere between India and the UK non-stop. They lived in a haversack, never got their mail and on the whole were a pretty hard-worked lot.

We set up an overnight laundry service on the hotel roof by which, for sixpence, a man could hand in all his dirty things at seven o'clock in the evening and have them all back, clean and ironed, by seven next morning. There was nothing like it anywhere else in the Med and soon the staging post at Catania became a very popular stop. I could not have rebuilt the airport buildings, nor started up this service, nor brought up the standard of the cooking by employing civilian Sicilian cooks in the mess, without the fluent Italian I had acquired before the war. When Witney came through on his flying visit we could give him a lunch he couldn't get anywhere outside Cairo. He seemed pleased and after nine months promoted me Wing Commander and moved me up to Bari to form a new staging post ready to move into Athens when the Allies reoccupied Greece.

I didn't want the job. I was forty-five, a lot older than most of my officers with whom I had little in common. A CO has to remain a little aloof. He is never really off duty. So he is bound to be lonely and I missed my home comforts and my beautiful new wife. However, I was soon so deeply immersed in the complexities of my new command that I had little time to mope – and anyway I was under orders.

It was a cockeyed set-up. Half the unit was to move up from Cairo, the other half down from Bari. We should not meet till we got to Athens. Officers, men, transport, radio equipment, mobile workshops, etc. were about equally divided between Italy and Egypt and the complications of who and what was coming from where was a sort of jigsaw puzzle that we never really sorted out until we had been some weeks in Greece.

The squadron to which I was attached in Bari operated night-flying Dakotas whose job was to drop liaison officers and all manner of supplies (including gold) to the Greek resistance. From their intelligence officers we got a rough idea of the Greek political set-up. It was, like most things in Greece, somewhat complicated. There were two main resistance organizations, the EAM operating in the western sector and the ELAS, with strong Communist affiliations, in Attica. Both, of course, professed hatred of the Germans, loyalty to the Allies, and abundant patriotism; but both had salted away most of our supplies and money for their own ends, which were, of course, to take over the country. The Allied units sent in when we reoccupied the country were in no sense fighting men. They were all concerned with rehabilitation: units to rebuild roads and railways, to reopen postal, telegraph and tele-phone services, to revitalize the economy; in short to do everything possible to help Greece, one of the oldest of the British allies, to get back on her peacetime feet. But when General Scobie, the GOC Greece, invited the resistance to lay down their arms, beat their swords into ploughshares and get back to civilian life, they at first demurred, then argued and finally attacked the people who had come to help them!

It was a very tricky situation, for which (in spite of warnings) we were quite unprepared. It never occurred to the High Command that Greece would not welcome her old friends with open arms, co-operate in every way with those who had returned to help her and be ready to re-establish the pre-war set-up, welcome the King back from exile in Claridges, and return to those democratic principles which she had first established in the Western world 500 years before the birth of Christ. But war throws everything into the melting pot and the only certain thing about it is that nothing will return to what it was before.

———

To show the flag an RAF HQ had been set up in Athens with a couple of squadrons of Spitfires. So to relieve the pressure on the coastal airstrip (now Athens Airport), I had moved my unit to receive transport aircraft out to Tatoi, a secondary airfield with no proper runway, near the Royal Palace some miles north of the city. I had requisitioned a hotel in Kifissia for the men and a villa for the mess – all this a couple of weeks before the crisis. I was faced with the same conditions as in Sicily: no accommodation, no water, blown-up, looted buildings, a general shambles that had all to be sorted out and made good. In addition, owing to the administrative muddle, there was no money – the printed paper money having been lost *en route* – and no supply of food. After a month in Greece we were still living on emergency rations, biscuits, tinned meat and boiled sweets. However, morale was high, the men liked the Greeks and though the position was critical, nobody could really believe in the threats that grew more and more ominous as the days went by.

At Tatoi, about 8 miles north of the city, my unit of a little over 200 men and 18 vehicles was out on a limb, quite isolated from everyone else, and I well remember the morning when the laconic voice of the Senior Air Staff Officer, Bob Foley, came over the line. 'Might drop by and see me, Lewis, will you? The balloon's gone up.'

It took me some time to get into RAF HQ in the Grande Bretagne Hotel. The road had members of the resistance posted at intervals along it. They were real brigands, crossed bandoliers full of ammunition, revolvers on each hip, knives, rifles, they looked as if they meant business; but they made no move to stop me. Indeed, one begged a lift into town. I thought the sight of him sitting in the back seat might deter any of his pals from taking pot-shots at us. In addition, it was now November and very cold. No fuel was to be had and all along the roads were streams of Greeks pushing prams and handcarts. They were on their way out to the royal forests beyond Tatoi to cut them down for firewood. I counted 600 of them before reaching the city.

The imperturbable Bob refused to talk business over our biscuit and corned-beef lunch, but afterwards he gave me a brief resumé of the situation. Nobody knew exactly what the partisans might try, but there were several thousand of them around and they were pretty touchy types. Any vehicle would certainly be a temptation to them. Out at Tatoi I could not possibly defend myself. There might be valuable aircraft on the ground. 'So,' he said, 'better pack up and get your lot into Kifissia by sundown. Send a flight down to Hassani. Keep the radio channel open. Tell them to look after any aircraft that get in – we've put a stop on all visitors by the way – and warn them to keep out of the centre of the city as they come through. They're liable to be pooped at.'

It was a hectic afternoon's work, but somehow we managed it. The narrow road between Tatoi and Kifissia was perfect for an ambush, but for some reason or other all the brigands had disappeared and the convoy pulled into Kifissia without mishap. The Air Officer Commanding the RAF in Greece, Air Commodore Geoffrey Tuttle, was the finest CO I have ever served under. Crisp, alert and efficient, he had an exceptionally likeable and friendly manner with officers and men, never losing authority, yet never standing on it. But now he was in a spot – we all were. The 600 men under his command were in one hotel, my 200 were in another. The RAF Regiment – the only men trained to fight – were only about 100 strong and poorly equipped. We had two light armoured cars, and four Bofors guns. To defend a residential suburb like Kifissia would have taken several thousand men. Besides, to defend it against whom? No enemy appeared. In the villas were many Greeks, people who were friendly to us. We could not turn them out. Only our Greek servants, pointing to some faceless man in a mackintosh strolling by, would say, 'That man is a member of the ELAS. I know him well.' It gave us a creepy feeling.

The men were unhappy and mystified. Only a few days ago everything had been perfectly friendly and now suddenly they felt cut off, besieged by people against whom they had no animosity whatever. It was our first experience of guerilla warfare. There was no front, no back, no sides. Attack might come from anywhere. The feeling of being constantly under observation, and yet unable to locate it, was very odd. Morale fell quickly. None of us had anything to do and idleness is a subtle enemy in situations like this. We had no means of defending ourselves, no arms or ammunition and nothing to do but wait.

But the news that filtered through to us grew more alarming hour by hour. The Piraeus had been overrun and occupied by the ELAS. Supplies, stores, food were being looted. It was not safe to move about in Athens. A machine-gun mounted on top of the Fix brewery made every vehicle coming into town from the airfield an easy target. There were ELAS groups throughout the city. A fifteen-pounder was taking pot-shots at the top brass in the Grande Bretagne and nobody could locate it. The Spitfires were out flying sorties, but had no proper targets. You couldn't turn machine-guns or rockets on people who might be friends.

I begged Tuttle to let me get my unit back to Hassani as quickly as possible. The operational squadrons had no time to deal with all the miscellaneous aircraft that had begun to pour in to investigate the situation. My flight down there already, one officer and fifteen men, was quite unable to cope. He agreed and we put through a convoy of ten lorries and about fifty men with our two light tanks at the head and tail of the column. They were fired on, but got through safely. Next day I went down myself with Tuttle in one of the armoured cars and another convoy. Again the sporadic fire in the suburbs, but no damage. But when Tuttle returned he found a six-foot stone wall built across the only road! Kifissia was cut off.

A few nights later the place was attacked. Charges of dynamite blew holes in the side of the hotels. Six hundred men and officers were rounded up by a horde of partisans (with young women prominently in the lead) and were driven off in our own vehicles somewhere towards the north.

Hassani airfield was now our only link with the outside world and the situation looked really dicey. ELAS held the Piraeus, controlled all movement in Athens. There were only four 'thick-skinned' vehicles in Greece. One well-sited machine-gun on the slopes of Mount Hymettos (behind the airstrip) could have riddled all the aircraft wings and put them out of action. Then we should be back to the beaches with only a flotilla of motor torpedo boats to rescue us. But luckily ELAS missed this vital opportunity.

By now it was December. Bitter winds blew down from the north and, if we lived in discomfort with no heat, no light and field kitchens, what was happening to our own chaps, the prisoners, being murdered for all we knew, at the hands of men with whom they had no quarrel?

Tuttle was everywhere. Quick, practical and always in a buoyant humour, he flew in and out of Kifissia (until it was overrun), landing his Auster on a hillside, bringing out my orderly-room clerk and best cook – perhaps the two most essential trades in running any unit. We improvised field kitchens, got up tents, fixed tarpaulins over half-finished huts, scrounged a lighting plant and vehicles. We had managed to keep our radio channel open and still had a skeleton cypher staff. We dug slit trenches to defend the airfield and watched, beyond Faliron Bay, the trajectory of tracer fire from our MTBs curling into ELAS strongpoints on the slopes of Kastella. Meanwhile, in addition to a state amounting to siege of the airfield at Athens, I had two detached flights, one up in Salonika and the other down in Crete. They were absolutely cut off and, if ELAS was at all organized, might be taken prisoner any day. There was no way of reaching them except by air and no means of getting them out.

Then Alexander flew in to see what was up. He had to wait two hours before one of our four armoured cars could be got out to Hassani to run him into Athens. But his reaction was immediate: 'Send in a division.'

The arrival of that airborne division was, I think, the most exciting and inspiring episode in my RAF career. Top-secret signals began to pour in: 'Forty Liberators arriving!' 'Twenty Wellingtons arriving!' 'Fifty Dakotas arriving!' For the first three days these aircraft all turned up at precisely 11 am. I have never seen anything like it. The sky was thick with aircraft.

All normal landing procedures were scrapped. The boys played it by ear. Stacked up one behind the other, wheels and flaps down, it was nothing to see six on finals at the same time. A bewildered aircraftsman at the head of the runway fired volleys of red lights to space them out, of which the pilots took absolutely no notice whatever. One burst tyre or one faulty landing and there would have been a monumental pile-up. But it was a magnificent display of airmanship. Coming in hard on each other's tails, so that before one aircraft was off the runway the next had touched down, they rolled in perfectly, and followed the jeep with its chequered flag to their parking position. An army lorry slid alongside from the rank of 100 we had organized, the load was transferred and the pilot moved on to the prepared park for take-off.

At this pitch of over 100 aircraft arriving simultaneously, the airlift lasted for three days. Then they got it organized. Arrival times were spaced out and the heat was off. But even so they were terrific days; organizing scratch meals for 400 aircrew was a strain on our resources. The night when the weather clamped in Italy and 100 aircraft crews could not get back was the climax. They thought they might all be shot up before morning. This amused us greatly, for we were used to the conditions and couldn't believe we were in much danger – which was far from the truth.

The airlift troops were not slow to go into action. Systematically they began to winkle the ELAS partisans, first out of the Piraeus and then out of Athens itself. The resistance forces were not able to compete with an organized sweep of regular seasoned troops and the result was a foregone conclusion.

But it took some time. Then the press, as usual, began to arrive, indignant at this attack on our allies. Was it liberation to impose a military dictatorship in Greece? Why shouldn't the Greeks arrange their own affairs? It was up to them to form their own government and so on. It was a typical stirring of the pot indulged in by people who had no idea of the actual conditions.

But the clamour was serious enough to bring Churchill out on Christmas Day. Greece would certainly arrange her own affairs when the country was normal and free elections could be held, but it was no part of Allied policy to allow the Government to fall into the hands of a communist-inspired minority, who aimed to take over the country with no mandate from anyone but themselves.

The affair died down. When those of my men who had been taken prisoner returned practically unharmed from a frightening ordeal, they had, many of them, white hair. They were sent home at once. The unit, brought up to strength again, settled down to its normal routine. Spring came. I was given a week's leave and recommended for the OBE (which I didn't get). Then came the Normandy landings and the end of the war in the West. As I was forty-six years old, Group 5, I was demobilized within a month.

———

IT was even more obvious this time that the end of the Second World War, though we had won it, though it was an enormous relief, brought no sense of finality. It was more like a recovery from a nervous breakdown. The patient might seem better, but the symptoms remained. We had all somehow become infected by contact with the disease we had defeated but not destroyed and the condition could recur any time in an aggravated form.

The disillusion I had felt as a young man in the First World War that the machinery of our civilization simply did not work, could not cope with the needs of society, returned with renewed insistence. The technological advances might make life more convenient and comfortable but they were bound to make it more complicated. Radio communication and air transport had telescoped space and time, but these fantastic novelties only bred more restlessness and impatience.

Was it desirable that everybody should go everywhere, know everything? Would it only make people more restless and fill them up with a lot of information they did not really understand and could not digest, make them more and more the slaves of 'experts', pundits and commentators who did not understand it either? There seemed to be a growing gap between what was really happening and what was said to be happening. What was reality? It was one of the key questions and, though I couldn't define it, I felt a strong urge to probe in that direction, to try to understand the 'sense and aim of my existence'. Was there any purpose in life? Had I any responsibility other than my own pleasure and profit? If I had a duty to my neighbour, what was it? In all these big questions I saw I had no sense of direction, no compass, no aim.

———

HOWEVER, now it was 1945 and the war was really over. For the second time in my life I was 'demobbed', turned in my RAF uniform and got back into civvy street. It was a marvellous feeling. The long years of constriction and service, of being under orders, doing what I was told, going where I was sent, were over. I could actually do what I wanted, go where I liked, and get on with my life!

The first and only thing I really wanted was to get back to the Rupi, my villa in Italy. I wanted to know how it had come through the war, see how everything had grown in six years and how my friend's villa next door had fared.

So it was wonderful to find Adolfo and Onorate and Rina in good shape. We had a wonderful reunion and found our friend's villa had been let to a rich Milanese for the war period and was well kept. Peace gilded everything and seeing it all again, enjoying scents and smells and the taste of Cinzano, meeting up with old friends, bathing, taking trips and indulging in all those peacetime pleasures of which we had been deprived for six long years, it seemed that life had never been so good and we positively wallowed in it!

There was extra gilt on the gingerbread for me in making the acquaintance of an attractive man who was staying with my friends. I grew to call him the mystery man beause, besides playing a powerful game of tennis and beating me easily at chess, he had the knack of changing the direction of conversation and somehow lifting it into vistas of thought and speculation I found fascinating.

His ideas weren't exactly religious, as I understood the meaning of the word, but they evoked exciting and compulsive responses in me to something – and I didn't exactly know what – but towards which I felt an immediate and instinctive affinity. So, putting questions and getting answers which did nothing but stimulate my curiosity and interest, I fell under the influence of this man and determined to see him again.

So when I got back to London I got in touch and was invited to meetings at a little studio near South Kensington Station where I met a number of serious-looking people who had evidently been as attracted as I was, and came every week to study his ideas. I suddenly realized I had found something that was changing my attitude to life and was vitally important. But I recognize *now* that if anyone had asked me what it was that had called me *then*, I should not have been able to give any understandable answer. I had, as it is said, 'heard a bell without knowing where the sound came from'.

I had certainly heard this bell. Was it an echo of childhood, my father's teaching, the Sermon on the Mount, the Lord's Prayer? Was it the jolt to my thinking on reading Shaw's socialism, man's place in society, in life, in the world? Or was it something in everyman's search through the mysterious vistas of beauty, the nameless longing for perfection, the call of El Dorado, over the mountain, beyond the stream? Whatever it was, all this whirling in the head of a boy of seventeen hurled into the massacre of the Somme, had left enormous questions, longings.

Over the years such thoughts had smouldered, slowly built up, almost unobserved. Now, suddenly, here was something unexpected, marvellous, an answer, or the promise of an answer, and being by nature a jumper, without knowing where I should land, I jumped.

I had come out of the war with no job, no idea of what to do except write books, which I didn't think would support me lavishly, but none of these things seemed to matter. I would leave life to look after itself, keep close to the 'Work' as we grew to call it, and everything would be quite all right. If ever a middle-aged man leapt blithely on to Cloud Nine, it was I!

15

Seen from Africa

IT seems that now is the moment to pause and take stock of my situation before setting out once more into something new. I hope I have entertained you with my life. It has been full of adventure and excitement and I have dashed through it all with great gusto and enjoyment. Actually, inside me, there has always been a counterpoint to this gaiety, a 'call', a half formulated search for something to believe in and live by.

It was now, in my early forties, I knew I had found it. I had come upon it unexpectedly – a set of ideas so basic, compulsive and simple, I began to wonder why I hadn't found them out for myself! I took to them with an enormous surge of attraction and excitement. The holy, the sacred had come alive, within reach. They began to guide me then and still do today.

However my account of the inspiration for all this, the extraordinary Gurdjieff, may not attract the reader in the same way as these pages he has read so far. His new ideas upset old ways and make demands on attention and habits of thought. Some people find difficulty in thinking about 'serious' matters. But I do not want to lose you now, you who have come so far with me. I beg you; try to follow, stay with this apparently topsy-turvy trip into the unknown! Who knows it may turn out to be the most valuable thing you ever did for yourself!

This book is an account of my life. If it had not gone on growing and changing of what value would it be? My last fifty years have been devoted to deepening this 'sense and aim of my existence'. The struggle and the fruits of it are on view. They leave me full of wonder at having been given such a glorious life! I humbly give thanks for it in joy and gratitude. Join my enthusiasm for it and hear me out, to the end!

Who was the man who had inspired these improbable aerobatics (and kept on doing so) in quite a number of people, who seemed ready and eager to put their lives in his hands? His name was John Bennett. To the everyday world he was a Director of the Coal Board and had a large house on Kingston Hill. This was the 'centre' where those who were close to him and his ideas lived. But name and address gave no idea of his personality and the magnetic quality of what he had to say and teach.

In stature he was a tall, good-looking man in his fifties, and had the air of being used to command. He spoke several languages, was widely read and seemed as much at home in philosophy or psychology as he was in higher mathematics. But all this variety was, so to speak, hidden beneath genial conversation and an evident open-hearted generosity of nature. He met all problems with assurance and authority, was never at a loss for an answer and though, in fact, he had only received a limited part of the Teaching he brought to us, it was quite enough to draw us to it and later, when the source of it all appeared, for him to seem to know it already.

The Teaching that had attracted and inspired him came from a man who was himself a mystery, a legend and probably dead. His name was Giorgi Ivanovitch Gurdjieff.

All Bennett had remembered of this Teaching was contained in a slim hand-bound volume of double-spaced typescript. Not much. Beyond this there were only rumours and mysterious hints of meetings with Gurdjieff in Constantinople and Berlin, of the mystical powers held by this extraordinary (and rather intimidating) Greek, who was the source of it all. But all this was misty, vague and out of reach. Bennett had met Gurdjieff, believed in him, and everything he told us about him and taught us of his work was more than enough to make us eager to understand it better and learn how to prepare ourselves to receive it.

———

THE sense of sharing in the foundation of a hidden Teaching which could bring renewed hope to the world led me to a whirl of questions and speculations at the weekly groups which I was allowed to attend. I found it all immensely exciting and stimulating. It seemed the answer to all the world's ills and the solution to all its problems. At the same time, Bennett confessed that he himself faced an awesome responsibility. P. D. Ouspensky, one of the earliest of Gurdjieff's pupils, had died. Gurdjieff himself had also disappeared and was believed to be dead. He, Bennett, alone remained as the custodian of these tremendous possibilities, which were Gurdjieff's legacy to the world. How could we preserve them for posterity?

The international situation at the end of the Second World War seemed far from stable. Many considered that hostilities could all too easily break out again and there was a grave risk that, in the next conflagration which might soon be upon us, these ideas might be lost for ever. Some safekeeping, some haven must be found where they could be protected and could grow.

With practically no further investigation, or what would today be called a feasibility study, Bennett swept us all off our feet by deciding that something must be done at once. He suggested that South Africa was our best choice and somehow convinced us that this was a wise, simple and logical solution to finding a refuge for our El Dorado. A nucleus was formed of those who trusted him and were ready to uproot their lives and set up this survival centre in a strange country that none of them knew, but which – such was the faith and hope Bennett inspired – was to become the taproot of this sacred trust placed in our hands. Because of its very nature it would be bound to succeed.

My part in this adventure was typical, exciting, romantic and quite unnecessary. My second marriage (taking place in war-time) had never been properly celebrated. The beauty of my new bride (half Burmese, half French) deserved something special. I decided to buy an aeroplane and fly to South Africa. It wouldn't be exactly a honeymoon, but it would certainly be something to remember.

I have described elsewhere (*Gemini to Joburg*) how I actually completed this wonderful 600-mile cross-country flight without incident, sold the aeroplane in Johannesburg at a profit and completed the reconnaissance with Bennett by car.

Certainly the site of this 'other Eden', when we had found it in the Eastern Transvaal, was an inspiring challenge. A magnificent lonely valley, unspoiled by any 'civilization' and complete with river and hundred-foot waterfall, it seemed ideal for our purpose. Our advance party was practically a family affair and consisted of my wife, myself, my son and his wife, my daughter and a friendly family of weavers plus an enthusiastic local spinster. My son and I set to work to plan and build the foundations of the new community with a will. We built communal living and eating facilities, bathrooms, kitchens and a fine big mill for weaving – which was to be the centre of our money-making activity. All this, it seems now, forty years on, took place smoothly and easily. Our hopes and our morale were high.

But pioneering, as all who have tried it know, is a rough road. Believing in 'ideas' is one thing, but living them, day by day, soon exposed our fallibility. We found, when we were really on our own, faced with crisis after crisis, that we had not enough understanding and faith to rely on the Teaching or each other. Something far deeper was needed to hold us together and keep the work alive in us. Soon we faced a miserable end to the trust that had been placed in us. We saw what we were worth – and it wasn't much ...

Then, utterly unexpectedly, came the good news! Gurdjieff was not dead! He was very much alive and working with groups in Paris! This was a bombshell which put us all into a state of bewilderment. The discovery that the author of these ideas which had motivated our beliefs and our daring, if rootless escapade, was alive came as an immense relief. The future did not depend entirely on us. Why struggle with a pale imitation of a Way when its originator is living and active? All we wanted was to get back to the Source.

————

THE first taste of Gurdjieff's own Teaching (as distinct from what Bennett had given us) reached us while we were still in Africa. It consisted of a typescript, the English translation of his masterwork *All and Everything*, and arrived in chapters, laboriously typed by devoted people back in Paris, who had undertaken the daunting task of putting the rough manuscript into a form that could be printed and which was eventually to turn into a book over 1000 pages long.

Reading this in a dribble of typed pages was an adventure in itself. It was couched in a strange sort of language in which even the grammar taxed our attention. The first chapter was called 'The Arousing of Thought'. This ambled on in a light-hearted sort of way in a long chatty introduction on Gurdjieff's ideas about life in general and when, at last, you got to the story, it seemed to have nothing whatever to do with 'religion' but was about three men in a 'spaceship' travelling between various planets in our solar system!

This was about the last thing we'd expected. All we had been taught about the conflict in our inner lives, our lack of values, stupidities and shortcomings, seemed insignificant and unimportant when set against this detached planetary scale. It had the effect of showing us our place and preparing us (far later) to try to begin to understand our limitations, possibilities and needs.

The Teaching itself, when we began to see that it was a teaching, took on extraordinary forms. There were stories of the distant past which the storyteller, Beelzebub, had witnessed, which spoke of migrations, of remote and forgotten times and peoples, a sort of history of the development of life in our solar system in spiritual terms. It told how human understanding had gradually evolved, how people at a 'higher level' had long ago made mistakes, taken wrong turnings and left spiritual legacies hard for mankind to overcome. Peppered throughout all this were impartial observations which showed how our ill-fated planet had been bedevilled by disasters, many self-made, and must struggle through suffering to learn the laws of God and live by them.

But to reach such a perspective was beyond us then. It was not until we had settled down to work that we began to see the scope and majesty of Gurdjieff's vision and where it could take us if we were prepared to drop our old ideas and grapple to understand life in a new way.

———

I T was after we had left for Africa and Gurdjieff had been found to be alive that the pioneer leaders in his ideas were invited by him to come to Paris. They were Dr Walker, Jane Heap and John Bennett in England and the remnants of Ouspensky's group (under the bed-ridden Mme Ouspensky) in America. What the European leaders taught their pupils had naturally varied, since they were all, in various ways, working on half-understood ideas about a teaching picked up from scraps that Gurdjieff had taught years earlier at the Prieuré (his property near Paris), and interpreted in their own ways. Only the Americans had a complete picture of what had been taught, but this dated from way back in 1917 and had been compiled by P. D. Ouspensky.

What these pioneers began to understand on their trips to Paris was revolutionary. All they had previously taught had to be renewed, given a new balance, which the groups had first to absorb and try to understand as they could. All this took time. That it was done at all was largely due to the remarkable influence of Mme de Salzmann, a French lady who was known to speak for Gurdjieff in many ways and took over the delicate job of reconciling the difficulties the leaders had in giving up their old ideas. Later she assumed the tremendous responsibility of holding the growth of the Work together in Europe and America after the death of its leader.

The picture that the Americans had of Gurdjieff's teaching according to Ouspensky (*In Search of the Miraculous*) provided a further complication. It revealed an altogether different view of what Gurdjieff had taught earlier. The American group, which had been working from it for some years, regarded it as more valuable and practical than Gurdjieff's *All and Everything*. Ouspensky's work (now generally known as *Fragments*) was a powerful and detailed primer of much that his Master had taught in Russia during the First World War.

It was the work of an outstanding and devoted pupil and its point of view was throughout logical and practical. Higher levels of understanding would come later when those who were prepared were ready for them. They were indicated but not expounded. Ouspensky was an intellectual. He did not feel he could speak with authority about higher states which were not easily passed on in written form. Nevertheless his work was so powerful and detailed that it provided many with all they needed.

So, at Gurdjieff's death, when for the first time he allowed his work to be made public, there were these two quite different versions of it. In a way they were complementary. Ouspensky's was a teaching manual which, for all its indications of higher worlds, remained firmly anchored in this one. Gurdjieff, on the other hand, seemed perfectly at home in worlds of any level and moved between heaven and earth impartially. His work grew like some gigantic myth, omniscient and timeless where man, dust as he was, could move into immortal regions and take his place there.

IT is very difficult for me to write about the months that followed the 'resurrection' of Gurdjieff, of all our curiosity and hope and wonder at what he taught, and then the sudden shock of his death, a year and a half later.

After fifty years the sense of bewilderment still persists. This morning when I settled down once again to read through all those letters that were written to us from Paris and London during that last extraordinary year of Gurdjieff's life, the same feeling came back – words were simply no good to try to pass on what was really a different kind of life at a different level.

How could they convey the strange atmosphere of a man, at once godlike yet intimate, infinitely distant yet perfectly homely, a wonderful host, father of the family, cutting up food, sharing titbits all round, with demanding eyes that glowed and challenged and at the same time evoked such love and trust that the memory of it would last for ever... No wonder people were lost, bewildered, as if they were in another world – as indeed they were.

They had been asked to write to us in Africa and try to keep us in the picture, and try they certainly did, but all the superlatives, all the protestations could not pass the thing they were groping to pass and could not – the presence of the man himself.

It is only going over it all again that I can also see the depth of the emotional upheaval they were going through themselves. They could not convey what was happening to them, let alone pass it on to us.

Fortunately, I kept all these letters and it would be quite easy to digest them into a coherent précis of what reached us over many months – long, lonely, frustrated days when we felt left out and could do nothing but hold on. But those letters reached us, one by one, shots fired half across the world, and this is the effect I would like to convey – how they arrived in the valley, incoherent, failing to answer questions, leaving out important bits and so on. This is how it was. Today maybe we could put it all together; then we could not.

So what follows is more or less as we felt it, then.

From John Bennett, Coombe Springs, 14.8.49

I am writing this on the eve of our journey into the unknown. At this time tomorrow Polly and I will be in Paris and we shall see G on Friday.

Two years ago I told people that a new phase was about to open. At that time I had no idea that Ouspensky would be dead and Gurdjieff alive or that I should find the wheel turned full circle. It is twenty-five years ago to the month that I set off to Paris to see G at the Prieuré and from that moment began my direct contact with supernormal experience.

Today, I feel like a new boy creeping timidly into the Great Hall of some ancient school – where even the other boys seem to be supermen and all about is a mystery. Somehow I cannot bring myself to realize that, at last, I have come to the possibility of real guidance and help . . . I will write to you from Paris.

We think of you battling with Nature in the distant South and we here struggling to keep our minds clear. There are times when I wish you were not so far away for I would dearly like to talk to you more about these things. But it makes me very happy from your letters to see that you truly struggle to keep the work alive. And so long as one does that, the work will take care of us.

From B. T., Coombe Springs, 13.10.48

Mr B. came back from Paris last night and talked with us over late supper about aim. G says it is sufficient to have aim to die honourably and not perish like dog, to have done one's duty with life before it is too late, to have made something imperishable in oneself before one's planetary body dies. . . He also said that only man who had aim – and could always be brought back to it by someone who knew how – could really be helped. . . Mr B is not going to America 'til November, so some of us may get the chance to go to Paris. . .

From John Bennett, 18.11.48

The truth is that everything is so exciting here at the moment that hardly anyone can bear the thought of being separated from it. At the same time if and when disaster strikes, the very people who are reluctant to do anything to share in building up a home for us to go to, will be only too ready and anxious to take advantage of what has been done . . . I am equally certain that within two or three years we shall enter that period of acute nervous tension which Beelzebub called 'solioonensius'. Such periods induce intense incentive to work in those who are capable of it, but they engender madness in those who have lost touch with the real aim of life. Whenever the process of solioonensius occurs on earth, a state of tension is created in which it is impossible for people to exist quietly like cows. They have either to work on themselves or they begin 'to destroy every-thing within sight'. As I understand it, the next solioonensius will be the most intense of all. As an outcome, either mankind will change to a different mode of existence or there will occur the most terrible process of mutual destruction.

So our decision to seek a place in SA remains just as valid as it was three years ago.

From C. M., Paris 20.10.48

The night our party arrived, as we came out of the hotel, Rina stopped us and said: 'You see that old gentleman there: that is Mr Gurdjieff.' We saw an elderly, rather shabby foreign-looking gentle-man going up the road. We hung back. He stopped at the corner, spat very deliberately into the gutter, and then crossed the road slowly. He did not appear to see us: he was a very impressive old boy, but I had the uncanny (and unemotional) conviction that he knew we were there. He then went off along the road and we went on our way.

Later in the evening we went to the flat, No. 6 Rue des Colonels Renard. It is a little flat on the first floor. As soon as you open the door your nostrils are assailed by a smell of herbs, not the ordinary 'herby' smell, but one quite special to No. 6. You go quietly into the little hall. . .

To maintain the story line I add here how, later, when we got back from Africa, I went over to Paris to meet Mme de Salzmann and she allowed me to visit Gurdjieff's little flat, to which all the letters written to us in the valley at this time refer.

The first thing that struck me about it was how small it all was. We had read about those meals with thirty or forty people present. But the dining room in the flat could not possibly seat more than eight. And the amount of food that came out of that tiny kitchen! The letters had spoken of people standing behind the table the plates being passed in from the kitchen, the crowding, the impossi-bility of getting out once you had got in. All the same those who had had the luck to feast at that table were starry eyed at the memory of it. The magic that hung over it.

Somehow I had imagined it all on a much grander scale. Mr Gurdjieff's private sanctuary lined with shelves of bottles and jars going up to the ceiling was little more than a pantry. And it was so dark! We were told the shutters were always kept closed; you couldn't tell night from day. That, and the awful collection of pictures that covered the walls, the tatty ragbag of stools and cushions; it was all offhand, well used, homely, personal: but, at the same time it was unique, absolutely 'his'.

People had tried to tell us something about the rituals of the meals, the drinking of toasts, the 'science of idiotism'. It all sounded mysterious, unexpected; we couldn't understand it. Apparently it came from some Sufi tradition. They said that all their pupils were idiots, struggling to escape the world of illusion and become their real selves. At the same time they were idiots in the world's eyes for having such ridiculous ideas. So either way they were idiots. Everybody was different, a different kind of idiot, but each could decide what sort of idiot he thought he was. Once chosen, he had to stick to it and, when the special feasts were held to celebrate the ritual, he could be toasted by all those present in the hope that he would really grow to be his real self. The toasts were drunk in alcohol, not to get drunk, but for each to strengthen his wish to *be*, and the amount to be drunk was strictly laid down.

Gurdjieff insisted on the ritual. There was a 'Director' to call the toasts, another to pour the wine and several others who had duties or honours in the course of the meal. This was all repeated twice a day, at lunch and supper, and it was during the calling of the toasts that Gurdjieff spoke to his people.

Naturally, back in the valley, all this was unexpected, extraordinary. We wanted to know more. We wanted to know what sort of idiots there were, in what sort of order they were given, what it all meant. So we were very glad to get a letter giving us more detail.

————

From Coombe Springs No date.

I expect you are wondering about the Idiots. So here is the order in which they are toasted:

1. Ordinary Idiot
2. Super Idiot
3. Arch Idiot
4. Hopeless Idiot: to which is always added 'both subjectively and objectively, to those who die honourably and to those who, early-lately, will perish like dogs. Then G will call on someone, usually Elizabeth, to add: 'By the way, it is important to add that only those who work on themselves will die honourably, while those who do not, will inevitably die like dirty dogs'. And to this toast we all say: Amen.
5. Compassionate Idiot. Sympathetic. Antipathetic and So-so.
6. Squirming Idiot – and to all hysterical women, present company included.

That is the First Series. Then comes the Second: the Geometric Idiots.

7. Square Idiot. Sometimes not an idiot: there are corners where something can get in.
8. Round Idiot. That is all sides idiot. Morning, evening, all the time.
9. Zigzag Idiot. To those who have five Fridays in the week; to all hysterical people – and to the 3 sexes.

Then, if dinner is still going on, all sorts of idiots get toasted: Enlightened Idiots, Doubting Idiots, Swaggering Idiots, Remorseful Idiots. . . Gurdjieff says that he is No. 18, but before anyone gets to him everyone is under the table – except him, of course, so he never gets his health drunk. Nobody knows who is 19 or 20.

From E. B., Paris. No date.

I didn't tell you about the food in Paris. We all eat jammed round the table with our elbows in each other's tummies almost. The meal always starts with so-called '*salade*' – too disgusting, floating about in a little bowl. 'Not such *salade* never was' – and indeed I hope so. Then there is usually meat or bird with rice and a big dish of radishes, onions, etc. passed round to eat with it. Then a sweet – always very sweet and syrupy – and fruit, melon, grapes, etc. Sometimes coffee, sometimes not. Throughout the meal he passes round oddments of food – apparently quite indiscriminately, so that one may easily find oneself eating sprats or bearmeat with one's sweet, sheep's meat from Bokhara, camel sausage from Kayseri – one never knows what to expect. Once he broke up fish in his fingers and then held out a fistful across the table, saying benevolently 'Who not squeamish?' The last evening we were there one of Brynn's goat cheeses was handed round which G described as 'special Scotch cheese from Scotland' and enveloped us all with a baleful stare, defying us to deny it. All this is washed down with, mainly, red or white vodka for the toasts, but there is also Mare, Calvados, Armagnac – most things . . .

From C. M., Paris. No date.

After the meal is over we go into the salon and settle ourselves on the chairs, the divan, the stools and the floor. G sits in his chair and Lise brings him his little portable organ which he rests on his knee playing with one hand while he works the bellows with the other.

He then makes the strangest music – the most wonderful music. He says it is 'objective' – that is, the vibrations he produces have a definite effect on people, both organically and psychologically. It affects people in different ways, tough business men and scientists sit with the tears streaming down their faces, others are merely bored or puzzled, others again are moved but do not know why.

Dr Bell asked him about this music, saying she found she did not listen to it with her ears. He said: 'Ears are no good for this music, the whole presence must be open to it. It is a matter of vibrations.' Then he added, 'But tears must come first.' He also said he had to put the whole of himself into these vibrations, it was very difficult for him. He is always exhausted after playing. Often he does not play. Then we play the records of the music.

This is the end of the session. The lunch session lasts from 1.30 to 4.30 or later; the evening session from 10.30 to 2 or 3 in the morning.

From C. M., Paris. No date.

The first room on the right is the reading room – very small (about 14ft square). Next to Mr G's chair is a cupboard full of dolls, little china figures, puppets and so on. Behind this is a large cloth like a stage curtain with various ornamentations including two large enneagrams in gilt sequins and braid. The walls are covered with pictures as odd, assorted and frightful (according to our notions) as any could be ... Well, into this apartment go all. We find seats – some on the bed, covered with dark cloth but not at all disguised, some on the settee and the rest on canvas stools, little cocktail bar stools, on the floor.

On the first night when the reader has been reading a quite short time, G came in. He is a shortish man, giving a most uncanny sense of power. He had, when I first saw him, been in this frightful motor smash four weeks ago. He is 82. He has no wrinkles, looks like a very well-preserved 70. Before I left he had begun to look 60! He has a bald skull, on which he wears a fez, or on grand occasions a black astrakan cap. He had on an old loose, gray sort of a 'housecoat', very unpressed, very shabby. He has very good features in an eastern Mediterranean way – but what strikes you first – and all the time – are his extraordinary eyes – deep brown, always changing, full of expression like a young man's, laughing, full of affection, blazing, watchful and caring for people. To complete the picture, a marvellous pair of twirled Hercule Poirot moustaches! I have never felt for anyone as I feel for Mr Gurdjieff. I see I have never trusted anyone before – and never loved anyone as I love him. You cannot help it – the strong hefty young Frenchmen, who do the movements, speak about their feelings for G quite openly with no considering. All one's centres know him.

Now a personal note – to me it means something important. One night at supper, G gave me a huge piece of beautiful white bread and said: 'Eat tomorrow with *café au lait*.' I said indignantly, 'There is no milk in Paris.' 'Oh, yes there is,' said G, 'tomorrow you have with your *café au lait*.' Well, I took it home and in the morning when my hell brew of black and white barley coffee appeared, I ate my white bread. Then I spent hours tramping about Paris looking for rooms for visitors – and came home to my own hotel to telephone and the proprietress said: 'Mademoiselle is looking very tired. Permit me to offer you some coffee.' And there was a tray with coffee and a jug of milk! – but I had not had faith.

From R. H., 30.11.48

I had been at the Fontainbleau Battle in the beginning (1921). We were digging the foundations of the Study House – I have never even seen it – to me it means trenches and loose building material . . . I wondered if they would remember me at all, after 25 years. However they were very, very good to me – though I was put through it! I was M'sieu Egout every meal except one!

Then I was taken into Mr Ģ's little room with John and the one-armed Michael Corah. Mr G played his curious little accordion, while discussing with John and Corah the latter's desire to be a musician. I naturally took the playing to be for Corah: but it tore me to pieces – me, who can't tell the different between one piece of music and another and to whom most music is a noise – Mr G turned to me and I said how much I was moved, and how strange it was, because music does not generally affect me. But now I had a very profound emotion such as I had never had before. He smiled. 'Of course.' And then, surprisingly, that he had played 'only for me'. I was astonished. He then told me some of the effects he could get on different types by his music – I don't wonder. It was overpowering. He told me to see him again before he went to America.

P.S. G has changed almost beyond belief. My 25 year old picture was of a sort of tiger-tamer, with a whip in one hand and revolver in the other. I could scarcely think of Gurdjieff without expecting a look or a word to make me jump. Now there is a much older man who has built up something that is essentially 'good', who has suffered very, very, much. Then we were the material from which he was making something for himself. His business was not to do anything for us. Now he is helping in a godlike fashion. Not that the tiger-tamer cannot be called up. I am sure he could put on a role that would shake the streets. But that is not his work now.

———

From R. H., 10.12.48

Mr B has just returned from seeing Mr G off on his trip to America. He described the scene at the Gare St Lazare. How all the French Group were there – about 150 of them – and their children – and Mr B and Mr G leant from the train and spoke to them. He told them of the tasks they were to do. The practical work of getting Beelzebub ready for publication in French immediately on his return – and of their own practical work on being. And in the midst of all the usual boat train confusion they became an island of quietness. . . As he talked I could see and feel it all – the importance of this moment when, after 50 years, Mr G's work is coming to fruition. This wonderful year when groups all over the world have sent people to Paris and Mr G at last publishes his books and goes out to visit the groups – first to America – to show the Movements and to guide them in all their 'subjective tasks'. . .

News of the death of Mr Gurdjieff came to us in Africa as suddenly as his rediscovery. One day he was a myth come to life. Another he was a life returned to the myth out of which he came. Both events were shocks to us; but they were not the personal loss that was felt by those who had been touched by his living presence.

In London, Paris and New York the feeling of loss was so deep and devastating that nobody had time to write to us about it. So I have no record of what reached us in Africa. I seem to remember a telegram giving us the bare news. The end when it came was swift and sudden. He seemed to withdraw from his body. His strength ebbed. In three days he was dead. Yet even right up to the end he was joking. The very last time Mme de Salzmann was to see him he was still *en vein*. 'You know what are galoshes?' he asked her. 'Now I put you in the biggest galoshes that ever existed.' It was not a new joke: to be put in old Jewish galoshes was one of his favourite ways of saying you were in deep trouble. But spoken on his death bed! What a way to bring her to accept the tremendous burden she would have to shoulder for many, many years.

———

From Elizabeth Bennett *Idiots in Paris*

We arrived at the chapel a little before six. I had not wished or meant to see his body. But after a moment's thinking I decided to go in. I am very thankful that I did.

I was overwhelmed by the force that came from him. One could not be near his body without feeling unmistakenly his power. He looked magnificent. Composed, content, intentional, for want of a better word. Not simply a body placed by someone else. He was not disguised. Nothing was concealed from us. Everything belonging to him, his inner and outer life and all the circumstances and results of it were there to be seen, if one could see. What force was in him then! I have never seen anything in any way like it. This, I think, was what I had dreaded. I could not bear to see him with the force gone from him. Yet in fact I saw his power for the first time unobscured.

16

Work in Progress

WHEN a key figure disappears from the scene it leaves a terrible shock, a huge void which it seems nothing can fill. However much the situation has been foreseen and arrangements prepared to meet it, there is a feeling of emptiness, of everything being without purpose, of not knowing what to do, where to go. It takes time to find a new balance.

To us in Africa Gurdjieff's death seemed a full stop. Nobody without being there can imagine the scale of that continent. To me it was alien, primitive, empty, 'foreign'. My roots were in Europe, cultivated, small-scale, civilized. I could not adjust to the vast emptiness of the African *bundu*.

Besides that, my wife and I were penniless. We had literally given the Work all we had. Willingly. Now our slender resources had been spent. The Work had cheerfully swallowed everything. What had it given us? I began to ask myself the question.

Since we had been cut off, on our own, the mix-up of half-understood, half-digested ideas called the Work had grown more muddled still. By a sort of conjuring trick Gurdjieff had suddenly reappeared and then, just as suddenly disappeared. His work had acquired more mystery, more scale, but, to us, even less meaning.

But when I came back to the question of what it had given us, I found a very definite but quite unexpected answer: silence.

It had happened the first time I went to a group. I walked into a room. Several people were there already, sitting. Some looked at me, some were looking down, some had their eyes closed. Nobody said anything, welcomed me, or gave any sign of knowing or not knowing me. It was strange, but I felt welcome. It was such a rich, silent silence. I sat down. It was like sliding into deep water, being

151

enveloped by something, received by it, sustained by it, becoming part of it. Wonderful.

It took me some time to settle down. I had never felt such a sensation of other people's presence before. I had heard about people trying strange secret games like 'table turning' or having 'experiences', feeling things, being enlightened, uplifted, opened, and all that. I didn't like it. It was the fag end of something that once had been sacred. I didn't want that. Maybe some people had acquired strange powers, but to me they were suspect, with a questionable background of power or money. Here there was no feeling of that whatever. I was just sitting with some other people, at rest, in peace. I don't know how long it lasted. There was no time in it.

When we got back to England it was wonderful to find this again and when Mme Yette (Henriette) Lannes, who had come to London to take charge of the English groups, allowed me to join one of them, I considered myself very lucky. Somehow or other I had lost touch with John Bennett. In some strange way my admiration for him had faded. In fact I never saw him again and only watched from afar the bizarre developments in his own spiritual path.

To all who delve around in the misty no man's land of spiritual archaeology his writings were of great interest because be brought to abstruse and difficult questions his own particular brand of articulate clarity. Gurdjieff's masterwork *All and Everything* is a baffling testament to the inner growth of Man but, after reading it over and over again, I found at a certain point I was baulked by the verbosity of his language which seemed to have the deliberate intention of 'muddling and befuddling' the reader. His writing, peppered with all sorts of made-up words and phrases, ends by infuriating the reader if they cannot decipher or understand it.

Unravelling the wool which Gurdjieff had effectively pulled over our eyes and reknitting it all into new depths of understanding is one of the real gifts that Bennett brought to his master's work.

But all this only appeared much later. Those first days on returning from Africa now seem in retrospect a series of crises. The Work was still unorganized, still 'coming to life'. It was the end of an era, after all. Gurdjieff had died. His Teaching had never, up till then, been more than a personal cult, believed in and followed by a select, selected, few. Now, for the first time, it was to be made public. His work, *All and Everything*, and Ouspensky's *In Search of the Miraculous* (of which we had never heard) were to be published worldwide. Centres were to be set up where people could study. Money had to be found for all the practical everyday things, necessary bases from which to spread the ideas, to help the world to see their value, to find a new way to live.

If there is anything obvious to any reader of accounts of life with G, it is that the last thing he valued was anything resembling organization. Thoroughly to disorganize, shock, surprise, dismay, upset everybody around him was basic to his nature. New ways of living, thinking, feeling, were the life, the spirit of everything he taught. How could the new get in if the old were not thrown out?

Also there was something different, magical, other-worldly about the atmosphere of the life he conjured up. In his company the future was known, coincidences were normal, dangers melted away, surprises were always fortunate – so it seemed. Nothing could touch those who believed in the Work. They were 'protected'. But, behind all the frantic bustle of the day-to-day bubble and squeak of readings, sittings, movements of that last tremendous year, Gurdjieff was himself working according to plan. He knew exactly what had to be done to meet certain needs, fulfil certain obligations under his own time schedule of the months or weeks of life that remained to him.

———

Is it possible now for us to make any objective assessment of the Teaching of Gurdjieff? Reading and trying to begin to understand the perspective and scope of his masterwork, *All and Everything*, it often seems to me it is not a work that belongs to the immediate future, that it is left as a guide to prove useful to people when they have understood far more, for days and centuries far ahead.

When a new teaching appears it rises from the root of what has been taught before. The truth is the same, what attracts us is the way the new teacher cuts away the old growth and shows us the hidden shoots springing from beneath. This apparent novelty is received with joy by the pioneer truth-seekers and repudiated with fear and disdain by the establishment which dreads the changes that seemingly new truths will bring.

So all our interest in Gurdjieff had been centred on these new

shoots, on the excitement and attraction of their novelty. The
Work had been seen and written about as a very 'modern' thing
from which we, individually, hoped to gain something. But beneath
it all the roots went very deep. Now our enthusiasm for the
novelty could begin to be matched by deeper understanding of the
nature of the roots from which it sprang.

Those who read the Bible and study it from a historical point of
view find a great deal of information on the past history of Jewry
and the suffering its people went through to preserve the truth as
they understood it. When, with the passage of time, the value of
these truths began to run down, they were given a new lease of life
by the appearance of Jesus of Nazareth. Christianity blossomed on
the roots of Judea. The New Testament follows on from the Old
and both are contained in our 'Christian' Bible. The Gospels
would lose their weight, their roots, if they were published alone.

Underlying all Gurdjieff's work, as we study it more deeply, we
find accounts of the remarkable detail into which he went to
uncover the roots of lost and forgotten religions. Out of these his
own truths began to emerge. His journeys had much more than
personal aims. An aspect of the growth of all human aspirations is
contained in his lifelong research into what may be called psycho-
logical archaeology, digging out the truth with personal as well as
communal aims. What he brought back to the pages of *All and
Everything* is the distillation of a lifetime of research. It is the
result of a fantastic personal effort made, objectively, for the
world. The value of all this is still hardly recognized. For those
who care to look, *All and Everything* is the new Bible.

This raises the question: what preparation did Gurdjieff make
for the future of his work? The ideas he brought back from his
long journeys in unknown parts of the world were rich and
strange. With them he returned to Russia at a time of enormous
upheaval, the birth of the Communist Party. Law and order was
being abolished. Nothing had taken its place. A huge nation was in
total disarray and in this mad incalculable situation, Gurdjieff had
not only to try to extricate himself and his scattered family from
being obliterated in the wanton killing that went with the chaos,
but also to rescue to the comparative safety of southern Russia the
first pupils he had left in his Moscow and Petrograd groups. It was
a time of incredible day-to-day danger and difficulty. No time, one
would have thought, in which to reflect and restructure whole

areas of religious belief and hope and reveal ways to open up new possibilities to mankind.

With all this Gurdjieff struggled, first as the head of his large family, then as the leader of those who followed him and loved him. Miraculously he succeeded in bringing a large part of them through it all to the comparative safety of southern Russia, to regions where the Revolution was less violent and less organized. Finally, after enough danger and adventure to overfill any ordinary life, he reached Constantinople and the prospect of escape to Europe.

Throughout all those years when 'other-worldly' ideas might well have taken second place, at every opportunity for rest and recuperation, he immediately flung himself and his followers into frenzied projects to set up groups to study his ideas and his sacred dances, which quickly developed into ballets, plays or demonstrations of great complexity and cost, arousing general widespread attention and interest. But as soon as the place, or its situation, was threatened, the whole project was abandoned and the groups moved on, narrowly missing being engulfed in the maelstrom of events.

The fire of these outpourings of belief had an almost demonic power over those who took part in them or saw them. Yet in a sense they were wasted, abandoned; valuable only for what people had 'learned' through the tremendous efforts in which they had been involved. Gurdjieff was looking for the technique of spreading his ideas, his teaching. It was to take him many years to reach the only possible way.

———

ALL we had learned before going to Africa would be, we thought, discarded, thrown into the background by the tremendous impetus set up by the appearance of the Master's own work. But, in fact, many of us took a long time to read all the thousand and more pages of *All and Everything*. It was too strange, too complex, too difficult. Only after a second or third reading did we begin to grasp the true meaning even of the title, far less of the extent of the book's originality, depth and power. Much we felt was quite beyond us and only after a change in ourselves could we hope to catch a glimpse of where it was leading us.

Yet, understood or not, there was a fascination about the book. The extraordinary stories, the strange words, the variety, the humour; we found that we read, put it down, shook our heads and then picked it up and read on. It was a book of revelation all right, but what it revealed was so much beyond us we couldn't 'use' it, we had to let it sink in, come across strange links, allegories, myths, uplifting truths of how the world might be – and pray to be worthy of the hope it gave us.

But, after all the big talk, the myths, the promises, the exhortations, what is the root, the cornerstone, on which the whole Teaching is built? What do we, personally, have to do to take a first step into this 'other' life? It is to accept a basic truth, similar to those to be found in every sacred teaching, but never stated so baldly, so uncompromisingly as by Gurdjieff:

> We are born in sleep, live in sleep and die in sleep.
> Our only hope of salvation is to wake up.

Well! (I can hear the reaction). This is obviously a piece of absolute nonsense, besides being a blatant lie. It is an insult to human reason to suggest that anyone in their right minds could make it. As for discussing or accepting it ... words fail me! However, believable or not, the shock has one great merit: it divides the sheep from the goats, divides those who are open-minded enough to hear what may lie behind such an outrageous statement and those who shut their minds to it.

What is the state of sleep? It is the condition in which the whole organism has lost touch with those parts of it which are responsible for directing its life. It is assumed that when the organism 'wakes up' it will obey this direction; what else can it do? But what does it actually do?

Take a very simple example: to look at oneself in a mirror. There I see a reflection of myself. I brush my hair, fix my tie, take a look at myself, sigh and decide that it will have to do. *I have indulged in my first act of self-observation.* For a moment I looked at myself. Then I lapsed back into my normal un-self-observant behaviour and 'got on' with my life.

Looking at myself, seeing myself, this was something quite new to me. I had never really seen the reflection in the mirror as *me*. I saw how other people looked, how they felt, even sensed their 'state', but never looked at myself like that. I rejected the idea. It threw me off balance, baffled me. Being outside myself, looking at myself, was unnatural, fairy-story stuff – Alice Through the Looking Glass!

That was it! Exactly. And it took me years to see what it implied. To 'see' myself was more than just looking at my image. It meant seeing my 'moods', comparing myself, how I was now, how I was then, even how I matched up to some ideal I had of myself. That day when I 'saw' how badly I had behaved, another when my pride had not left me with a clear conscience. All this, little by little, began to shake the old opinion of myself, that I was more or less perfect. All those different 'I's, changing every five minutes. 'You nothing but taxi.' I was scared. I stood before a cold impartial world in which I was nothing.

Of course it didn't hit me all at once, as it does now I write about it. It came over me, bit by bit, a slow dawning of recognition. This inexorable computer I had in my head that went round and round forever throwing up new combinations of old ideas. Of course it all depended on how closely I looked, how deep I was prepared to go. I couldn't (then) face myself all the time. That was never asked of me. But now, many years later, looking back on the long perspective, I have reached a point where I can sometimes see how everything is linked on a stairway that began with the first decision just to look at myself! That, over the years, had developed into this long pilgrimage to find a new world.

But how to get there? That was still in shadow. The standard ways, though I had been brought up in them, did not seem to fit. The man-made morality, the religious rituals of the day meant nothing. It was to find something I could believe in and live by that had brought me to the Work.

The Work was exciting. But where would it take me?

In my first days of study with Bennett I do not recollect that this aim of 'waking up' – and remaining awake – was central to the Teaching. The first idea I remember – and I remember it vividly – was ancilliary to it. We called it in those days, 'multiplicity'. We were not, we were told, just one person with many moods, but a sort of centipede, walking on dozens, hundreds, of different contradictory legs, each of them called into existence by reacting to what other people said or thought (hence the multi-headed hydras and dragons' teeth of the old legends).

This idea that we were not one person or, like Walter Mitty, had

different 'sides' to us was far from new. Plays and books galore
had been written exploiting the theme. But exploding the whole
idea, saying there was *nothing* permanent, central in our lives, no
basic 'I' to which we always returned, this was too much. It
undermined our feelings of self, the basic idea of personality,
belittled us into mere talking boxes, chatterers, sounding off into
dozens of contradictory opinions, beliefs, likes and dislikes. That
attacked the roots of our egoism. It was rejected as absurd,
ridiculous. But, of course, we in our earliest attempts at self-
observation had already caught ourselves in these different roles.
To us, personality was a troop of shadow boxers, always arguing,
contradicting, changing from for to against, yes to no, right to
wrong, endlessly, interminably – no wonder the world was in a
muddle!

Of course, the categoric 'all or nothing' command of Gurdjieff,
'Die honourable death, not perish like dog', had reached us in
Africa. But everything that reached us there was so far away, such
a dream of something we had never thought of, hoped for, that we
really didn't take it in. Perhaps such a decree could only be given
from the level of those who gave it. To those who taught me, on
my return from Africa, the tremendous power and urgency of the
impossible was watered down and expressed in a far more accept-
able form: 'Remember yourself always, everywhere.' That might
be within reach: it was worth a try. So those first snapshots of
self-observation soon became moments of self-remembering, the
beginning, for those who had it, of that 'instinctive need' given by
Beelzebub as one of the Five Obligatory Strivings that should be
part of the honourable life of a man.

But this trying to be 'there', to be 'conscious', though it was
evasive, ephemeral, brought an enormous enrichment to life, a sort
of key to character. This is what people really were, not what they
seemed to be. You could see it in little children – they were all
essence – before they had learned to copy their parents, grow
personalities – and lie. Now, they showed only the root of what
they would one day be 'like'. We all had these roots. They were a
sort of bodyguard, the guardians of my 'very' self – the self I could
call I – when I saw it was the kernel of my essence. But to reach
that firm ground and stand there might take a lifetime.

I submit that to have come to all this through just looking at
oneself in the mirror is an extraordinary metamorphosis, an

example of the immediacy and power of Gurdjieff's teaching –
and how all teachings that have the same root are one and illumin-
ate each other. The further you go, the simpler it becomes.

———

HARDLY had I – and a lot of other 'beginners' – begun to grapple
with this new view of ourselves than we were faced with another
idea just as 'new' and just as unexpected.

I remember very well how I received it. I was sitting reading
Bennett's book – all he could remember of Gurdjieff's teaching
(this was long before going to Africa or the discovery of Gurdjieff
still being alive) and was stopped by being confronted with an
empty page, with nothing on it but an equilateral triangle. The
three bare lines in that compulsive shape had an 'equals' sign
against the apex and at the left and right lower corners a 'plus' sign
and a 'minus' sign respectively. The effect was so strong, so vivid,
so complete, I looked and looked and looked at it, as if there had
never been anything like it in the world before!

This was my introduction to the Law of Three, the second
fundamental cosmic law of the Universe. It stated that there were
three independent forces which were manifest in everything, everywhere, from molecule to Milky Way. These forces were called – to
use Gurdjieff's own words:

> First, the Affirming Force or the Pushing Force or simply Force-Plus:
> second the Denying Force or the Resisting Force or simply the Force-
> Minus and third the Reconciling Force or the Equilibriating Force or
> the Neutralizing Force.
>
> *All and Everything*, p. 1132

While we lived in our 'sleeping', imaginary world we did not
notice this third force, but it was always there – as the Holy
Trinity reminded us – a ghostly presence. But when we 'woke up',
gave any situation our attention, we could see that our duality was
not enough. Yes and no, black and white, right and wrong, were
just generalities until they were defined. To have meaning there
had to be a third ingredient that specified *what* was real, black or
white, right or wrong. Without that, no event! But we were third-
force blind. To see it we had to 'wake up'.

Life consists of a series of 'happenings' – random hopes,

disappointments, troubles, desires, worries, big and small, stream through our thoughts, overlapping, appearing, disappearing, vanishing, all of them dreams without substance until the third force enters to make us say: 'This or that, was real, it actually happened!'

It was many years before I really began to see any of this, to be able to stand back enough to watch it going on. Then what was really at stake in wars, politics, human relationships looked quite different, richer and often more terrible for being seen more clearly. It opened up possibilities in all sorts of invention, research and any situation where progress was blocked or hung up. Surveying the problem, looking for the third force, would allow solutions to appear. Seeing the third force was the key to seeing reality.

If we start to look for examples of the Law of Three at work, we can find them all around us. The earth's orbit round the sun is held precisely as it is by the third force – the gravity between them; dough, yeast and fire make bread; composer, artist and instrument make music; man, woman and love make children. Only three forces, coming together in the right proportion can bring a result.

———

GURDJIEFF comes up with a striking analogy to see the Law of Three at work in us, to show us what Man is really like. Taken as whole, figuratively, he suggests Man can be seen simply as a cart, horse and driver. His body corresponds to the cart, his feelings to the horse, and what is called his intelligence to the driver.

There should be a fourth party – the owner of the whole thing. But unfortunately, owing to the life-style of the young, he never turns up and the whole contraption has become a

> broken-down hackney carriage, which has long ago seen its day, a crock of a horse and a tatterdamalion half-sleepy, half-drunken driver whose time designated by Mother Nature for self-perfecting passes while he waits on a street corner, fantastically daydreaming for any old chance passenger. The first who comes by hires him and dismisses him as he pleases, and not only him but his horse and cart as well.
>
> *All and Everything*, p. 1193

Gurdjieff gives a scathing caricature of the average driver, his laziness, his poor education, his smattering of information which passes for knowledge, his self-indulgence in food and drink and women, his preoccupation with material things, his readiness to flatter and lie and even to gratify these weaknesses by stealing money that should have been used to feed the horse.

Meanwhile the poor horse, owing to the negligence of those around it and to its constant solitude is, so to speak, locked up within itself. It is kept tied up and nothing has ever been done for it except to abuse and beat it. Instead of oats and hay, it has been given straw, which is totally insufficient for its needs. So, at the least sign of interest or affection it is ready to surrender itself completely.

As for the cart, the situation is even worse. It is made of many different materials and was evidently designed to carry heavy loads and stand the shake-up of travelling over rough roads. Its greasing, for instance, relies on the jolting from such travel which it does not get on smooth asphalted roads. The driver, of course, knows nothing about greasing and oiling, with the results that soon the cart begins to creak and rattle, bolts get loose, bearings rust and journeys rarely end without considerable repairs. . .

Gurdjieff develops this wonderful analogy in considerable detail (What part do the reins play? What is the function of the shafts?) and leads us to his conclusion that as long as our life is a 'taxi' at the mercy of every chance passenger, there is no hope for it. Therefore every man should aspire to be master of his cart, horse and driver and to have his own 'I'.

———

I think most of us were surprised to find what it means to work in a group. We had come this far largely by our own personal efforts and studies. We had picked up some of the basic ideas on which Gurdjieff's work is founded. We saw wonderful vistas opening before us – a few of which I have touched on in these pages. Now we were beginning to work regularly with others – mostly strangers – who had all got to the same place, stood more or less on the same level. Progress from now on would be group progress. The Work brought hope.

We were all given the same question, the same task. Over a given period we met weekly to discuss what we had seen. It was astonishing to find the effect of the same question on others. Each, it seemed, had seen the task differently. To some it had meant almost nothing, to others it opened up a new world and set them thinking in quite a different direction. So, in unexpected ways, each broadened and deepened his own understanding of what the word understanding meant. Feelings began to come before thoughts.

We began to see how narrow our personal opinion (of which we had always been so proud) was. To me, a chattering know-all, it was already an experience just to sit and listen and salutary to find some quiet little body I hadn't thought much of coming out with thoughts that made me look childish. What we gained from others so enriched our own work that even from those early days we began to change ourselves. This was how change came about, by listening, reflecting, taking something home and perhaps bringing it back next week, a bit more deeply understood. So we grew by listening, sharing, being together. The group had a mind of its own – 'One hand washes the other' G had said and, as usual, it was deeply and practically true.

There were other bonds in group work which only appeared as we experienced each other. People began to respect and trust one another – and to see that it was the first time in life they had ever done so! We began to take to obligations, worldly obligations, as we would to old friends. Worldly tasks became work tasks as well. All this, to me, was a quite unexpected bonus. It made higher things homely family things and no less sacred for that.

At the same time this group relationship was something quite special. It did not spill over into daily life. We were close to each other and yet at the same time separate. We did not think of making friends with others in our group. We looked on the Work as something very private, very new, very much a secret which we were privileged to share and which set us apart from everybody else. Of course, a lot of this was nonsense and gradually broke down as we began to see how we were posturing before each other and before life. But I can still see the 'holier than thou' expressions on people's faces on meeting and the pretence of working when we were merely covering up. It took some years for this to break down, to admit to others and to ourselves that we were not, and were unlikely immediately to become, conscious men and women and we might as well face our limitations – and begin to live in truth! It was a very real step in understanding to have reached this point – we could actually admit that we could not remember ourselves and not get thrown out of the Work!

━━━━━━

ALL this I do not think would have been possible at all without the being, the level of help, that was brought to it by Mme Yette Lannes, who presided over the growth of the English groups until her death, more than 20 years later. She was French, a member of Gurdjieff's closest Paris group and I suppose the most striking thing about her was her devastating common sense!

As it was to her that I owed almost everything I had been taught about the Work, I feel I must pause to say something about the life of this remarkable woman.

She came of peasant stock from a small village near the Pyrenees. Her father had died during her childhood leaving her and her mother to tramp the countryside humping heavy bales of cloth to sell to the neighbouring farmers. She saw there was no future in that. So, to help her mother and better their lot, she determined to get out into the world and earn money. She coaxed the village mayor to let her learn to type, using the old machine in his office during the luncheon hour. Having mastered this, she set off for Lyons to become a secretary. There, finding that the duties required of her were not entirely secretarial, she almost starved. After some months of this a stroke of good fortune occurred. Her village priest was offered a modest post in Paris and invited her mother to housekeep for him. She went along.

From there she never looked back. By diligence, formidable intelligence and a peasant capacity for hard work, she soon began to make her way. She formed part of that strange international group that participated in the Spanish Civil War. Shortly after her marriage she happened, by chance (as it always appears), to meet Mme de Salzmann. 'What has that woman got that I have not got?' she asked herself – and determined to find out. Her study brought her to Gurdjieff himself and from then on her life became devoted to his work.

To it she brought not only a natural endowment for the endless struggle it implies, but a shrewd, intensely practical grasp of fundamentals. She was not one to get lost in philosophy or theory. To everything and everybody, while constantly watching herself, she brought an everyday common – or more properly uncommon – sense of what was necessary. If the three inner circles of humanity can be described as the philosophical, the theoretical and last, the practical, she stands firmly rooted there.

When you have seen such growth with your own eyes, it cannot be forgotten. Growth is possible, change is possible. Here before you is the proof. It is open to you. Maybe you cannot go so far, but you can enter the path and follow it as far as you can, this is the way, as Gurdjieff put it, to die an honourable death.

———

GURDJIEFF signs off the introductory chapter of *All and Everything* by describing himself as being 'simply a Teacher of Dancing'. The 'dancing' he taught took the form of 'the Movements', to which oblique reference has already been made in these pages.

The Movements are simply a series of postures taken up by the human body which, when they follow in a certain sequence and a certain rhythm, result in what are called 'sacred gymnastics' or Sacred Dances. Such dances have, from ancient times, been used as a means of transmitting hidden truths.

Gurdjieff gave great importance to these Movements and put special efforts into teaching those who showed particular feeling for this aspect of his work. He brought back, it was said, hundreds of these Sacred Dances which he had learned in those faraway, hidden monasteries about which we, at that time, knew nothing. Some of these were of great complexity and difficult to perform and even the simpler ones which we learned at our weekly classes set much importance on a high level of attention, on accuracy of posture and rhythm and to assuming the exact poses we had been given.

These Movements have to be seen to feel their value. They are quite unlike any usual gymnastics or ballets. They need a special quality of attention because, although they seem simple, they follow none of the 'usual' sequences of positions which we tend to take up automatically. To those who perform them they bring a wonderful feeling of being part of a perfection of togetherness in movement and, in some of them, in a sense of deep inner silence and calm. I always felt it was a privilege to take part in them and they left in me, afterwards, a heightened state of being alive, while to take part in one of the rare demonstrations was to be uplifted by a sense of being held in a moment of holiness and beauty.

———

MEANWHILE, wrapped up in all this, I was back in London with my family life to lead, treading water. The little carpentry business I had started was a failure. Africa had been a failure too. The Work had given me a new attitude to life, but I couldn't see how to adapt my 'ordinary' existence to it. Everything had happened too quickly, been too much for me, turned me upside down. I couldn't see. I was stuck! Then, suddenly, out of the blue, came a message from Mme de Salzmann: 'Would you like to join a House of Work in America?'

The idea of going to America always brought hope. My last trip before the war had been wonderful. Now the possibility of joining the famous Ouspensky Group (as this House of Work turned out to be) was the sort of thing that inspired me. Didn't I say the Work took care of you? Here was a sure sign of it.

A month or two before this, Mme Lannes, who had been a sort of mother to me through all my first years of study, had already been sent to the Ouspensky Group and it was she who had suggested to Mme de Salzmann that I came over to the States to join her.

When Mme Lannes had left, all of us in London had felt cut off. So the chance to be with her again was a joyful prospect. I should be among friends. In all this sugar there was only one pinch of salt, rather a large one: I must find some way to pay for our tickets to New York, for my wife, of course, was coming with me.

It was a dilemma. I had no reserves left. Africa had swallowed all my worldly goods. I had even had to part with my beloved Rupi, my villa in Italy, to try to get the Transvaal farm on its feet. That had failed too. Africa had cost me £10,000. Not much now; all I had then.

Now I should have to scrape the barrel. My last treasure, my Shansi chests must go.

Way back in my Peking days, twenty years before, I had come by four Shansi chests. These were part of the marriage dowry that was carried at wedding processions and contained everything the wife brought with her to the marriage. Mine were beauties and must have been part of an important wedding for they were most beautifully painted all over, especially the doors, which were small masterpieces of the art of that period. These wonderful chests had 'made' my living room in various houses and flats I had lived in all these years. In Peking they had cost me £5. Now I saw them go for £250. (Five years later, I priced one of the four, specially mounted, for sale at 500 guineas!)

Mme de Salzmann was delighted I had got our tickets this way. She said it was part of my 'revaluation of all values'.

17

Time to Retire

W E arrived in New York to find Mme Lannes on the docks to meet us. We adjourned to the flat of a friend for lunch, after which we should be driven down to Mendham where the group was situated. It was at that lunch that cold shivers began to run up and down my spine.

From the moment she began to talk, I realized that Madame was facing another of those situations almost too heavy for her. She went over all the people working in the house, giving us a vivid insight into their characters. At the end of each one, she turned to me with those deep searching eyes: '*Méfiez vous, Cecil! Méfiez vous!*' Only one or two in the whole household escaped her warning to watch out! There was something seriously wrong somewhere. If she could hardly cope, how could we? The house took on the air of a prison. What had we got ourselves into?

The house itself was a large well-built place which had at one time been the Residence of the Governor of New Jersey. It stood on a hilltop surrounded by woods and ornamental gardens now sadly neglected and overgrown. Around it at a lower level were barns, workshops, outhouses and about 400 acres of arable land.

The house itself had three storeys and a basement. Ample reception rooms and kitchens occupied most of the ground floor. The first floor (complete with red carpet) was reserved for Work VIP guests. The top floor, originally the servants' quarters, had corridors with small bedrooms on either side. These were allotted to pupils who were there for Work and on whom the running of the whole place depended. One of those rooms was allotted to us.

The household consisted of half a dozen spinsters of various ages and two alleged 'farmers'. There were in addition, privileged guests, members of the Ouspensky family, old pupils of Gurdjieff

167

and occasional visitors. All these were VIPs who took no part in the running of the house and even ate quite different food from the pupils. There was, in addition – an important addition – a mangy savage Chow dog with a habit of attacking anyone who disturbed it. This creature held a privileged position – since it was supposed to provide opportunities for people to 'wake up'.

But what made the place unique and gave it its (to me) eerie and dreadful atmosphere was the invisible and menacing presence that directed it. Mme Ouspensky was an old Russian lady who for many years had assisted her husband in the running of such houses as this. When he died those closest to her naturally stayed on to help lighten her bereavement and she tried to continue her husband's work. When she fell ill and lost her powers of speech, the place should have been closed. But it was not. The bedridden old lady assumed the role and prestige of a teacher. When we got there her speech had deteriorated so much that only one or two people could understand her. These 'bodyguards' saw to it that everything that happened in the house was reported to her. Everybody reported on everybody else while Madame made her assessments on 'right' and 'wrong', upbraided one, praised another and issued her autocratic commands. Such secret service methods seemed particularly suited to the Slav temperament.

We, of course, were never allowed to see her. She was held in awe – and I think a good deal of fear – by all who came to the house. My reaction was a violent revolt against this travesty of Work which was evidently leading a lot of well-meaning but stupid people precisely nowhere.

We live in an age when it seems many are looking for spiritual direction. Once caught by some 'teacher', they are very easily duped, fall into a sort of hypnosis and lose all power of discrimination. We, in Africa, had been as perfectly sure what we were doing was right as, to quote Gurdjieff, 'a thoroughbred donkey is convinced of the rightness of his obstinacy'.

So, these good people had, so to speak, slipped sideways into a cul-de-sac. A House of Work must aim to be conducted and maintained at a level above that of everyday life. 'By their fruits shall ye know them.' A few days at Mendham showed the fruits all too clearly. The place was an absolute shambles. The farm buildings were crammed with rusty, abandoned agricultural machinery and implements. The wildest disorder prevailed in workshops and storerooms. Everything was run down, bodged up and heading for the scrap heap. The farm, as a farm, produced nothing. Although there was a large market garden, no fresh vegetables were ever eaten by the household. If there was an excess of such things as beans or peas, they were promptly sold, or bottled to be eaten perhaps a couple of years later. We took over a whole Stilton cheese as a present to the house. It was forgotten for a month. By then it had gone bad. Only after our protests was some of it distributed. The idea of eating anything fresh or 'good' was a sort of sin!

Being sent to Mendham and meeting very different Americans from those I had met in California cast the first shadow on my .idealism about the Work. These people had been indoctrinated with Work ideas, 'remember yourself everywhere', and presumably went about doing it all the time. But did they, or were they just pretending? I couldn't help seeing from the bored, slovenly way the place was kept that it was all utterly mechanical.

I was deeply shocked by this. What had happened to these people? Why had they given up — for that was what it amounted to? Somehow I vaguely glimpsed the idea, 'the impossible possibility', but some obstacle had come between them and their hope. I didn't believe it, of course. Everything could be overcome, if you worked on it. But the niggling thought remained for me to come back to later.

Meanwhile, everything they explained to me was a field for inner work — the outside did not matter. If there was all-round incompetence, waste and neglect, that was beside the point. What mattered was what they had learned through it. They had, supposedly, seen how incompetent, wasteful and neglectful they were . . .

Anyhow there it was and the 'holier than thou' household spy ring was at first bewildering and then produced in me a violent antagonism to the whole set-up. But for Mme Lannes it was worse. We had only to 'learn' and do what we could, but she had the task of trying to bring back a healthy work attitude to these lost people. And, of course, they did not want it. They wanted everything to remain as it had been. Her attempts were frustrated and thwarted at every turn. Conspiracies were set up to prevent her speaking. She collided, of course, head on with the invisible autocrat whose authority was being threatened. But doggedly and finally successfully she managed to set up, not at Mendham but in New York, groups among those who had in various ways managed to escape the Mendham monster. Then she begged to be allowed to return to Europe.

She left a month before the three months we had promised to Mme de Salzmann to 'try' America was up. Once Mme Lannes was gone, we were isolated, treated as outcasts, but I was perversely determined to see it out. Somehow I had to find a way to detach myself from the oppression of the place and, again, trust the Work. I believed the situation would right itself. It did. With my usual luck I ran into an ex-BBC friend who remembered my work there. He was now in radio at the United Nations and took me on to make a weekly radio programme for the Food and Agriculture Organization. I enjoyed the work and stayed on with the UN for a year before returning to London.

———

'THE change in some people is extraordinary!' said Mme de Salzmann, looking at me and smiling. It was, I suppose, forgiveness for my poor showing in America and her welcome on my return to London.

I was deeply grateful. I had not been able to see any future for myself in America. So when London friends engineered an interesting TV opening for me and I was accepted, it was a real lifeline. I was soon profitably involved and it really was extraordinary how all the negativity and protest of my Work days in New York simply melted away. How slender and shallow are our impulses! It is not simply that we shrink from suffering, it is that we simply don't see the value of it and slide out. Few people in Paris labelled themselves 'squirming idiots'. I think it takes a lot of seeing.

Anyway, in the warm 'home' atmosphere of the London house all the old impulses returned with enthusiasm at the promise of serious Work. It really was a second chance. I saw how weak I had been in America, how I had not been able to separate myself from my circumstances and keep the inside steady and detached whatever went on outside. Another failure! It was time to begin to see that my failures there, in Africa and in everything, were in me, not in my circumstances.

Now, forty years later, reducing all those years into these pages, I am sure the reader also must have felt the rush of events coming through. Ever since I had met the Work everything seemed to have been taken at a gallop. Someone with deeper roots could have done better. Mine were shallow. So ... there it was, as it was. I had to live with it.

This return to London was the turning point, the start of another more reasonable and becoming way of life for me – the start of serious Work.

SERIOUS Work! I suppose what I really mean by that is the same old question: how to wake up! In a way I knew it already. I knew about self-observation, self-remembering, looking for a more positive attitude to life and so on. But knowing these things and actually carrying them out, finding the way, all this needed more effort, needed help from those who had been through it all, knew the difficulties and pitfalls and, more than that, knew how to encourage and sustain me. Although it was this, as a vague, wordless longing, that had called me in the first place, the excitement of the African adventure, the flying, the pioneer work in the veld, all this had masked it. I had pretended, as usual, to know more than I did. Now it was time to make up for lost time.

Most of the original people who had started study with John Bennett, Jane Heap or Kenneth Walker had now amalgamated. Those who had studied with Maurice Nicoll had joined us. The Gurdjieff Society had been founded in London and was under the care of Mme Lannes, with weekly help from Paris from Henri Tracol and Maurice Desselle, with Marthe de Guigneron directing the Movements. Nothing more generous could have been given us to start us on our way and, looking back, it seems to me that, although we were serious and had a good attitude, we never realized the quality of the help we were given in those days by our French friends and what we owed – and still owe – to the lifelong devotion of these good people – and, of course, Mme Lannes – who, all their lives, had been so close to Gurdjieff himself.

Although the aim of our study never varied, the weekly progress of it is difficult to see. Some weeks (from what I know in my own group) it was heavy, lifeless and stuck, then progress revived. My own memories are full of gratitude to what I owe to others in the group. They held me up through empty (for me) meetings, helped me to see what I never could have seen alone. We started off a lot of people on a bus going in the same direction, now we were a group, sharing the same aims, even if we weren't going at the same pace. There was, under it all, a hidden feeling of unity. Wonderful days!

Seeing ourselves! What an extraordinary thing it was – and is! To me there is always this feeling of space, of being free to look about me, see where I am. My situation is not what it usually is, part of the breathless rush and tumble of daily life. I have stopped! Seen it! I am different! Awake!

And what did I see when I 'saw'? A focus. On myself, as I was in that moment, perhaps my voice, my pose, my attitude, my feeling, separated, distinct and real! It was this that remained when I was back in the millstream. It was this – my state! How you always are – and how you could be.

So, slowly, I began to get this, rather lonely, picture of myself. Cutting myself down to size brought an immediate desire to get closer to others because I had seen my own weakness, my own need of them. I am my brother's keeper – whatever the Bible may say!

In all this I am compressing almost twenty years of study into a few paragraphs. There were long patches of dreary emptiness in which nothing seemed worthwhile and the whole thing a sort of obstacle to living a more 'normal' life. Then, without really appreciating it at the time, I began to cut out these 'normalities'. Somehow, slowly, I began to see, I had once lived like these people and now had, as it were, seen through it. There was a curious and surprising feeling, not of being 'better', but of love, sympathy for a world which was somehow blind to its condition and could not, would not, see it.

All around us, the world over, in those years, (I add this much later), there were huge convulsions in whole societies. Tremendous 'wakings up' had occurred and were occurring, but these, though certainly in the right direction, seemed like miraculous flashes of clarity between nightmares. From Communism to democracy, from slavery to freedom, from left to right, always the same dualities! The opposites could never solve anything. And there, down the ages, stood the Law of Three, the Holy Trinity to tell us how to get the result! The Middle Way was the answer to every-thing.

The world was deeply asleep, had woken up with a cry, only to fall deeply asleep again. Could nothing be done? Was it the world's fate to suffer its own self destruction? Was humanity a failure because it was blind?

———

FOR some time the Gurdjieff Society had wanted to acquire some property outside London where it could start a centre for crafts and gardening. Rita Thorburn, who had been closely associated .with the African adventure, eventually found, near Maidenhead, an abandoned chicken farm, originally owned and now being sold off by Lyons, the caterers.

It was a large derelict set of wooden buildings with asbestos roofs set round a courtyard, a broken-down sewage plant, a dozen wild cats and an overpowering stench of chicken shit left by the previous owners in a series of deep ditches which ran beneath the buildings where the thousands of luckless birds had been housed. There was also a small house for the manager, some outhouses and a few acres of nettles. We acquired the freehold of all this for, I believe, somewhere in the region of £14,000.

It turned out to be just what we needed and wonderful, pretty primitive, material for mend and make do! Long hours clearing those dreadful ditches, getting the sewage working, putting in drains, water and electric power supply and services, redesigning the layout, cleaning the whole place up and cutting the nettles, occupied teams of devoted men and women, hardly any of whom knew anything of the technical side of this work, on their Satur-days and Sundays for over a year. Nobody, seeing the place today, can have any idea of what it has grown to be from what it was. When at last it was finished and opened for the crafts to get working, I remember a sense of real accomplishment and satisfac-tion that we had brought off the whole undertaking. It was a triumph of what working together could mean.

Now printing, bookbinding, carpentry, weaving and pottery are only some of the activities covered by the weekend teams. The chance to develop useful skills while keeping the aims of the Work alive presents a wonderful opportunity to broaden the base of the effort — and also to learn an attitude, a 'trade', which could be valuable through life. Study, besides being a set of spiritual, intellectual concepts, becomes a practical way to set the hands working for the spirit and the spirit working in the hands. Gurdjieff was the most practical advocate of using life for work. Head, heart and hands can be our personal Holy Trinity in action.

———

IT was one day after lunch and Mme de Salzmann was talking to us. Somebody asked her a question: 'How can I help people? I often want to help, but I don't know how to, don't know what to say, do the wrong thing. I feel it ought to be easy, but it isn't...'

Mme de Salzmann sat silent, then she spoke in that very clear voice of hers: 'You are quite right. It isn't easy. The impulse of love — that is easy. But, knowing how, feeling the need of the other person, knowing by instinct, training or experience what to say or do, being impartial, that is very difficult... That can be genius...'

She broke off, smiled reflectively, then: 'I will tell you a story. One day Mr Gurdjieff happened to be lunching alone at a small Paris restaurant. His attention was called to a table nearby where he saw a couple, clearly very anxious about the boy sitting with them. He seemed almost like an animal greedily eating the food before him. He was fat, very fat, far overweight. He ate like an animal. Mr Gurdjieff overheard one or two remarks the couple were making and knew they were talking Armenian. Now it happened that he had a great weakness for Armenians. He said they were a wonderful people of great antiquity. They had not let their country be overrun by Western civilization. They had kept up their old customs, particularly the roots of their language, which was full of old sayings, old customs of the past, and this kept their people clean and unspoiled by the slime of the West.

'When Mr Gurdjieff spoke to them in Armenian, they were clearly surprised and delighted. They got into conversation, he joined them at their table and, of course, being Mr G, it wasn't long before they were treating him as an old friend. Only the son went on eating, taking no notice. Mr G explained he was a Russian, a doctor, a child specialist, but of course unknown in Paris, where he was still making his reputation. They arranged to meet again and Mr G succeeded in getting their confidence and hearing more about their deep anxiety about their son.

'He told them that, in his opinion, it was their love that had spoiled the boy. His condition had become a disease. It was quite well known in Russia, where parents were often over-indulgent to their children. It was fear of starvation really. They had known terrible days of famine. Their children must never know that, so they encouraged them to eat and eat well, with the result that some of them could not stop and the thing became compulsive, serious . . .

'He was very busy, he told them, and it was only because he had a weakness for Armenians that . . . well, he would make them an offer: "Give your son to me. I will cure him. It will take about three months. But there are conditions. You must not see him, write to him, or come anywhere near him during this time. Your absence is part of the cure." They were a bit doubtful about this, adoring their son and never having been parted from him. "Besides, three months . . . that's a long time . . . what will it cost?" Gurdjieff brushed all this aside. "It will cost what it costs. Whatever it costs, you must promise to pay it without question. Your faith in me is part of your son's cure. . ." Well . . . finally they agreed. Probably it was only because Mr Gurdjieff was what he was that such an extraordinary arrangement was possible. . .'

Mme de Salzmann paused, looking round at us all. We were breathless, excited. Seeing, as any good storyteller can, that she had got us, she smiled again and went on.

'The first thing was to gain the trust of Sarkis – that was the boy's name – his trust and affection, that was all-important and not difficult. He had a naturally open and affectionate nature. Gurdjieff started by painting a pitiable picture of his own state. A terrible thing had happened. "Just today! Just when I was going to take off on holiday with you!" he said. "I was robbed! In business." The man would be caught, of course. He would be rich again, but for the moment he had nothing. They would have hardly enough to eat. But soon everything would be better! (He kept on inventing these 'bad luck' stories). But tomorrow never came, they had hardly enough to eat, but now they trusted each other, shared everything, it would be bound to come out all right.

'Well, Sarkis believed him and began to adore him and over the next weeks, getting used to starving without noticing it, he grew into a healthy young man, ready to do anything and everything Gurdjieff asked of him. The money never turned up and they were always very poor, had to work, had to struggle to make ends meet, but together they would make it. This regime went on for weeks, Gurdjieff putting more and more work on Sarkis' shoulders, with the excuse that he himself was getting weaker, older. . .

'At last, at the end of a long day when they had climbed all the stairs up to the top flat where they were living, Mr G, accidentally, tripped over the trash can and sent the whole lot — it was full — cascading down the staircase and landings below. Starting in at once to pick up all the mess, piece by piece, and get it back in the bin, without the least sign of any blame or irritation at Mr G's carelessness was a climax. The boy was cured, both in body and mind. Gurdjieff threw his arms round him. It was over!

'At the family reunion the parents, overjoyed at their new-born son, now an athletic and normal young man, almost timidly asked Mr G for the bill. Mr G showed them the itemized account Sarkis and he had made together of what they had spent. Every detail was shown. The total was so small it looked ridiculous. . .' She tailed off, sat silent, looking at us. 'So you see what it is, impartial love.'

———

IT is generally agreed that behind the temporal world we know, there is a 'something', a 'Being', (whom we, of course, think of as a 'human' being) who exists in a dimension we cannot apprehend, called eternity. This Lord of the Eternal we call God, and it is He, who, for reasons we cannot know — just as a fish cannot know the nature of the earth — created the temporal.

All this mysterious part of a 'different' life has always remained vaguely untouchable, prohibited, and huge playgrounds of 'make-believe' have sprung up around it. Visions, revelations, legends, beliefs, hidden sects claiming divine authority, have taught a naïve and trustful world to believe endless fantasies about the nature of God, the origins of the universe and the relation of the temporal to the eternal.

It remained for someone with the right kind of mind and the right kind of curiosity to delve into these challenging and un-known areas and bring new order into this mystical mess. During his years of travel into remote corners of the world, Gurdjieff met people with links reaching back into the remote prehistorical past and had been given accounts of what had been found there. Passing this through the filter of his own unique insight resulted in the first comprehensive outline of the mechanics, the structure of the universe.

His discovery, as it may well be called, contained nothing new, nothing that, piecemeal, had not been known before, but bringing order into it, seeing it as a related whole, with all the implications that derive from it, that was discovery indeed.

One of these basic discoveries was the Octave of the Ray of Creation, the backbone of the Teaching that Gurdjieff opened to those first pioneers he taught in Moscow at the time of the Bolshevik Revolution. And it should not be forgotten that this remarkable step forward occurred amid a whirlpool revolution of hysteria and blindness which had perhaps never been equalled in the world before. The time of one of the worst 'backslidings' in the history of the human race was also the time of this deep new insight into the true nature of the structure of the Creation.

Here is Gurdjieff's Octave of the Ray of Creation:

Absolute
All Worlds
All Suns
Sun
All Planets
Earth
Moon

In its beginning, the Absolute, the Creation, bursts into life and the order of its development is *upward*. The moon is the growing tip of the Creation, as the twig is to the tree, not the end of everything as the magnitude of the actual size makes it appear. The whole basis of life is growth.

We have no difficulty in accepting this in everyday life. The conception of some new product is easy, but its production passing through smaller and smaller processes grows more and more complex. At last, beyond all these complexities appears the product, the new life! The end is the beginning.

The greater part of *Fragments*, Ouspensky's masterly exposition of Gurdjieff's ideas as taught by him in 1917, grows from this basic Octave of the Ray of Creation. For all its deep insight into the nature of things, it is only a simplistic scaffolding into the outline, the structure of the whole.

This was the scale of the ideas we set out to study on these first years of serious Work in 1951.

The idea of an octave, of a stairway, up or down, between different levels or categories of things was new to me; but it was clear that things could be related this way. Life on the moon (if there was any) was quite different from life on earth. That was clear anyway. The nature of all the planets was not the same as ours and yet for all their differences, they were tied to the sun, his children, so to speak, and that gave him their own level, their own special position. It was pretty well impossible to conceive of any kind of life (as we knew it) on that great fireball sun round which everything turned. Yet, since the sun gave us life, it must have life itself of some magical incandescent kind – and share it with all the other thousands of suns we could see twinkling in the vaults of heaven. And all these suns, after all, must have their own families, as we had ours, dark presences circling round them. So there was this fantastic multitude of 'all worlds' with their silent ghostly orbits populating the universe, an altogether different level of life from any we could ever imagine.

Although the whole idea of levels in a living universe – for this is what it was – was too vast for us ever to be able to grasp, I did see something about the level of All Suns that I felt I could relate to. How had this eternal, so unknown, so hypothetical, got into life, I asked myself. There must be a place, a sort of fountain, a gusher, through which the eternal, the Creator, poured himself into the temporal world. This divine wellspring, this entry of all life and love and creation into time, must (I suddenly saw) come by way of the suns, all suns, our sun.

Coming to this, by myself, through pondering over dry pages of a book, was a marvellous moment, a sort of confirmation that the divine Origin of Everything created on earth was the sun has never since left me. I knew it had been common knowledge, ever since the days of Ahknaton. But what of that? Finding it for myself had made it mine.

All those years, seen from this later perspective, seem to have made a full satisfactory life, a time of uneventful but necessary effort. Though I know it was a period when I was maturing in various ways, I have no sense of special moments of understanding or discovery. It was as if I began to absorb the whole tapestry of the Teaching and take it in, almost by a sort of osmosis, aided by closer relations with all the others who were being renewed by the same changes in themselves.

In the outer material world there had been similar signs of growth. Generous gifts had resulted in the acquisition of a fine house to become the London home of the Gurdjieff Society. To this a beautiful studio for Movements was added later. Bray, our country centre for crafts and other practical activities, was developing steadily. More people were drawn to the Work, numbers increased and there was a general (dangerous) feeling of success and status. A centre had been developed where those who wished to come and study Gurdjieff's work would be welcome.

Hitherto all 'religious' ideas have issued from laws, commandments, truths given divine authority by having been pronounced in the remote past. Gurdjieff does not deny such truths, indeed he reinforces and adds to them. But he offers a new, experimental way to approach and reach them. The world of *All and Everything* is so vast and yet so interrelated that wherever you touch it you are inevitably led back to the one God who created and illuminates the whole.

In these days when all the old patterns of life are being discarded and reshaped it is time to verify the validity of this new approach, and to come, study and, in studying, begin to understand what is difficult to simplify into headlines. These pages are not an attempt to 'teach' Gurdjieff's work. That is a task far beyond my capacities. They are just the record of a sort of pilgrimage made by one maverick pilgrim, blessed by its 'taste'. All I dare do is examine one or two aspects of his work and say how I have understood them in the hope that this may interest the reader enough to make him want to find his own way deeper into such questions. His time will not be wasted.

———

EARLIER in these pages I spoke about the Law of Three and said it was the second cosmic law of the universe. The interested reader may have wondered, if the Law of Three is the second law, what is the first?

Reference in the preceding paragraphs to the way human

development could be thought of as a process brings me back to the first cosmic law of the universe – the Law of Seven.

If the Law of Three may be called the law of events, the moment of crisis when things actually happen, the Law of Seven directs the process, the steps through which they must pass to make them happen. So the two laws, the Law of the Event and the Law of Process, govern the working of the whole universe. Or, better to say, since this is something beyond human understanding, this is a blunt and limited approach to fundamental mysteries which must always remain beyond us.

That the Law of Seven actually exists, evidently belonged to ancient knowledge, can be seen for example, in our seven-day week. The octave is certainly a widely accepted seven-point notation through which music can be created and passed on. Every student of science or medicine comes across the way processes of renewal or creation seem to fall into sevenfold periods, of which Mandelief's Table of the Elements and the colours of the rainbow are common examples.

In *All and Everything*, Gurdjieff gives the Laws the prominent place they deserve in his long and complex analysis of their place in the structure of the universe. Ouspensky elaborated it further in his working out of it and called it 'the System'.

It was a remarkable work, as far as it went. He was an excellent spiritual plumber. But *All and Everything* was something entirely different. It was a fantastic myth of Beelzebub's banishment to the slums of the universe and the redemption he had found from his work there.

There are aspects of the Law of Seven which are not concerned with time. We have spoken of the Ray of Creation and the Seven, only partially connected with time. But there are, of course, many, many processes in which time is an essential element.

Over the years I have devoted a great deal of study to the Laws, trying to understand them better. I never got very far. But there was one thing that offered hope – the Enneagram. It is a symbol which, in some way that I can't explain, seems to epitomize and draw together and disclose all that the thousands of words about the Laws don't convey. The Enneagram holds the mystery of both of them – if you can find it. . .

ENNEAGRAM

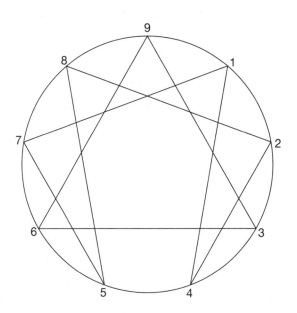

THE Enneagram is a symbol showing two interlocking arrangements of lines within a circle. The circumference of the circle is divided into nine parts and these are numbered on the perimeter, clockwise. If we designate the Whole as 10, or multiples of 10 and divide it by 7, we get a recurring result: 1.42857. If we divide it into 20, the answer is 2.85714 recurring; if into 30, 4.28571; into 40, 5.71428; into 50, 7.14285; into 60, 8.57142. Mathematicians may be able to explain why this particular form of division gives this six-figure recurring result – always the same six digits in a sequential order from a different starting point. But to the rest of us it is a mystery. What is it telling us? Why should six figures arranged in a particular order seem to hold such a world of possibilities.

Taking the basic sequence, 142857 and joining the points on the circle by lines in that order we get a six-pointed figure. In addition, joining the points 3, 6, 9, forms an equilateral triangle, point 9 being the apex of the whole diagram. There are thus two interlocking diagrams, representing the Laws of Three and Seven contained within the Whole.

Gurdjieff says that he has been permitted to reveal this sacred symbol whose origin lies in the remote past. There is a certain fascination in the complexity of the whole Enneagram and on examining it more closely, it appears that the six-point diagram is divided into two halves, right and left. These are, so to speak, loosely tied together at the top 7–1 and 8–2, but leave a noticable gap at the bottom between 4 and 5, while the three-point triangle weaves in and out through the whole. We have already briefly examined these two basic universal laws, the Laws of Events and Processes; the Enneagram clearly shows how their interactions permeate the Whole. It is a symbol of everything existing.

In order to examine the Law of Seven a little more closely the simplest way is to put a process on it, to see if we can find the progressive steps (1–8) in action, so to speak. Let us take ourselves as the guinea pig. We are in a process, after all, the process of trying to perfect ourselves. Our aim is to be conscious beings.

How do we start? How do we get to the diagram's 1? Somebody talks to us, gets our attention, we think it worth exploring the ideas put forward. We like them and, after a while, we decide to study. So we meet the Work. We are at 1.

Now the diagram becomes a question in itself. Can you imagine yourself walking along one of the lines in it? If you can, then your life within it and what happens to you as you move about within it is real, you can take part in it all. So, if you can, join me at 1.

There, at once, (assuming a linear forward motion from 1 to 8) we come under the influence of a teacher, 7. Our interest and enthusiasm grows very strong. We see what we have to do and can't wait to do it. Our first practical efforts are successful and we imagine ourselves well on the way to getting a grip on the whole thing. So we shoot down the road to 4 and think when we get there, we shall really understand everything and have arrived.

But time goes by and, in spite of continual help from 7, the more we learn the more complex and difficult it all seems to get. The depth and majesty of the Work awes us and we realize 4 is a long way off. All our own difficulties and weaknesses begin to show up. We often feel quite lost and despondent. Should we give the whole thing up? In fact we have sunk back to 2 – the most difficult and challenging point in the whole journey.

Now the struggle begins. There are shocks. Up and down the

roads between 1, 4 and 2, we may spend many years. If it were not for the constant help from 7 we should have chucked it years ago. In despair, we sit at 2 and send our prayers and longings and hopes across to the Master at 8. There is help there too, if we know how to ask.

There always is. The road is not one way. Our questions to 7 strengthen his efforts to give us more. Our prayers to 8 return to us in consolation and determination, buoying our will. Love and hope flow through the whole. The whole process is sacred, self-renewing, divine.

But at last there comes a day when we feel we have somehow gravitated to 4. The Work has worked in us. We feel 'different'. We are 'old hands'. We have suffered a good deal learning to understand ourselves, to get to where we are. We know too that 4 is not the end. It is the place where we see the Whole more clearly, see that there is something beyond the personal. The Work exists, objectively, in its own right. There, across on the 'other side' are those who serve it. And it calls us.

So, excited and humble, full of joy and doubt – and a big push from 'outside' – we take the great leap into the unknown, across the chasm of the personal, and arrive at 5.

Here everything is different. We begin to feel the power of the wish and longing of others who come to us for help. Trying to remember how we once felt, we struggle to go deeper and deeper into ourselves to find the answer that will help that person at that moment. Their failings and hope mirror our own. The love of the Master at 8 is closer. It comes down to us, feeds us, we feel deeper, more real. We see we lack the simplicity and purity at 7. We see our own failings every day, yet, because we are needed we go on. . .

Here I must stop. That is as far as I have got. To go further would be to step into lies, imagination. But I think this is enough to show an aspect on which the Law of Seven is built.

OUR different reactions to these studies soon made us notice that people, as a whole, fell into categories, seemed to belong to different 'types' and, mulling this over every week at the group meetings, naturally led us on to another of Gurdjieff's ideas – a basic idea, as it turned out – that people were not all on the same level, that there were definite levels of life.

He told us there were seven different levels possible to 'three-brained beings' on this earth. The first three took care of the vast majority of what are called 'ordinary' people – the thinking man, the feeling man, and the practical or mechanical man. Although, at first sight, this seemed a rather arbitrary way to classify people, after thinking it over and talking it over at length, it did seem that everybody could be seen as a mixture of these three types.

Man No. 1 lived mainly in his head, Man No. 2 in his feelings, Man No. 3 in his habits, that is in the mechanical pattern of his life – which played an enormous part in everything he thought and felt. All these three basic types lived as they were born, part of the normal, 'sleeping' humanity of the world today.

Man No. 4 was born Man Nos. 1, 2 or 3; but began to differ from them because he had joined some teaching or begun to follow ideas which had become central to his life. This gave him a permanent centre of gravity, a direction, an aim. He knew where he hoped to get to and was, in fact, a man in transition, struggling to become Man No. 5.

Man No. 5 had arrived at the point where he was no longer a slave to change. He had his own permanent 'I', and all he had belonged to it. He had been called 'the just man made perfect'. His only aim was growth.

Man No. 6 had acquired levels of knowledge and understanding which may be classed a superhuman. But he was not 'perfected', he could still make mistakes.

Man No. 7 had access to all knowledge. His birth was miraculous and his life given to the world. He appeared to have been sent. Periodically his presence had become necessary to save mankind from itself. He is the Living God.

As usual Gurdjieff's picture of Man's possibilities took in a whole octave, a growing process going far beyond anything we had imagined. We had vaguely seen that there were saints and, above them, great spritual leaders who had founded religions and given new values to the world. But for practical purposes our interest and attention lay in Man Nos. 1, 2, 3, 4 and 5. We saw we were all Man Nos. 1, 2 and 3, struggling along in a corridor, marked Man No. 4. Would we ever get to Man No. 5? This was our key question. Could we complete the journey? Suppose we didn't make it? At what point along the corridor could we expect to 'die honourable death, not perish like dog?'

———

IT is very difficult when you think you have understood a bit more to remember how it was when you understood it a bit less. There is a sort of 'limit' we put on our understanding but, it seems to me, it always recedes as we add another bit to it. I was told that after fifty a man never adds to what he knows, he just goes on repeating himself. I don't find it true at all. At ninety-four, hardly a day passes but I feel I understand things more fully, more deeply – that is to say more simply – than I ever did before.

So where had I got to – or, more properly, where did I think I had got to – in the Work at that time? I thought then that I had got beyond it.

It sounds now, as I write it, to be a monumental bit of self-important stupidity; but then I felt there were huge areas – love, pity, sorrow, suffering – which Ouspensky's Gurdjieff did not touch at all. I had purposely read nothing about contemporary thinking. I didn't want my view 'dulled' by reading anybody else. What I had was enough. But now, feeling a bit lost, when I did begin reading how others were thinking, feeling, writing, I began to see where this 'gone beyond' feeling came from.

Those extraordinary days in 1917 when Gurdjieff had at last returned from his explorations, his journeyings, he evidently needed to speak about (and probably put together as he spoke), his amazing picture of what may be called a scaffolding of the form and evolution of the universe. Nobody had ever revealed such a 'blueprint' before and, in Ouspensky, Gurdjieff happened to have the most remarkable and gifted pupil, who grasped what he was getting at, saw all the implications clearly and, using inverted commas to give it all Gurdjieff authenticity, spelled out this 'teaching' which, in a way, he usurped as his own.

It had a ring of authenticity, that was true, but it was not the whole truth. As far as it went, it was remarkable, unique, but it did not go far enough. *All and Everything* shows this clearly; but at that time, we were not studying, not being taught, what Gurdjieff had said, but what Ouspensky *said he had said*, thirty years before.

———

'SERIOUS work! I have the feeling that those who have come so far
with this book must be more than a little perplexed and irritated by
not having been told simply and clearly what Gurdjieff really taught.
What is the core, the source of the teaching? So far we have had a
lot of miscellaneous ideas, generalities, principles, etc; but all this
needs to be simplified, summed up, put together, before most
ordinary readers can regard it as anything more than another of
these mystical hobbyhorses a few dotty people get caught up in.

How do we see 'our' world? It is a very self-centred place where
everything stems from our human point of view. We have been
told of general theories and principles which explain the way the
outside world functions; but these are remote and theoretical; not
many feel them to be interesting and important. They are marginal
to our personal lives. The real focus is the way we live and get on
with other human beings around us.

Gurdjieff suggests that the more we study and try to understand
the two fundamental cosmic laws, the Law of Three and the Law
of Seven, the more we shall be able to find our place and relate to
the outer and inner worlds in which we live. These basic principles
emerge in a perfectly practical way in the experiments, the exer-
cises, we are given to verify how we are related to these worlds. All
this is part of what Gurdjieff calls living an honourable life.

He also gave us general aims by which to live in the Five
Oblignonian Strivings. Here they are:

The First striving to have in their ordinary being existence everything satisfying and really necessary for the planetary body.

The Second striving to have a constant and unflagging instinctive
need for self perfection in the sense of being.

The Third: the conscious striving to know ever more and more
concerning the laws of World-creation and World-maintenance.

The Fourth striving from the beginning of their existence to pay
for their arising and their individuality as quickly as possible in
order afterwards to be free to lighten as much as possible the sorrow
of our COMMON FATHER.

And the Fifth: the striving always to assist the most rapid perfecting of other beings, both those similar to oneself and those of other
forms up to the degree of the sacred Martfotai, that is up to the
degree of self-individuality.

All and Everything, pp. 385–6

Throughout *All and Everything* there is also what seems to be a
deliberately off-putting hurdle – the challenge of a strange form of

language, verbose, complex, difficult to read, designed perhaps to deter those who think they can 'dip into' things that are not and cannot be lightly available. The reader has to meet and overcome this difficulty as he can. As a break to easier, livelier stuff he can turn to *Meetings with Remarkable Men* – snatches, parables, if you will, taken from his own youthful search.

But finally the root of this new Dictionary of Life lies in six lines – the Epitaph for his father – which sum up the essence of all worship:

> I am Thou.
> Thou art I.
> He is ours.
> We are both His.
> And all shall be
> For our neighbour.

THE set pattern of daily life continued through the sixties, but I was ageing and the question of retirement came up. *The Daily Mail* – with the generosity of that great organization – employed me until I was sixty-eight, then gave me a pension to which I was not really entitled, and turned me loose into my Golden Age.

During those years I had acquired two new 'life' responsibilities, an old country cottage and a new (third) wife. The cottage was a gem and we spent seven years in it, making a garden, only to find when it had matured that poor weather prevented our enjoying it. So, reluctantly, we sold and, after an autumn trip in a caravan to look Europe over, decided to settle in Corfu.

Then for the second time my young man's irresistible challenge of adventure popped out. In my forties it had been quite unnecessary to buy an aeroplane to reach South Africa (but what a flourish it gave to the end of my flying life!). Now it was just as extravagant to buy a motor cruiser and take three months to get to Corfu when an aircraft could have put down there in three hours.

However that is what we did and what splendid 'never again' trips they turned out to be. It is a bit late in the day to go into the details here, but I have done books about both these episodes (*Gemini to Joburg* and *Turn Right for Corfu*) for those who want to fill in the gaps.

My third wife was also a gem, but did not take seven years to mature – though some of her friends, hearing she had decided to take me on, had the gravest doubts about her maturity. After all, my record in the marital stakes was dismal; my means were, to say the best of it, meagre; my prospects, as far as anyone could say, were nil and, as a bonus, my heart was medically suspect while she was twenty years younger with a heart as big as all our tomorrows.

However, out of this 'happy go lucky' life, the result I suppose of trusting in God, together we have built over thirty years of lively happiness and content, which among other things have left me free to write these pages and say something about thoughts and ideas which have dominated my insignificant life and bless the partner in it – a blessing which, I must add, derives chiefly from the fact that she considers time spent on higher things largely wasted and relies on her instinct to keep us both on an even keel. It seems to work very well. So when all's over, I think we may be forced to admit that God has known very well what He was doing and to bless the Old Chap for keeping such a benevolent hand on us.

18

The Fifth Way

STARTING again! On an island that was new to us, with new places, new faces, new laws, new money, new shops and a new climate, all this was an exciting stimulus. Every day seemed a challenge, and a happiness. Finding a bit of ground to build on, clambering all over the steep hillside we found. Dashing down to Athens with the plans of our wooden pre-fab. Seeing the house arrive, three months later, all on one three-ton truck. Watching the five carpenters putting up the whole place complete – unbelievably – in four days, and walking off, singing drunk from the farewell bottle of whisky I gave them, without saying goodbye, leaving us gasping!

Dealing with what Gurdjieff called the First Oblignonian Striving, that is 'to have all that is really necessary for the planetary body' fully occupied us for our first year in Corfu. The Greek way of life was still, in many respects, very primitive, on the peasant level, but it had all the virtues (now rapidly disappearing) of simplicity, generosity, gaiety and goodwill that more than made up for lack of 'facilities'.

So there, at last, it marvellously stood, our little house, gleaming with varnish, six inches above the ground (the concrete floor was in no respects level) with no drains, no plumbing, no light and needing, so we were told, five coats of paint over all the hardboard and three-ply it was made of. The local workmen were gay and charming, utterly incompetent, and took the whole thing as a joke – they had never seen a wooden house before – but somehow or other, after what seemed a century, we stood on the terrace, between the two great olive trees, as we had planned, looking out over the whole island, the mountains and the sea!

And with it all went wonderful water, wonderful fruit and

vegetables, wonderful fresh air and the limpid companionship of the Greek seas. The exhilarating living of life, which had become so automatic, so dull and depressing at home, renewed itself daily. No need to wake up to life. Life itself did more than its share in waking us up to splendid sunshine and mornings like the dawn of the Creation. All this was a sort of bonus to life, something we did not deserve, a blessing given us free, daily, to thank God for and rejoice in.

Once the building of our home was finished we began to get the 'feel' of this new way of life. There were moments when we could pause, reflect and compare how we were living now to the way we had been living then. The first thing was a sense of freedom; partly this was the novelty of it, partly the simplicity, partly the climate. But more than all this was the feeling that what I would call the pressure of life was less. There seemed to be more time for everything.

What a lot of pressure, for instance, I had given to keeping up with the Work. I had always had a sense of obligation, of duty, never to miss anything, never to let any 'life' obligation take precedence over the Work. But behind all that, far deeper and more troubling, was something I had not wanted to face at all – my growing sense of failure in it. Whatever I found out from now on, would be my own.

———

THOSE who have read this far will already have seen clearly enough that the root of all this inner striving is self-observation, seeing yourself, seeing your sleep. From this comes the idea of waking up, then the crescendo of demand to be more and more awake, and finally the goal of being always awake, a 'conscious' being.

Now, after twenty years of steady daily effort, I had reluctantly come to the conclusion that I was not going to reach that goal. I had reached moments of being awake, I had known a conscious state was possible, but holding it, keeping it up, living in it all the time, that was – for me – impossible.

There was quite a lot of pressure put on everyone to work for this impossible. 'Remember yourself always, everywhere' was the command; 'Die honourable death, not perish like dog', a threat;

'Two hundred conscious men could save the world', a hope. This was the urgency that Gurdjieff gave to it – and there was absolutely nothing new about it.

'Be ye therefore perfect, even as your Father in Heaven is perfect.' All true religions in various ways, teach the same thing. The reasons they give vary with the people, the period, the country; but the world's saviours have always called for the same effort and the world has consistently refused to make it – or rather, perhaps being 'normal' human beings – unable to make it.

At first, when I saw this inability (which I construed as inferiority), it gave me a feeling of guilt. I was 'unworthy' because I could not do it. But, as time went on, watching the behaviour of others around me, I began to suspect that they too were in the same boat. They too were failing in this central effort to do what they had set out to do.

So why did they go on? Unable to admit failure to themselves? Considering better the opinion of their friends? Fatalism? Nothing to do? There must be something more positive with which to meet such a centrally important part to many people's lives?

And of course there was. I had felt it, known it myself, in the first moment when I had felt this urge, when 'something' had called me to follow up, find out what 'it' was. But when it came to analysing it? I do not remember having any of the 'usual' religious ideas – being 'immortal', going to heaven or anything like that. But there was an instinctive need, wish, longing to find my way to something different, special, secret, reserved for people who 'knew', were 'initiated'. That remained, and although vague and unspecified, took me through all the first exciting months, years, when others were there, when Gurdjieff's ideas began to be made known, were ignited, organized into practical work. But then? Somewhere along the line must have come the test between having an idea and making it come true. My head says I can; my body says I cannot; my heart says I must.

Why did we want to be 'better'? Why weren't we satisfied to be human, as God made us, as Nature designed us to be? Why all this running about after some will-o'-the-wisp of another life? What was it all but an encyclopedia of fantasies, fairy tales, futilities, with no co-ordinates but dreams, no existence without belief, no destination beyond hope?

And then the bigger question – what motivates us, all of us? The majority seem to have no other motivation than a purely material, temporal one – to make money, marry, raise a family. Some do have the idea that there is this being called God, who lives some-where above them, whom you 'go to' in church and who is, maybe, a good idea. But it doesn't make much difference as far as ordinary life is concerned. And finally there is a small minority who believe in God, sometimes fanatically, and put pressure on others to do so. Out of these comes the phenomenon called religion which has caused more suffering, grief and war than all our other vices and which, today, in spite of continued protesta-tions of peace and love, continues to do so.

———

IN the very early days when I first met the Teaching of Gurdjieff, I remember how I talked excitedly to some of my friends who were interested in such things and they began asking me pertinent questions: Who was this man Gurdjieff? Where did all these ideas derive from? Was he a Buddhist or a Sufi or some sort of odd ball with ideas of his own?

I really didn't know the answers and I didn't much care. There were so many wonderful things going on. I knew they were spiritual ideas and they helped me to see myself and make some sort of contact with the endless, inner world around me. That was enough – for the moment, anyway.

But later on we were given the idea of the Stairway and the levels on which people could live and grow. I have referred to these ideas earlier in these pages – the different types of men and women, the way that having an aim towards Work could change them.

Later on, pondering on the way the world was going and won-dering if there were any possible sources of help, I came back to the idea of levels – the ordinary Man Nos. 1, 2 or 3. The struggling Man No. 4. Up to Man No. 5 it was fairly straightforward. One could see the growth that was open to us.

The levels of Man Nos. 6 and 7 seemed superhuman, quite out of reach. Man No. 7 was the image of perfection: God made flesh. But Man No. 6, as I understood him, was an unperfected perfec-tion, standing between fallible humanity and infallible godhead, a man who knew what was necessary to perfect our imperfections, but had not himself quite reached it and was still struggling up to the level beyond all struggle.

All this was, of course, just the wiseacreing of an ignoramus, but the idea lay about in my head and now, after many years, it seems to me there may be some sense in it.

Perhaps Man No. 6 is the level at which Gurdjieff stood. His terrible dichotomy: ineffable tenderness, pity and love of humankind on the one hand flashing over to intolerance and violence at its blindness and stupidity on the other. The battle rages daily, hourly, throughout his life. Endless curiosity, courage and persistence in the search, endless patience and impatience as a teacher, every lovable human and distressing human quality, the big stick, the 'language of the smile', to some an idol, to others black Devil.

At the end of it all, Gurdjieff leaves us with a tremendous legacy of understanding and help, an unvarnished picture of mankind, of how we are and could be – and takes a thousand pages to do it.

But Jesus Christ has only to leave us the Beatitudes and the Lord's Prayer to bring half the world to its knees. That is the difference between help and worship.

Both are necessary.

———

AND yet ... and yet ... worrying back and back at the question, there is this basic instinctive desire in every living creature to reach perfection; its own perfection, the climax of its growth, the orgasm of its life. All life is recreated in moments of ecstasy. And the ecstasy is the moment of immortality. The new life is created in the image of its creator. God so loves the world that He cannot prevent Himself from creating it again and again, forever new, and forever in His image. If ever there was a need of proof that Divine Love is life itself, here it is.

And still we have not reached the end. For to mankind there is this terrible dichotomy: his double life. Every other creature lives to recreate its own life in its children, in this world. But for man there is this other deeper longing added – the urge to recreate the essence of his best, his 'holiest', in a new life in another world. This sits like a raven on the shoulder of man's intelligence, for this 'other' life cannot be found or placed in time and space, cannot be described except in images, and yet presents to those who believe in it something definitely there to be desired, lived and died for. Yet those who reach it are very few.

So what remains for the rest of us? That is the question I brought away with me from all those years of study. If what Gurdjieff called 'the Fourth Way' – the way of self-consciousness – is beyond us, is there a Fifth Way within our reach?

A Fifth Way! This new idea had come out of me in a moment of inspiration. It was clearly something beyond anything I could do more than dream of. But it came from the urgent need for change which is sweeping through the world today. It is as if the whole planet (and perhaps the whole solar system) were passing through a poisonous area of space to which the earth has reacted by catching grave nervous disorders of all kinds. Gurdjieff said it was a recurrent disaster called 'solioonensius' and had been prophesied from long ago. It faces mankind with a need to revalue all values. So now while we turn back to God, knowing Him to be the only safe refuge in times of chaos, there is a deep feeling that our worship has become empty. We must bring something more. Only new attitudes, a new purity, a new contribution can renew the faith, hope and love that will be sought desperately in the disasters that, alas, seem to lie ahead.

It is the extraordinary leap in the speed at which everything is changing that is proving too much for us. In the old days power, Church and state set up organizations to teach and tax and although laws were unjust and there was much inequality and suffering, there was no means by which the people could rebel or seek to alter the form of life to which they were subject. Their voice could not be heard.

Today mass communication is such that everybody can hear everybody else. The result is not the universal harmony and peace on earth that was hoped for and forecast, but ferocious enmity and greed. This loss of honour and conscience must inevitably be followed by general chaos and the most dreadful mass destruction, suffering and starvation before a new order can emerge to save the dregs of an exhausted mankind – if indeed Man can survive the universal holocaust that, alas, must follow on the present uncontrollable trends.

Is such a recovery possible? Can miracles happen? Can there be some sudden revulsion from mankind – the self-styled 'Lords of

Creation' – at its subhuman way of life? Some way of throwing
Satan to oblivion? Who will rise up and shout to the hero in us:
Now! Enough! Who dares to set the world on fire for God?

———

IN the middle of writing these pages came the news, over the
phone, that Elizabeth Bennett, John Bennett's widow, had died,
tragically of cancer. She was so much involved in those early days,
so close to many who were there, I felt I could not let the moment
go and must make a memorial note and include it, just on the day
it reached me. . .

So Elizabeth is dead. I am glad – for her. I had heard vaguely she
was ill. Not serious. I was abroad. I did not hear the dreadful
details: there is nothing to be done. The sentence: three weeks to
two years . . . No reprieve? After such a life! Such devotion, such
courage, such love. No favours for the faithful? I suppose not.
Only gratitude and prayers.

I am no close friend. Just someone in the background – with
a memory of Elizabeth. What do I remember – after fifty
years?

Coombe Springs. The big gardens. People wandering about.
Sitting. Working. What is it, 'working'? Just more sitting. Many
young women; some young men. John in the background. Always
deeply into something. Elizabeth, white blouse, golden hair, a
smile . . . Nice girl, something to do with the house . . . Never
forget that house. Feel of important work going on. . .

Africa! The *bundu*! The track drops down steeply over the
shoulder of the mountain into the valley. There we are, alone.
Pioneers. No roots in the splendid landscape. Just there to be a
bolthole for the Work – when the world breaks up. When will it
break up?

Then wonderful news! Gurdjieff is alive! Wild jubilation! Letters.
Presents. What can we do? Send something from Africa. Avocados!
A tray of avocados! Airmail. Weeks go by. No news. Did he get
them? Must find out. Ask someone. Someone reliable. Elizabeth.
'Yes. Sending present.' A present from Gurdjieff? Impossible!
What present? More weeks go by. Then a big parcel arrives in the
valley. Three great pots of Russian caviar! What a gesture! What
generosity! Only he could have done it! Elizabeth must have sent

it. Dear Elizabeth. I kept one of the pots – the only thing his hands may have touched – sort of relic. . .

Then all those years – extraordinary years – for her. Marriage must have meant a sacred oath, a vow to John: wherever you go, I will follow. I will be there. With you. Until death.

And when she had kept that vow through all those extraordinary, greedy-for-God years, when he had gone home, leaving her, when she was alone, she kept trust with those that were left, those who had followed him, loved him and returned to them, the world over, even to us for a few days, keeping something alive, part of her vow, her love for him and what he had stood for.

Now there is this last letter:

Thank you for stretching out a hand to a cancerous old woman – apologies for the writing, the pain is bad today and I am not securely in control. . .

Oh Cecil, I am so free, so happy, so grateful. Time to compose myself internally, externally, time to heal old wounds, time to overcome weaknesses, time to be happy and grateful and free. I have had such a wonderful life. And you there, at the end of it – kind, humorous (very important, that!) and there!

Much love, old friend.

19

World to Come

THE shock of Elizabeth's death was her last great gift to me. It was a sharp reminder to make me reflect once again who I was and where I stood in the everlasting question of life. Once again I had to reflect about Gurdjieff, about Beelzebub. I knew I had not absorbed a hundredth part of the mysteries and questions it could answer. But I had tired of the endless catalogue of disasters, of the age-old mistakes and failures of mankind, of the near-impossibility that anything could ever come right for our beloved earth. I didn't dispute the weight of the charges, but I rejected the death sentence implied. What about compassion, about love and forgiveness?

And then one day with an actual shout of wonder and delight I suddenly realized that Beelzebub's 'impartial, objective criticism of the life of man', *All and Everything,* was only half the unfinished picture that Gurdjieff had left us! Why had I forgotten *Meetings with Remarkable Men*? Why had I missed what was under my nose?

Here was the positive way to live, to fight our way through these dreadful days of despair and lassitude. Here was an outstanding, original and moving account of the exceptional 'honourable life' lived by Gurdjieff in his youth, from fifteen to fifty. It takes us into a world we can only imagine today, the life of the small Transcaucasian country town of Alexandropol. Here Gurdjieff was born, lived with his family and began life.

He was brought up in straitened circumstances by a father who, observing the honourable customs of the time, ruined himself in the service of his neighbours and became a simple carpenter. His son was therefore used to hard work and poverty and was already, in his childhood, beginning to help the family's finances. Even in those days it becomes clear he was exceptionally intelligent and

197

ingenious in finding ways of earning money – making popguns to
sell to other children and becoming quite expert in embroidery –
and this aptitude at being able to turn his hand to anything,
coupled with a fantastic ability to pick up all sorts of trades and a
memory that never forgot anything, made him evidently a young
man with a future.

But added to all this was something else – an insatiable curiosity
to find out the 'why' of things, which grew to be a central feature
in his life. The first we hear of this is in boyhood. He was sitting
one afternoon in the shade of a tree working on a piece of
embroidery. It was an open place and some boys nearby were
playing together. Suddenly he heard a cry, so strange and fearful
that it must have come from someone in deep fear or danger. The
young Gurdjieff jumped to his feet and ran out to see what was the
matter. What he saw was a strange little boy among a crowd of
others, screaming because he was trapped. He was trying to get
out of – but did not seem to be able to get out of – nothing! Just a
circle one of the boys had made by dragging a stick around him in
the dust. The other boys were standing round, jeering and
laughing: 'Yesidi, Yesidi, can't get out!!' What did it mean, 'Yesidi'?
He kicked away the dust from the circle and the boy bolted
through the opening and ran off crying, terrified. Gurdjieff stood
there, transfixed. What had happened? Something very strange . . .
A mystery. . .

Later one of the boys told him how the Yesidis were a small
tribe where wrongdoers could be imprisoned in a circle drawn
round them on the ground until it was broken or one of their
priests uttered the magic formula that released them. Gurdjieff still
stood there. That was magic. How was it done? He must find out,
must find out!

It was this thirst to find what lay behind all sorts of coincidences, so-called miracles and strange inexplicable things he
happened to witness in his youth that led Gurdjieff into a series
of remarkable journeys into remote and distant corners of the
world, which are the subject of these Meetings. The mysteries
turned out to be far deeper and the secrets better hidden than he
had thought.

This aim to seek the truth is common. We all have it. There are
many truths, large and small, but it is clear before you get very far
in *Beelzebub's Tales* that Gurdjieff's aim is not a passing fancy. It

is perfectly clear and simple. It is man's ultimate aim – to find God.

Many, I think, have this aim in youth, but lose it later. It is too big. Easier to conform to some faith, believe in God and go to church. Others think that finding something new, some sect or guru, will fill their need. Still others make it a career and become professional God-seekers. But all these believers, of all shades, serious or trivial, are 'into' something and follow some existing established line. Gurdjieff does not reject any of this, but he suggests that more awareness and understanding are necessary. Tomorrow's man really needs to find a new way to come to all this and follow it faithfully far beyond the casual place it holds in our world today.

It was this burning need, so sacred and, at the same time, so practical, experimental, scientific that drew others to Gurdjieff in his youth and gradually formed a band of self-styled Seekers of the Truth. Its members were youngish men from the most unlikely backgrounds, soldiers, priests, thieves, old school friends, archaeologists, travellers, noblemen all devoted to go to any lengths to get to the heart of the mystery.

It also seems that the quality he brought to the search, the urge behind it all, added a glow to the whole enterprise. Gurdjieff admits that while still a young man he had acquired powers of telepathy and hypnotism which gave him possibilities of influencing and helpng others in an exceptional way. This led to sudden and unexpected intimacies. Whatever the situation he seemed ready for it. He was an expert in ju-jitzu and fiz-les-loo and loved a good fight, never of his own making and preferably against the odds. But something valuable always seemed to come out of these escapades. In one case it saved a man's life (he was being mugged by four thugs), in another taking part in a brawl against British sailors earned him and a friend free passage on a British cruiser from Smyrna to Alexandria.

As this fascinating story unfolds in the most diverse and unexpected episodes, a curious similarity seems to grow between the men and their aim. The more persistent and determined they became, the more they learned by what they went through, the more they saw the nature of their search. It was a life-absorbing labour of love and when the journeying days were over, it led Gurdjieff to set down, many years later, in *Meetings with*

Remarkable Men, the record of the fruits of it all – still leaving us plenty of room to find more – and passing on to us his passion for the search.

————

To give some idea of the quality of the search here is part of the story of perhaps his last great adventure into forbidden territory. After spending more than a year learning ancient Persian chants and old sayings, necessary to protect their identities, he set off with his old friend Professor Skridlov on a long journey. It includes a magical interlude in it on a steamboat up the River Daria.

As the river was very unpredictable, the steamer was often delayed by sandbanks on which it ran aground. During these delays, all the passengers went ashore and camped on the banks alongside, sometimes for several days, till the water was deep enough to allow the boat to proceed. Gurdjieff pauses in his narrative to paint a Breughel of the scene:

> In this picturesque and motley crowd, merchants predominate; some are transporting goods, others going upstream for supplies of cheese.
>
> Here is a Persian, a merchant of dried fruit, here an Armenian going to buy Khirgis rugs on the spot, and a Polish agent, a cotton-buyer for the firm of Poznansky, here a Russian Jew, a buyer of caracul skins and a Lithuanian commercial traveller with samples of picture frames in papier mâché and all kinds of ornaments of gilt metal set with artificial coloured stones.
>
> Many officials and officers of the frontier guard, and fusiliers and sappers of the Transcaspian regiments are returning on leave or from their posts. Here is a soldier's wife with a nursing baby, going to her husband who has stayed with an extra tour of service and has sent for her. Here is a travelling Catholic priest on his official rounds, going to confess Catholic soldiers.
>
> There are also ladies on board. Here is the wife of a colonel, with a lanky daughter, returning home from Tashkent where she has taken her son, a cadet, to see him off to Orenburg to study in the cadet corps. Here is the wife of a cavalry captain of the frontier guard who has been to Merv to order some dresses from the dress-makers there and here is a military doctor's wife, escorted by his orderly, travelling to Ashkabad to visit her husband who is serving in solitude because his mother-in-law cannot live without 'society', which is lacking where he is stationed.

Here is a stout woman with an enormous coiffure undoubtedly of artificial hair, with many rings on her fingers and two enormous brooches on her chest, who is accompanied by two very good-looking girls who call her 'aunt', but you can see by everything that they are not at all her nieces.

Here are also many Russian former and future somebodies going God-knows-where and God-knows-why. Also a troupe of travelling musicians with their violins and double-basses.

The members of each of these groups began to regard and to act towards the passengers belonging to other groups either haughtily or disdainfully or timidly and ingratiatingly, but at the same time they did not hinder one another from arranging things each according to his own wishes and habits, and little by little they became so accustomed to their surroundings that it was as though none of them had ever lived in any other way.

In the morning the life of the passengers resumes the rhythm of the day before. Some build fires and make coffee, others boil water for green tea, still others go in search of solsaul poles, get ready to go fishing, go to the steamer and the shore or from one bank to the other, and all is done calmly and unhurriedly, as everybody knows that as soon as it is possible to go on the big bell of the steamer will ring an hour before departure and there will be plenty of time to get on board.

WHEN, at last, they reach the hidden monastery they have been seeking and are mysteriously met by a monk and received into it, they are glad to rest and remain there some time, coming under the care of one of the brothers, Father Giovanni, with whom they have many long talks on questions that are important to them.

Here is a short example:

Our brotherhood has four monasteries, one of them ours, the second in the valley of the Pamir, the third in Tibet, and the fourth in India. Two of our brethren, Ahl and Sez, constantly travel from one monastery to another and preach to them.

They come to us once or twice a year. Their arrival at our monastery is considered among us a very great event. On the days when either of them is here, the soul of every one of us experiences pure heavenly pleasure and tenderness.

The sermons of these two brethren, who are to an almost equal degree holy men and speak the same truths, have nevertheless a different effect on all our brethren and on me in particular.

When Brother Sez speaks, it is indeed like the song of the birds of Paradise, from what he says one is quite, so to say, turned inside out; one becomes as though entranced. His speech 'purls' like a stream and one no longer wishes anything else in life but to listen to the words of Brother Sez.

But Brother Ahl's speech has almost the opposite effect. He speaks badly and indistinctly, evidently because of his age. No one knows how old he is. Brother Sez is also very old – it is said three hundred years old – but he is still a hale old man, whereas in Brother Ahl the weakness of old age is clearly evident.

The stronger the impression made at the moment by the words of Brother Sez, the more this impression evaporates, until there ultimately remains in the hearer nothing at all.

But in the case of Brother Ahl, although at first what he says makes almost no impression, later, the gist of it takes on a definite form, more and more each day, and is instilled as a whole into the heart and remains there for ever.

When we first became aware of this and began trying to discover why it was so, we came to the unanimous conclusion that the sermons of Brother Sez proceeded only from his mind and therefore acted on our minds, whereas those of Brother Ahl proceeded from his being and acted on our being.

Yes, Professor, knowledge and understanding are quite different. Only understanding can lead to being, whereas knowledge is but a passing presence in it. New knowledge displaces the old and the result is, as it were, a pouring from the empty into the void.

One must strive to understand. This alone can lead to our Lord God.

———

AND then – when we have been taken up into the heights by these inspiring journeys, for which the truth seekers had been preparing themselves for months and even years, to reach forbidden places where no European had ever been, we are suddenly brought down to earth with a thump by the obvious practical question: where did the money come from? Such journeys cost money, even a great deal of money. But money is never mentioned. It is always assumed there is plenty of it. Nothing seems to be put off or given up for lack of funds. But who had it? Who held the money bags?

It was only at the end of his life, on a trip to New York when an American who had come to listen to him and hear about his travels asked Gurdjieff directly: 'How was your work financed?' that we got the answer. It was the first time anybody had dared ask the great man such a question. By then he had acquired such a reputation as being with higher powers and superhuman faculties, nothing so mundane as money was of any importance.

It was therefore a mouth-opening shock when Gurdjieff began to answer the question seriously. His answer took the form of a long and almost unbelievable saga which later became known as The Material Question and now forms the last chapter in *Meetings with Remarkable Men*.

What emerges is that there never was or had been any financing, any funds, nor any Djinni in the background who provided million after million out of devotion to Gurdjieff or his aims. What there had been was an astonishing cornucopia of ingenious, and often hilarious, ploys Gurdjieff himself invented to make money! And make it himself, usually out of the naïvety and gullibility of people.

His resourcefulness, originality and detachment from the whole thing has a sort of magic about it. Fortunes could be made from barrels of bad herrings or out-of-fashion corsets. If money was needed, then he would make some; dive for coins dropped from passing tourist ships in Constantinople, set up as a shoeshine boy in Rome, make paper flowers or snare sparrows and paint them up to pass as American canaries or start a 'universal workshop' and make millions! Nothing was too bizarre or unexpected to serve his turn and be dropped the moment its usefulness was over. He remained free of it all. Money-making was just another tool to get you where you wanted.

So the wheel turns full circle. This hidden life, passing almost unnoticed while it was being lived, turns, now it is over, into a legend. The legend of what treasure the will and search of one man can bring back into life from its own depths to renew, in a desperate time, some hope for the life of the world to come.

———

SOMEHOW I feel every man ought to take up his stance before these questions and say: I don't understand the mystery but here I am before it. I owe it to myself to have a position from which to confront it. I have been given gifts of courage, curiosity, sensitivity – tools with which to challenge the unknown. I owe it to myself, to my fellow men, to take it as far as I can, to confront the mystery. David and Goliath.

There had been, after all, a time of perfection, a Golden Age. Not a myth, a dream. There are records of it, this age before man existed when, for millions of years, Great Nature had been slowly and painstakingly created out of primeval slime to become the miracle that it is – a complete world entity, a society of almost infinite variety, growing, recreating itself and maintaining a divine state of balance and unity which resulted in the perfection of our primeval dreams – a harmony of heaven on earth. And this harmony persisted, for probably 10 million years!

But there came a day when the Creator decided it was time for Nature to take a step forward. In our temporal world everything must be born, live and die. Perfection has to be continually re-created. So, to sow discord and effect this forward step, the Creator decided to send down Satan, his son, the arch irritant, the everlasting troublemaker, the perpetual destroyer, a threat to Himself, to all life on earth, but the only one who could provide the spur to the world's re-creation – or destruction.

Again and again I have stood before this insoluble 'why' of the Creation. Sometimes thoughts come up which seem to bring the answer nearer.

Suppose we go back to the very beginning and say we are creatures living on an insignificant planet called earth, satellite to the centre of a minute solar system, whirling in a sea of stars. This earth has somehow acquired a protective and transforming veil called the atmosphere and beneath its shield a phenomenon called life has appeared. It is a sort of fungus, a very thin and delicate film, which has evolved on the surface of the earth. It is referred to as organic life or Great Nature and Man is an animal, part of it. This part is known to Man as life, 'his' world, in which he is almost wholly absorbed. At the same time he is aware of being related to other worlds above and below him, but the difference in scale is so vast it is almost impossible to realize the relation – zero to infinity.

How should Man relate to time, which varies with every level of creature that lives in it? How should he relate it to the living cells of which he is composed and conceive of them as beings, with an individual life, place and purpose, a cycle as real to them as his life is to him? Or how should he relate time to Great Nature as a whole, as a single living being, with its sickness or health, its needs and desires, its growth and decay, its lifespan and destiny among suns and comets, as far beyond Man as are his cells within him? And, as for the earth, immeasurably beyond both Man and Nature, what relation can time possibly have with this itching skin which has recently grown on its surface?

Yet these different beings, living in utterly different time scales, each part of totally different worlds, are yet all inevitably inter-dependent, interrelated, co-existent, one. This is the miracle, the enigma of the Whole.

SUPPOSE it had worked out differently. Suppose God had invented Man, this elegant baboon, with his priceless gift of intelli-gence, as a sentient creature, with a *feeling* for life, not obsessed with *thoughts* about it? The whole evolution of collective life would have been different. Alas, He did not. He remained impar-tial and waited to see what would happen.

There was the possibility that somewhere along the line wise men would appear and warn their fellows that if they were seduced by thought-dreams, imagined they were lords of the crea-tion and set up a society of imitation supermen they were doomed to become inframen and destroy themselves. Thought was no more than a decoration on feeling, a willing, amusing and inven-tive servant; but one who, given the chance, would dream up a scientific madhouse bound to destroy the Utopia it promised.

From then on, having made the decision to trust the head, the inevitable followed. Reason bred argument and argument division. Right and wrong were born and from them, the whole quagmire of ownership evolved and mushroomed until today the partition and care of rights of possession have become the first interest in the world's life. Practically and realistically whole societies have sunk to little more than guerilla gangs murdering for power and profit. Compared with what had been hoped for Man, we have degenerated to subhuman levels. So – why should we not be superseded? Many other species have suffered the same fate.

WHY not? Why shouldn't the runt of mankind be superseded by a new race of men who live to serve the world and love it. What have we done to assume precedence and power over the rest of Great Nature? Who gave us the authority to regard the earth as our property? Who permitted us, ignorantly and selfishly, to interfere with the laws and rhythms of Nature? Caring nothing for her life or her needs how dared we proclaim ourselves lords of the earth and protest that we live to improve it when we consistently rob, mutilate and destroy it for pleasure or profit?

There are blessed and devoted men and women working among us today who live to discover and bring back to us miracles of ingenuity and adaptability by which all Nature's creatures, great and small, arrange to live and prosper among their fellows in mutual tolerance and love. They live off each other and destroy each other only for food. They have no enemies. Their Golden Age lasted ten million years until Man came to destroy it.

We watch as if it were a sort of fairy tale, the miracle of these peaceful lives being lived among us, and a burst of impotent grief and disgust surges up in us at the shame of the wholesale murder and thoughtless folly that exists side by side with it. This is the inescapable situation we have allowed to thrive amongst us. We enjoy murder for profit and shrug off disgusting brutality a thousand times lower than anything Great Nature could ever dream of – and we cannot, dare not, face it.

Our world has taken a runaway course, set for disaster. It is already out of control and cannot be stopped. All restraints upheld by morality and religion have been flouted and abandoned. Law and order rely on force. Civil disobedience on a national scale borders on civil war. International greed and irresponsibility are taken for granted. The whole world is in debt. But money is running out. When there is no more to borrow, no more to lend, what happens? A breakdown in banking, a threat to all organized society and, short of a miracle, the end of civilization, as we know it.

This is black reading, but it is a situation nearer than we dare think, for it is only an aspect of another world problem we have created for ourselves – the damage being done to the balance of Great Nature herself by the wanton destruction of the forests by which she breathes, the water she drinks and the air which is her life's blood. This is forcing her to show her displeasure by calling up her reserves: gales, droughts, floods, irregularities in season and climates.

A further aspect of this world crisis is the state of humanity's health. In spite of an overall growth in general knowledge of simple rules of how to maintain it, human health is deteriorating. The deadly habit of drug-taking is on the increase. Round this, incurable diseases and deadly infections have appeared, warning us of the wholesale destruction of blameless populations – the very people whose vitality and youth we were, unknowingly, relying upon to rejuvenate our satiated society.

But beyond all this lies the root of the whole matter, the final obstacle, seemingly unsurmountable, the inevitable growth of world population.

We do not yet understand that Great Nature is an entity, a being, which to live has (like every living creature) to maintain a delicate and carefully adjusted balance. This she has done over tens of millions of years, creating herself, a miraculous creature of infinite variety and beauty. The secret of maintaining this balance is to permit every creature to have its place, but to keep it within limits by the pressure of other creatures that surround it, all living off each other. Any attempt to take over a larger place is slowly and peacefully discouraged by neighbours. We can sometimes see this process working on a small scale in the countryside that surrounds us. The larger scale can be inferred from the way that – over the millennia – Great Nature has maintained a veritable Garden of Eden for us to live in.

What do we know of the will or wish of our Creator? All we can see is a general tendency to growth we call evolution. Perhaps it was necessary for the general life on earth that Great Nature should take a step forward, and this step should be the insertion into life of a new element, a creature living partly in another, higher, dimension. Of course it would disturb the smooth course of things as they had been. But it was a challenge. Could Nature absorb these new beings, could she adjust the whole to admit them, contain them and grow a greater world from their presence?

The success of the experiment depended very much on how these new beings behaved, how they saw the life around them in which they were developing, how they adjusted to it. They could co-operate with life or they could attempt to dominate it. Dangerous! But they must have their chance to learn, to see what restraints and disciplines were necessary to ensure the growth of the community. There would probably have to be tremendous crises. If they were too destructive, they would destroy themselves. But if they, or some of them, came through, they might be the forebears of a new generation and type of human beings who had learned humility and lived to love and serve, renewing life on our beloved earth.

———

WE have been warned by voices from the remote past that this was bound to come. There have been periodic crises in the life of our planet (and maybe in our whole solar system) before, when the earth suffered terrible shocks and changes to its very foundations. Now again it may be racked with violent storms, eruptions and earthquakes; Nature will produce unforeseen epidemics and diseases, life will be beset with every kind of discord and discontent. These terrible earth- and lifequakes have two quite opposite effects on human beings. They can no longer live quietly and peacefully with each other. Either they are filled with an urgent need and desire to work for the salvation of their souls or they are impelled to perpetrate every sort of violence and destruction on their surroundings and their fellow men.

It seems that we are now entering such a period of overall change and destruction. The signs are everywhere around us. We attribute this to all sorts of human failings, political ineptitude, social inequalities, poverty, hunger, crime, violence. Everything is 'wrong' and must be 'put right'.

Now we begin to see it, but we really do not know what to do. The scale is somehow beyond us. We lack the vitality to face it. Laws and legislation can do nothing against such instinctive forces.

Meanwhile there are hidden minorities which have seen the calamities ahead. These are small communities which have understood some part or aspect of truth and are working together with their own aspirations, believing that they hold the secrets which will save the world from itself. But they are wise enough to know their limitations. Small, they have learned, is beautiful. They hold together because they have understood the need to work together, that inner power is greater than outer strength, and believe there are higher powers whose sanctity and love they wish to call upon, emulate and live by. Those who have found this need in themselves and sought out these centres of God's hope may well turn out to be the seed of the world to come.

———

IN the past any attempt to escape from the huge mechanical mess of civilization has always been seen as something remote, a new life only to be reached by 'holy' men after years of penance and self discipline, reserving for them a special reverence and place in 'another' world quite out of the reach of the ordinary man.

But is it? These states of sleeping or waking which are the core of Gurdjieff's teaching, are not a 'deep' remote question. They are more physiological than theological, a matter of admitting another aspect of human intelligence to daily life, of permitting these hitherto 'hidden' thoughts to emerge from the dungeon of the 'subconscious' and take their place in the consciousness of the whole man.

Because this idea, the possibility of such an awakening, is so strange to us and its awakening so deeply buried under centuries of neglect and forgetfulness, a very relaxed and open attitude has to be found to begin to coax this other self out of hiding. We have to find the instinctive need for it to grow and, so to say, go into training to develop it and make place for it.

But finally the basic need is to SEE THE NEED to WAKE UP. This is the crux of the whole matter. Once seen it begins to have a life of its own and grow within us.

The more we admit it to our lives, the more there grows a need for a deeper, fuller understanding of what it means to become more conscious of our selves, the God within us and our place in the whole.

———

So, at last, I must come to the end of this marginal note on the tremendous days I have lived through and as I do so, I am conscious of a deep stirring about me and a sort of expectancy, as if the earth were holding her breath, waiting for the moment when someone would light a match and set the world on fire!

For, as you have read these pages, you must surely have said to yourselves again and again: but, of course, I know this. This is how I felt, this is just what I hoped for. . . But! What can I do, what can anyone do? The forces piled up against us are so huge, so deeply entrenched, clung to by so many, even if they are doomed. . . I know, I know. . .

But it does not matter because there is always the answer. It comes from the millions who have seen their lives wasted, drained away time after time by greed and lies, but who somehow get to their feet again, still believing in hope and love. But we now begin to get the measure of the enemy, his power, his skill and the ferocity of the struggle that lies ahead.

A stirring now begins to mass worldwide, it has grown to be more than a longing, a protest, it demands action from those the wasted lives. The dead, the dying, the starving, the millions outraged by the subhuman façade of irresponsibility and stupidity which has become the poisoned diet of the sleeping world.

To meet this it is necessary to WAKE UP! Not as some fancy, esoteric theory, but as a desperate need, which will soon be shouted across the world, too long fed on the promise of tomorrow. WAKE UP to the fact that day by day and life by life you are living and dying in a sea of lies and dreams.

You know it, but you have always put it off, never really faced it, never dared see that the root of all evil is the lie of your life itself.

Now is the time to think, to come together in small growing groups, slowly facing yourselves, slowly finding out the way, massing an alternative society, living not against their fellow men, but denying all that is tainted with the evil of too much self. There will be mistakes, excesses, desperate and terrible encounters – but the hope beyond! It is greater than all the stars! No longer a dream, but a possibility!

A new man in a new life in a new world!